Verbivoracious Press

Festschrift Volume Four

RIKKI

DUCORNET

VP Festschrift Series:

Volume 1: Christine Brooke-Rose
Volume 2: Gilbert Adair
Volume 3: The Syllabus
Volume 4: Rikki Ducornet
(Edited by G.N. Forester and M.J. Nicholls)

Reprint Titles:

The Languages of Love
The Sycamore Tree
The Dear Deceit
The Middlemen
Go When You See the Green Man Walking
Next
Xorandor/Verbivore
by Christine Brooke-Rose

Three Novels — Rosalyn Drexler
Knut — Tom Mallin
Erowina — Tom Mallin
The Greater Infortune/The Connecting Door — Rayner Heppenstall

New fiction:

Mirrors on which dust has fallen — Jeff Bursey

other Verbivoracious titles @

www.verbivoraciouspress.org

Verbivoracious Press

Festschrift Volume Four

edited by G. N. Forester and M. J. Nicholls

RIKKI

DUCORNET

"Like the moon, the novel is a symbol and a necessary reality. Ideally it serves neither gods nor masters. Philosopher's stone, it sublimates, precipitates, and quickens. House of Keys, it opens all our darkest doors. May the Pol Pot Persons of all genders and denominations take heed: to create a fictional world with rigor and passion, to imagine a character of any sex, place, time, or color and make it palpitate and quiver, to catapult it into the deepest forests of our most luminous reveries, is to commit an act of empathy. To write a novel of the imagination is a gesture of tenderness; to enter the body of a book is a fearless act and generous."

Verbivoracious Press

Glentrees, 13 Mt Sinai Lane, Singapore

First published in Great Britain and Singapore

by Verbivoracious Press

www.verbivoraciouspress.org

CONTENTS

RIKKI DUCORNET:

FESTSCHRIFT VOL. 4

Introduction

EDITORS

For the fourth VP Festschrift, we find ourselves captivated by the work of magical surrealist, postmodern historiographer, and multitalented artist and poet Rikki Ducornet. Among the responses are Warren Motte's take on the oneiric properties of Rikki's fictional worlds, exploring the "butterfly dream" aspect of *Phosphor in Dreamland*. Mary Caponegro ruminates on the dazzling range of monsters and innocents in Rikki's novels, from the fascist Septimus in *Entering Fire*, de Sade in *The Fan-Maker's Inquisition*, and the psychiatrist in *Netsuke*, to their counterparts Lamprius, The Fan-Maker, and Akiko. The *wunderkammern*, or cabinets of curiosity, are a vital component of Rikki's work, and receive two critical celebrations here, first from Michelle Ryan-Sautour, who focuses on *The Jade Cabinet* and limns the influence of Gaston Bachelard's "poetics of space", and other preoccupations from her two essay collections. The second, from Michael J. Emmons, showcases the wonders in a range of novels, including *The Stain* and *The Fountains of Neptune*. The personal responses include several short memoirs, from Allan Guttmann's time visiting Rikki and Guy Ducornet in the French village of Le Puy-Notre-Dame in the late 1970s, Steven Moore's experiences publishing Rikki at Dalkey Archive, Joanna Howard's breathless tribute to Rikki the writing instructor, and Lily Hoang's seasonal essay-memoir, filtered through brief words of counsel from Rikki at Cornell College. Other contributions include Tammy Dasti's interpretation of Rikki's criticism of the Catholic Church in *The Stain*, Brian Evenson's perspective on *Netsuke*, Ricco Barbels's creative approach to *The Fountains of Neptune*, Raymond L. Williams's essay on the influence of Latin American authors

(Borges in particular) on her works, and short homages from Laird Hunt, Robert Coover, and Eleni Sikelianos. Ducornet's voice can be heard in 'The Deep Zoo', included here from the titular collection, a 1996 interview following the publication of *Phosphor*, and in a long email chat with the editors. The festschrift also includes two fiction pieces, the first from Igo Wodan featuring an explosive twist on 'Fortuné' from *The Word "Desire"*, the second from Nadine Mainold in a piece inspired by *Gazelle*, exploring a complex relationship in an exotic climate and the impact of estrangement over the course of a daughter and father's lives. Our keen thanks to all those who contributed, participated, and generally made themselves essential in the creation of this festschrift.

Enchanted Watermelons

FORREST AGUIRRE

I t was at night. That much I can establish. The year might have been 2005 . . . or 2006. Season: unknown; month: unknown; day of the week: unknown. It was 1 AM.

My memory has failed me. The memory might not even be real. Might not even be mine. You see, my memory can't be relied upon: I was ensorcelled.

The enchantment had begun many years before, when I discovered Ducornet's *The Stain*, rummaged through *The Jade Cabinet*, and bloated myself on *The Fountains of Neptune* in rapid succession. Not long thereafter, I had the privilege of publishing her story 'Buz' in the World Fantasy Award-winning *Leviathan 3*. But most of the legwork there was done by my mentor and co-editor, Jeff VanderMeer. This time, I was speaking to Rikki on my own.

Of course, I had corresponded with her before. She sent marvelous letters, which I keep to this day, replete with strange comic drawings throughout. I read and examined them, words and lines, with something between amusement and idolatry. They were, in a word, charming. I use that word in the most ancient and pagan of ways.

My purpose in calling Rikki that night at 1 AM—or maybe it was earlier—was to ask her if she would be willing to send me a story for an upcoming anthology I was editing. I don't know if she ever said "yes," but a story did eventually come in the mail, somewhere down the timeline, I don't know where. Somewhere. Somewhen.

Rikki was as pleasant and as personable as I had hoped. I think she might have noted that I was both very tired and a little starstruck. I had spent the night before ripping up carpet until past the witching hour and the previous day sanding the hardwood floor in preparation for staining it. Or maybe I had stained it by that point. If so, the fumes didn't help my vertiginous thoughts. If not . . . it was late, and I was exhausted.

I wish I could have recorded that conversation. I would like to have known exactly what was said and when. I know we spoke about her collaborative work *Ubar*, which she was creating with Amy England and Catherine Kasper, a portion of which (Catherine Kasper's portion, to be specific) I had published in the *Leviathan 4* anthology. We touched on Angela Carter's works and our shared love of Borges, the conversation meandering, appropriately, through the labyrinths of literature. We spoke of whimsy and playfulness in writing, of the dreamlike quality of the works we loved.

At some point, the conversation became decidedly ethereal. We had been speaking for a couple of hours. My ear hurt from holding the phone against it too long. I was dozing. Not because Rikki was not captivating, but because she was. I was Trilby. She was my Svengali. After a time, I think she realized that I was slipping in and out of consciousness because she started to intersperse the word "watermelon" into random spots in her sentences. I kid you not. "Watermelon". Perhaps she was channeling Brautigan. But I think not. I think it was a test. A watermelon test. Or it was a way to help me to wake up, to realize that I was slipping into the realms of the nonsensical. Or, perhaps, she was burrowing into my unconscious, directly accessing the inner folds of my brain in an effort to stimulate my thoughts to awareness while simultaneously numbing my senses, leading me through the dream lands, to lucidity.

It was much like reading her work.

It was night. That much I can establish.

The Deep Zoo

RIKKI DUCORNET

> Writing is the uncovering
> of that which was unrevealed.
> —Ghani Alani, *Dreaming Paradise*

In the tradition of Islam, the first word that was revealed to Mohammed was *Igrá* (Read!). The world is a translation of the divine, and its manifestation. To write a text is to propose a reading of the world and to reveal its potencies. Writing is reading and reading a way back to the initial impulse. Both are acts of revelation.

*

The Ottoman calligraphers delighted in creating mazes of embellishments in which the text was secreted like a treasure. The text needed to be deciphered and the task proved the worthiness of the reader. These calligraphers' mazes remind us that if the text is the mirror of an exorbitant, mutable universe, it is playful too. The maze places the text within an intimate space, very like a garden, where the text hides, then reveals itself; perhaps it could be said such a text is irresistible. Writes Gaston Bachelard: "All the spaces of intimacy are designated by an attraction" (*Poetics of Space*).

*

The texts we write are not visible until they are written. Like a creature coaxed from out a deep wood, the text reveals itself little by little. The maze evokes a multiplicity of approaches, the many tricks we employ to tempt the text hither. The maze is both closed and open; it demands to be approached with a "thoughtful lightness" (Calvino). The powers lurking within it are like stars. Despite their age and inaccessibility, their light continues to reach us and to reveal us to ourselves.

*

A playful mind is deeply responsive to the world and informed by powers instilled during infancy and childhood, powers that animate the imagination with primal energies. A playful mind is guided as much by attraction as consistency and coherence—and I am thinking here of Lewis Carroll's Looking Glass world—its consistent tyrants, the coherence of its nonsense and the energy of Alice's fearless lucidity. The Looking Glass reminds us that the world's maze is attractive to eager thinkers. After all, playfulness describes as much the scientist as the artist (and Lewis Carroll was both).

The idea that the world was engendered by the spoken word comes to us from Egypt. Here language flourished, mirroring and delighting in the phenomenal world. Here Paradise persisted; the gods and their creatures dwelling together in good understanding or, phrased differently, in *knowledge* of one another. And if the world of nature and its book indicated the divine, it also provided a place of unlimited encounters. To name a thing was to acknowledge and evoke its primary potencies—religious, medical, and magical. Plants, minerals, and animals were not only animated by the divine breath (nous), they were its vessels. Each tree, bird, river, and star was an altar, the dwelling place of a god. To gaze upon the world's image reflected in the waters of the Nile was to gaze into and reflect upon a sacred face or body: Hathor the cow-faced goddess embodied by the moon, Horus, the falcon, perched among the reeds.

Deep in the desert, each fossil shell was seen as Hathor's gift, tossed to earth from the sky; the fossil sea urchin's fivepointed star needled to its back indicated its stellar origins and explains why such things are found placed near the dead in ancient tombs. To use a lovely term of Gaston Bachelard's, such a reverie—and to leap from stone to star can only be called a reverie—"digs life deeper, enlarge(s) the depth of life." Bachelard offers these lines from the poet Vincent Huidobro:

In my childhood is born a childhood burning like alcohol.

> I would sit down in the paths of night
> I would listen to the discourse of the stars
> And that of the tree.
> —*The Poetics of Reverie*

Such *sympathies*—the stone, the moon caught in the branches of the willow, the gods, the stars—are born of looking at the world and a deep dreaming. The ancient world of sympathies, rooted in inquisitiveness and informed by imaginative seeing, gave us marvelous aesthetic and scientific achievements; alchemy for example—that exemplary amalgam of science and poetry, that "immense word reverie" says Bachelard. It would be a mistake to dismiss such *sympathies* as mere foolishness, for they were born of qualities of mind that illustrate what Italo Calvino calls the "lightness of thoughtfulness" (*Six Memos for the Next Millennium*) and illumine his phrase: "Poetry is the enemy of chance." The moment one reaches for the star-struck stone, the reverie begins; the moment its star is recognized as a piece of the night sky fallen to earth, the poem begins. Chance gives way to a deep seeing and the recognition of a pattern that informs the mind with light, a pattern that incandesces and *burns like alcohol*. If poetry is the enemy of chance, it is also *the daughter of chance*.

If I have chosen to open this essay with an evocation of an ancient world and its *sympathies*, it is because the urgencies concealed within the maze of the mind that animate our imaginations, provoke incandescence on the page. I am not calling for magical thinking, obscurity, or preciousness, but for an eager access to memory, reverie, and the unconscious—its powers, beauties, terrors, and, perhaps above all, its rule-breaking intuitions, and to celebrate with you the mind's longing to become lighter, free of the weight of received ideas and gravitybound redundancies. If we were scientists and not writers, we would not waste our time reinventing gravity. Speaking of a poet he especially admires, Calvino says,

> The miraculous thing about his poetry is that he
> simply takes the weight out of language to the point
> that it resembles moonlight.
> —*Six Memos for the Next Millennium*

And Bachelard:

> For things as for souls, the mystery is inside. A reverie
> of intimacy—of an intimacy which is always human—
> opens up for the (one) who enters into the mysteries of
> matter.
> —*The Poetics of Reverie*

The mysteries of matter are the potencies that, in the shapes of dreams, landscapes, exemplary instants, and so on, inform our imagining minds; they are powers. For Bachelard they take the form of shells, a bird's nest, an attic; for Borges a maze, mirrors, the tiger; for Calvino moonlight, the flame, and the crystal; for Cortázar ants on the march and the cry of the rooster.

Potencies are never static but in constant flux within our minds, and what's more, they *fall into sympathy* with one another. For example, for Borges, there is an evident sympathy between the tiger's stripes, the world's maze, language, and the maze of the mind; for Calvino, between moonlight and the lucent transparency of clear thinking; for Bachelard, between attics and a love of solitude; for Cortázar, between the cock's cry and the knowledge of mortality, of finitude.

*

> The world of animals is an ocean of sympathies
> from which we drink only drops
> whereas we could drain torrents from it.
> —Lamartine (as quoted by Giovanni Mariottini in his
> essay on Aloys Zötl, *FMR#1*)

One evening years ago, a family circus set up its shabby tent in the park of a French village—Le Puy-Notre-Dame—I called home. As I approached the park, I heard the sound of a powerful motor and searched the sky for an airplane—a rarity at that time in that place. The sky was empty of everything, even clouds, and the thrumming I heard was the purring of tigers. An instant later, I saw the cage and two exquisite tigers, surely drugged; their contentment in such small quarters was uncanny. If I recall this distant evening, its circus and its tigers for you now, it is in the guise of an introduction to *potencies in the shape of beasts.*

For the first issue of Franco Maria Ricci's magazine *FMR*, Julio Cortázar was asked to write an essay on the bestiary of a little-known and eccentric nineteenth-century painter from the foothills of the Bohemian mountains whose name is Aloys Zötl. From 1832 to 1887—the year of his death—Zötl painted 170 achingly beautiful watercolors of animals inhabiting the ideal landscapes of his imagination. Years were kingdoms: 1832 ruled by fish, 1835 by reptiles, 1837 by the gentle tyranny of birds. André Breton called his bestiary "the most sumptuous ever seen."

Instead of describing Zötl's bestiary, Cortázar chooses to walk us through his own Deep Zoo. His essay is titled 'A Stroll among the Cages' and it is a parallel journey on a path *burning like alcohol* that generously leads straight to Cortázar's own holding ground of totems, just as it prepares our eyes for the sight to come: Zötl's lucent tigeries and tigered lucencies:

> And then a cock crowed, if there is a memory it is
> because of that, but there was no notion of what a cock

> was, no tranquilizing name, how was I to know that
> was a cock, that horrible rending of the silence into a
> thousand pieces, that shattering of space throwing its
> tinkling glass down on me, a first and frightful Roc.

This shattering of silence precipitates the infant Cortázar into a waking nightmare that would never abandon him entirely. It informs the beasts that follow—with a vaguely menacing shimmer.

"What comes next," writes Cortázar, "has a Guaraní Indian name: mamboretá, a name that's long and beautiful just like its green and prickly body, a dagger that suddenly plunges into the middle of your soup or drops onto your cheek when the summer table is set," and there is always an aunt who flees in terror, and a father who authoritatively proclaims the inoffensive nature of the mamboretá while thinking, perhaps, but not mentioning the fact that the female devours the male in the middle of copulation. And Cortázar recalls the terrible moment when the "mamboretá would become enraged" with him for past torments and look at him from its branch, accusingly. Barking frogs come next (Zötl, by the way, was especially partial to frogs, and the lion's part of his bestiary belongs to them), and swarming ants that "pass through a house like a detergent, like the fearsome machine of fascism," locusts whose devastation brings Attila to mind, and a couple of amorous lions, their bodies trembling "slightly with the orgasm." Cortázar fulfills his promise to us admirably: we have strolled among the animals, although to tell the truth, there were no cages anywhere. The vision is clear, unobstructed, and hot. Cortázar has given us totemic potencies; he has given us Aloys Zötl.

Now, because I cannot offer you Zötl's paintings, and because Cortázar chose not to describe them, the task falls to me.

*

The imaging consciousness holds its object (such

images as it imagines) in an absolute immediacy.
—Gaston Bachelard, *The Poetics of Reverie*

Immediacy is precisely the word that characterizes Aloys Zötl's bestiary. With few exceptions, he had seen his subjects in books only, yet painted them with feverish deliberation. I imagine it was chronic and unrequited longing that drove him on, for his bestiary surges with all the kaleidoscopic opulence of a mushroom-enhanced daydream. Spangled and lucent, Zötl's beasts have been conjured hair by hair; one can count their whiskers, their feathers, and their teeth. (One thinks of Borges's magician, dreaming hour after hour and one by one the infinite elements that make for a living man.) Zötl's creatures take their ease in gardens as lavish as wonder-rooms; he has packed his pictures with rarities, so that the overall effect recalls the haunting superabundance of Max Ernst's experiments with rough surfaces and sopping rags, those hieroglyphic landscapes haunted by hierophantic loplops. Or Borgesian dream gardens, which are the amalgam of all the gardens one has ever loved. Zötl's pictures provide a glimpse of paradise: it is a first glimpse, prodigal and unfettered. In other words, Zötl has painted the potencies of Old Time, when to name a thing was to bring it surging into the real. Even his scattered stones are poised for speech.

But—what about tigers? It seems there are none. However, there is a leopard, completed in April 1837. He is the same leopard that haunts the fables of the Maya and, as all the rest, he is meticulously painted *and he is very still.* Clearly he has heard a sound that has frightened him.

Perhaps he has heard, and for the first time, the crowing of a cock. And perhaps this is the writer's task: to make audible a sound of warning—which is also the sound of awakening.

*

The subconscious is ceaselessly murmuring, and it is by listening to these murmurs that one hears the truth.

—Gaston Bachelard, *The Poetics of Reverie*

Back to Egypt, where things and their names were not seen as separate entities, but were instead in profound sympathy with one another. These perceived sympathies are often very playful, as in this story of Isis and Seth.

Seth, in the form of a bull, attempts to overcome Isis. Fleeing, she takes the form of a little dog holding a knife in its tail and evades him. In his thwarted excitement, Seth ejaculates and his seed spills to the ground.

When Isis sees this she cries, "What an abomination! To have thus scattered your seed!"

Where Seth's seed has fallen, a plant grows called the coloquint (or bitter apple). In ancient Egypt, the word for "coloquint" and "your seed" is one and the same.

Within a writer's life, words, just as things, acquire powers. For Borges, *Red* is such a word, as are Labyrinth and Tiger. And if Beauty in the form of a yellow tiger or a red rose "waits in ambush for us" (*Seven Nights*), beautiful words are the mind's animating flame.

In his essay on his blindness, Borges recalls a cage he saw as a child holding leopards and tigers; he recalls that he "lingered before the tiger's gold and black." Nearly blind, he is no longer able to see red, "that great colour which shines in poetry, and which has so many beautiful names," but it is the yellow of the tiger that persists, as does its beauty and the power of its beautiful name. In his story "The Zahir," the Tiger *is* the Zahir; it is the face of God, God's name, the sound he uttered when he created the world, the "shadow of the Rose" and the "rending of the Veil" (*Labyrinths*). Tiger is the power that brings the unborn universe surging into the real and, what's more, it is the name of the infinite book you and I are writing; it is the letters of each word of this book; Tiger is the calligrapher's maze and also the text hidden within that maze.

It is the *shell* that tigers Bachelard—that lover of intimacy and solitude. A creature with a shell is a *mixed creature*; it reveals and conceals itself simultaneously. You will recall that in ancient times a fossil shell acquired the potencies of the moon. Stones of unusual shapes were empowered by Osiris also; they evoked the myth of his dismemberment and his own scattered limbs. In the myth, Isis gathers the pieces of her husband's broken body and makes him whole; she revives him. For Bachelard, "The fossil is not merely a being that once lived but one that is still asleep in its form." He is speaking of the "spaces of our intimacy, the centers of (our) fate"; he is speaking of our memories, those powers that, "securely fixed in space," remain coiled within us, ready to spring and inform our lives with immediacy and our thoughts with urgency.

In his *Poetics of Space*, Bachelard writes:

> We have the impression that by staying in the motionlessness of its shell, the creature is preparing temporal explosions, not to say whirlwinds of being.

And in *The Poetics of Reverie*:

> The passionate being prepares his explosions and his exploits in . . . solitude.

The shell, the yellow tiger, the crowing cock, the moon—these are the potencies in which time is compressed in the form of memories. To write is to engage a waking dream, to, in solitude, prepare a whirlwind. Says Bachelard:

> Daydreams illuminate the synthesis of immemorial
> and recollected. In this remote region, memory and
> imagination remain associated, each one working for
> their mutual deepening.

For Bachelard, Time has but one reality: that of the instant. The instant is our solitude stripped bare, stripped down to its essential potencies—its Deep Zoo.

*

> The shapes of time are the prey we want to capture.
> —George Kubler, *The Shape of Time*

When I was a child, I came upon the dead body of a red fox in the woods; it was early summer, and the fox's belly was burning brightly with yellow bees. A species of animate calligraphy, the bees rose and fell in a swarm that revealed, then concealed, the corpse. Yellow and black they tigered it, and they glamorized it too—transforming what otherwise might have seemed horrible into a thing of rare beauty. It is no accident that my first novel opens with the death of a creature in a wood.

If I have, throughout this essay, dwelled on the potencies of what I've been calling the Deep Zoo; it is because it is the work of the writer to move beyond the simple definitions or descriptions of things—which is of limited interest after all—and to bring a dream to life through the alchemy of language; to move from the street—the place of received ideas—into the forest—the place of the unknown.

But the Deep Zoo's attraction is not sufficient. We must take care that our books do not resemble those seventeenth-century wonder-rooms or nineteenth-century parlors, with their meaningless jumbles of stuffed bears, kayaks, giant lobsters, and assorted stools. In other words, just as the museum of natural history has contributed to, perhaps enabled, our practical knowledge of the phenomenal world—and do not forget that the development of the museum coincides with the exclusion of Christian orthodoxy from the process of scientific inquiry—so must the books we write be free of those restraints that impede aesthetic invention; so must they be enabled by the rigors of intellectual coherence. Again, if we are to be quickened by the prime qualities of the Deep Zoo, we cannot allow our books to be determined by excess or arbitrariness. Ideas and language deserve our chronic, acute attention. After all, a book is above all a place to think, and the lightness of thoughtfulness our way of approaching the truth.

It is our capacity for moral understanding that enables us to interpret the world and to act thoughtfully and with autonomy. As psychoanalysis demonstrates, knowledge of ourselves and the world allows us to heal, to transcend the moral darkness that suffocates and blinds us. The process of writing a book is similar as it reveals to the writer what is hidden within her: writing is a reading of the self and of the world. *It is a process of knowledge.* That is why the lost roads and uncharted territories of the world's maze deserve our interest. If a book is a place to think, it is a pragmatic place, a place of experiment and discovery, a *battleground* (Calvino's word) where the orthodoxies—religious, political, neurotic—that interfere with clairvoyance are dismantled and replaced by a new order. In other words, to write in the light of childhood's burning alcohol, with the irresistible ink of tigers and the cautious uncaging of our own Deep Zoo, we need to be attentive and fearless—above all very curious—and all at the same time.

In Maria Dermoût's *Ten Thousand Things*, a living sea snail in a box guards memories in the shapes of small, disparate objects. When the snail dies, it is replaced—a spiritual manipulation that is also an act of magic. Resurgent, the memories continue to inform the world with a playful, essential, and erotic mystery. Writes Borges:

> In my soul the afternoon grows wider and I reflect.
> —*Dream Tigers*

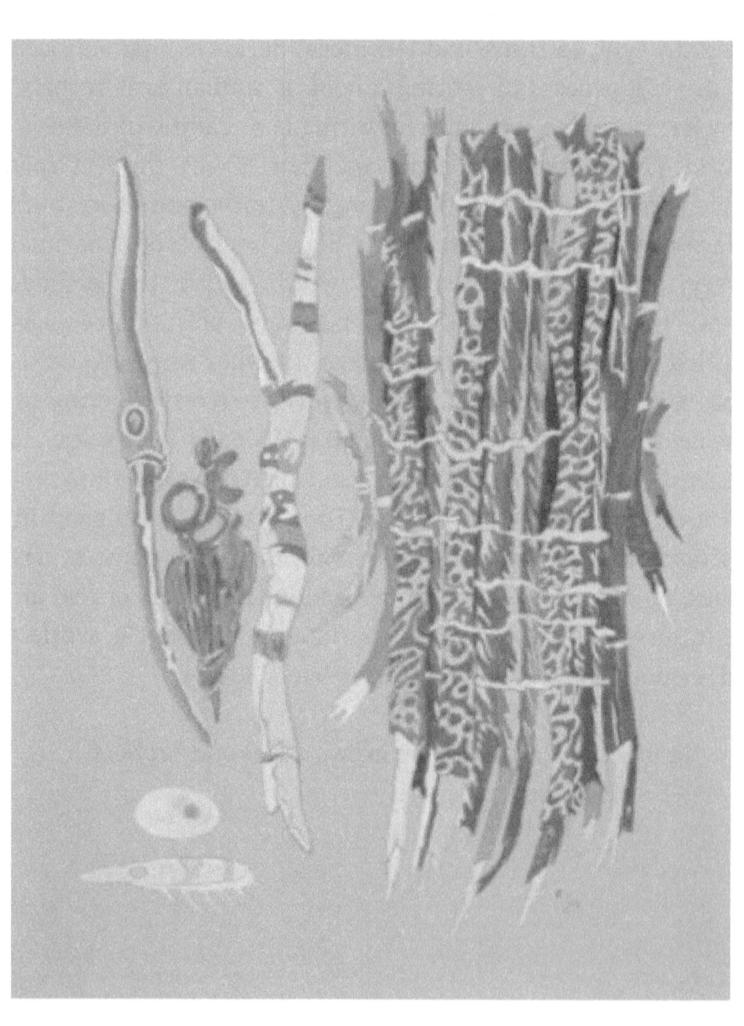

Dream On

WARREN MOTTE

One way to read Rikki Ducornet's writing is as a sustained meditation on the power of dreams, and on the way the oneiric shapes our notions of who we are and the kind of world we inhabit. "I will dream a book!" her Sade declares in *The Fan-Maker's Inquisition* (192) further musing, "What are books but tangible dreams? What is reading if it is not dreaming? The best books cause us to dream; the rest are not worth reading" (194). Clearly enough, for him, dream informs both production and reception, both the writer's task and that of the reader. And perhaps the sort of unexpected conjunctions that dreams enable so naturally afford a site for the creative articulation of writing and reading. For Ducornet herself however, it is not simply a matter of dreaming a book. In a conversation with Geoff Hancock, she remarks, "I rarely translate a dream into fiction. Rather, dreams *precipitate* my fiction" (23). The nuance is a critical one, I think, insofar as it underscores the importance of writerly work. That is, the dream is not the tale itself, needing only to be translated from an oneiric mode to a textual one; and the writer is not a mere translator. Instead—and crucially—the dream triggers a creative process in the writer, or quickens it, but it is not the only element involved in the creation of fiction.

Dreams and the lessons they convey can teach us a great deal about fiction and its uses. Notably, they suggest that worlds which we may have imagined as distinct and mutually impermeable—the dream world and the waking world, for instance, or the fictional and the phenomenal —in fact overlap in certain points of their reach, allowing us to migrate productively from one to the other, and back again. "The Surrealists tell us that our dreams can change our lives," Ducornet mentions to Hancock. "In certain existing aboriginal tribes, children are told to bring songs and images back with them from their dream journeys. And when a child has had a nightmare, for example, if he dreams that he is being chased by an animal who threatens to eat him—he takes a stick to bed with him, dreams he slays the animal and awakens unafraid. To awaken unafraid is to awaken *changed*" (26). Fiction offers us the same kind of prospect, at least as Rikki Ducornet conceives it. In order to awaken *changed*, it suffices to accept the possibility of that metaleptic gesture, that shift from the dream state to the waking, from the fictional world to the real. Moreover, we must see that gesture for what it is, not as a scandalously irrational act, but as a behavior that we engage in easily and spontaneously, whenever we let our imagination run free.

Considerations of that sort come to the fore most especially when Ducornet's fictions are not only *precipitated* by dream, but when they put dream itself on stage, and cause it to perform.

I'm thinking particularly of *Phosphor in Dreamland*, whose very title precipitates *us* into the realm of the oneiric. That realm, as Lynne Diamond-Nigh has pointed out, is a place where "transcendence can and does occur," (218), a utopian place, a place of dreams. Birdland epitomizes such a place in the novel, a site of marvelous possibility. It must be noted however that the oneiric is not merely a matter of theme in *Phosphor in Dreamland*; it is also (and perhaps foremost) a matter of technique. In other terms, if dream is very bound up in what is *told*, it is equally bound up in the *telling*. The narrator alerts us to that early on in the text, when in the Prologue he refers to his account of Birdland as "this *revery*" (3), patently inscribing his own narration under the sign of the dream. That remark inaugurates a speculative discourse that echoes throughout the novel, as Rikki Ducornet turns the notion of dream this way and that, examining it in different lights and perspectives, testing it in a variety of circumstances in order better to see what kind of results it may produce. She is interested, I think, both in the way we construct ourselves in the real world and in those other kinds of constructions that we conveniently refer to as fictions. More acutely still, she wishes to sketch conjunctive sites wherein the distinction of the real and the imagined becomes thinner and thinner.

Dream, deployed in the service of both theme and technique, provides a powerful tool in that regard, enabling the dreamer to break down barriers of different ilks, whether literal or purely notional. The most accomplished dreamer in the novel is its eponymous hero, Phosphor. But his dreams are not always good ones. To the contrary, he is sometimes beset by nightmares: "Fogginius was tyrannical and for the slightest infraction locked his stepson inside his sea trunk, which, as Phosphor grew, seemed to shrink. There, curled in a fetal knot, Phosphor would will himself to sleep, only to awake screaming, having dreamed of tombs and wells and pits" (14). In one sense, dream offers Phosphor a way of dealing with his stepfather's cruelty, recreating the actual situation in a virtual mode and purging the former, to some degree, of its terror. And despite its unpleasantness in the moment, the dream remains a creative act, one in which Phosphor can allow his mind to play, even though his body cannot. Fogginius himself is no stranger to nightmare, moreover, as he demonstrates shortly before he dies:

"The nightmare," Fogginius whispered, his voice fractured and thin, "is a cold wind raging within the mind. The nightmare is an amalgam. It contains:

> The sulphur of ingested rage
> The feces of fear
> The rosin of unrequited love
> The urine of ingested falsehoods
> The owls of unresolved quarrels
> The jackals of jealousy
> The knots and snots of perplexity. . . ." (106)

The recipe is a potent one, and Phosphor will take it to heart. Or rather, he will take its *poetry* to heart, for he knows that Fogginius has lost his reason. The poetry of Fogginius's description of nightmare is one element in a significantly plural and mobile conception of dream that Phosphor elaborates little by little, as he gradually matures and comes into his own as an artist. For it is legitimate to read *Phosphor in Dreamland* as a Künstlerroman wherein the principal vector of reflection upon art and its uses is oneiric in character. In Phosphor's case, at any rate, such reflection seems to have taken root very early on: "The idea that would haunt him for the rest of his days had begun to take form: that everything visible and palpable is light; that the world is but a seeming, and, above all, that *form is matter dreaming*—an idea he would not articulate for years but that would, once formulated, inform his creative life with an exultation born of conviction" (15).

That idea is a familiar one to us when it takes the shape of the dream argument, that is, the notion that the vividly sensual aspect of dreams should cause us to distrust the way we use our senses to distinguish between reality and illusion. That issue, as important as it may be in the philosophical tradition, is not a capital one for Phosphor, however. He is more interested in light itself, and in the process of illumination. Indeed his very name marks him cratylically as a bringer of light. "I believe there exists a connection between Phosphor's discovery of the capacity of light to steal from reality and produce counterfeits in the form of photographs," remarks the narrator, "and the real seized by the mind of the artist and reproduced by memory upon the walls of a cave —which is another sort of black box" (24). Here Ducornet gestures to a chain of speculation whose links are figures from Plato to Shakespeare to Nabokov. Clearly enough, it is a question of Plato's cave here, and of the play of light and shadow in that "black box", that darkroom, that camera obscura, that "sea chest", that womb with a view. Stealing light in order to produce a counterfeit is precisely the moon's crime against the sun, according to Shakespeare: "the moon's an arrant thief, / And her pale fire she snatches from the sun" (*Timon of Athens* IV iii). Further, one might easily argue that Vladimir Nabokov steals that "pale fire" from Shakespeare, putting it to use as the title of his novel—and, not incidentally, deploying it as the foundational idea of an ironic vision of art as imitation, recycling, and outright thievery. Nabokov underscores that kind of larceny moreover when John Shade seeks to name *his* poem: "But this transparent thingum does require / Some moondrop title. Help me, Will! *Pale Fire*" (*Pale Fire* 41).

Borrowings of that sort are crucially important in the construction and transmission of culture, without a doubt. Yet Phosphor also comes to understand their importance in the evolution of the individual, as well. In his own case, the way that he understands dream evolves as a function of affiliation and influence. Sometimes that process is collaborative, at other times it is clearly oppositional. In just such a perspective, it is revealing to compare Fogginius's definition of nightmare to Phosphor's definition of dream (as indeed the narrator of the novel invites us to to): "*She is an airy tincture of a fragrant rain, the brightest flowers, all the colors of China and Persia combined, the mystery of weather and shells breathing beneath the sea*" (108; italics in original). As Phosphor sketches it, the construct is dramatically illuminated right in its middle; and if that light is reflected from another source, what difference does it make?

One of Phosphor's recurrent dreams is curiously interactive in quality. Its chief figure is Extravaganza, Professor Tardanza's daughter, and it is highly charged with erotic potential:

> In his dream, Phosphor saw Professor Tardanza's daughter threading toward him as naked as a thing of Eden. Opening his arms to receive her, he pushed his feet into the nebulous mud upon which he was precariously standing, to keep from falling.
>
> She was hot. Before he touched her, he could feel how the air about her burned: she was poised at the center of a mandorla of fire. But just as he would embrace her, his rival Enrique Saladrigas slipped between them, and Phosphor was eclipsed by a body twice as tall and twice as broad as he. In despair he battered at his rival's back with both his fists and at the buttocks that now pressed against

> his face so that he could barely breathe. A terrific stench was upon the poet now, and the more he battered Saladrigas, the greater his rival grew. (66)

One could certainly say many things about this passage, about the vectors of Phosphor's dream. Allow me to focus on only one of them, the manner in which his approach to Extravaganza is *blocked*. For it is very much a question of blockage here, I think. In the first instance, it's a sexual blockage, and it causes Phosphor to swear that if he cannot win Extravaganza, he will abandon every other activity, with the exception of poetry. Significantly enough, he imagines that his poetry will be produced in dream: "He would no more clutter the universe with things but animate it with verses, dreamed in silence and in silence pressed to parchment" (68). Blocked in one direction, his desire will express itself in another. But to his current way of thinking, poetry is a poor substitute for the carnal.

Phosphor is not the only one who is blocked, however, for Extravaganza is incapable of dreaming (121). Indeed, as Lynne Diamond-Nigh has pointed out, the inability to dream is a curse that has afflicted her entire family (219). The problem that Ducornet sets up here is of course ripe with narrative possibility; and the way that she resolves it has a great deal to say about dream and its potential. For when Phosphor and Extravaganza finally do make love, Extravaganza dreams for the very first time, discovering thus both a new world and a new self. "It was true that Extravaganza was somehow transformed," the narrator remarks. "Her father looked at her, perhaps for the first time, with curiosity. But when he asked her to describe her dream, she could only blush and shake her head. You will not be surprised to learn that she had dreamed of love" (143). As to Phosphor, he too had dreamed of love, and more precisely "of a sexual extravagance so acute that he was, as he recalled it now, still shaken" (143-44). The mutual affinities of their dreams confirm the conclusion that a particularly saturnine figure, Rais Secundo, provides in his report to the Tribunal of the Holy Office of the Inquisition: "*Luste and dreaminge, I have ascertained, are inexorably joined*" (158; italics in original). Yet where Secundo offers that conjunction as one that is powerfully productive of sin and evil, we are invited to take it for something else entirely, because, as J. H. Matthews argues, "Rikki does not look upon eroticism as self-indulgent daydreaming. It appears to her just the way surrealism shows that it must be, a revolt against the human condition, a means for surmounting the limitations of pedestrian living and for asserting the irresistible power of desire to release men and women from oppressive contingent circumstance" (319).

Phosphor and Extravaganza dream together, then; and their dreams are significantly interpenetrable, just like their bodies. The manner in which Phosphor understands their lovemaking in retrospect, and his way of articulating it, are very intriguing indeed. For he frames that key moment and the events surrounding it in oneiric terms: "When he looked back upon it, it seemed to Phosphor that his marriage had taken place in a dream" (135). We are confronted, in other terms, with two ways of looking at dreams. On the one hand, dreams—and most particularly lovers' dreams—are mutually affiliative: Phosphor dreams and Extravaganza dreams, and in certain key sites their dreams may converse with each other. On the other hand, dreams are significantly projective: Phosphor dreams that he made love with Extravaganza, and that she dreamed of love. Let us consider those two modes a bit, calling upon a couple of other noted dreamers as we do so, and bearing in mind all the while the possibility that those modes may not be as different as they appear at first glance.

In some cases, dreams may nest within each other like Russian matryoshka dolls in a series of containers-and-contained that can be neatly parsed. But dreams are very slippery things; and the relations between those slippery things can never be quite as stable as we might wish them to be. Dreams facilitate metamorphoses and transformations, notably. Any dreaming subject is likely to find herself or himself turned into a dreamed object. Moreover, when it is a question of two subjects dreaming simultaneously, and in parallel as it were, the transformative potential of the dream is more pronounced still. Such is the lesson of the "butterfly dream" that the ancient Chinese philosopher Zhuangzi recounts:

> Once Zhuang Zhou dreamt he was a butterfly, a butterfly flitting and fluttering around, happy with himself and doing as he pleased. He didn't know he was Zhuang Zhou. Suddenly he woke up and there he was, solid and unmistakable Zhuang Zhou. But he didn't know if he was Zhuang Zhou who had dreamt he was a butterfly, or a butterfly dreaming that he was Zhuang Zhou. Between Zhuang Zhou and a butterfly there must be *some* distinction! This is called the Transformation of Things. (*Basic Writings* 44)

It is a humbling lesson, but also a very liberating one, if we agree to take it on the terms that Zhuangzi offers. For on the one hand it condemns rationalist readings of dreams to failure, while on the other hand it multiplies the interpretive possibilities that dreams provide and broadens their field of play.

Seen in another perspective, the "butterfly dream" is an example of what Lucien Dällenbach calls "aporetic emblazonment" in his study of the figure called the mise-en-abyme (*Le Récit spéculaire* 37-38, 51). He identifies therein three types of that latter figure. First, the simple emblazonment of like within like, for instance a play within a play. Second, the infinite emblazonment of like within like, for example, the Quaker on a box of Quaker Oats who is holding a box of Quaker Oats upon which there is a Quaker holding yet another box of Quaker Oats, and so forth. Thirdly and finally, "aporetic emblazonment" of like within like, in which the relations between the container and the contained are unclear and constantly shifting. When Dällenbach invokes the notion of aporia to characterize that latter kind of structure, he is taking his place alongside the rationalists, arguing that the phenomenon defeats our efforts to analyze it using our usual categories, taxonomies, and critical tools. And he is undoubtedly correct, as far as that argument goes. One wonders however if that is all we can learn from it, or if on the contrary that "aporetic" figure may have other, important things to say about how we dream and how we imagine ourselves in the world.

Let us consider a more modern cognate of the "butterfly dream." It occurs in the final chapter of Lewis Carroll's *Through the Looking-Glass and What Alice Found There*, a chapter entitled "Which Dreamed It?" Therein, Alice, in conversation with her kitten, says of the Red King, "He was part of my dream, of course—but then I was part of his dream, too!" (344). Her remark launches the question that the chapter title articulates, of course. But should any reader fail to recognize that, Carroll complaisantly concludes his chapter—and his book—with a question directed to the reader: "Which do *you* think it was?" (344). Where the kitten feigns to ignore the question and continues to lick her paws, I'm not sure that we have the same leisure. For we have followed Alice through the looking-glass; we have met the Red King and the other citizens of that looking-glass world; we have in fact inhabited that world for a time. Consequently, we may be loath to imagine that it was *only* a dream, whether that of Alice or the Red King. We might be tempted to reply that it was both Alice's dream and that of the Red King. And not only their dream, but Lewis Carroll's dream and ours as well. My guess is that it is in that articulative and intensely specular dynamic that we come closest to the truth of the matter.

Rikki Ducornet's familiarity with Lewis Carroll is a matter of record. In conversation with Sinda Gregory and Larry McCaffery, she mentions her fascination with Carroll during her childhood ('At the Heart of Things' 126-44), and the way she researched him thoroughly as an adult, when she was in the process of composing *The Jade Cabinet* (137-38). We can be quite certain, too, that she is familiar with Zhuangzi's "butterfly dream." What I am trying to point out here is not a record of influence, cultural borrowing, and allusion, but instead a matter of affinity, one that is bound up in a fundamentally similar vision of literature and its uses. Zhuang Zhou and the butterfly, Alice and the

Red King, Phosphor and Extravaganza—all of them dream together, dreaming *about* each other. Those dreams are powerfully performative, in that they cause the "other" to *be*, each in its instance, turn and turn about. Moreover, each of those dynamics is overlaid, intricated, and enriched by another, in which the dreamers are author and reader, respectively.

In that sense, fiction is a shared dream. Shared among the characters who populate the fictional world, certainly; but likewise shared (and more amply still) by author and reader. Among all of the many meditations that *Phosphor in Dreamland* puts on offer, that one is the most salient, I think. Fiction elaborates worlds where the categories of "inside" and "out" shift vertiginously in function of our angle of perception, like a lenticular image. The "inside-outness" of fiction is always complemented—and interrogated—by its "outside-inness." That is part of fiction's challenge; but it is also part of its fun and part of its fascination. Reading, we dream. Of Phosphor dreaming Extravaganza for instance, or of Extravaganza *finally* dreaming Phosphor. Or perhaps indeed we dream of both, together and simultaneously, just as each dreams the other, our dream enabled and largely conditioned by Rikki Ducornet's dream, all of us—you, me, Ducornet, Extravaganza, Phosphor, Zhuang Zhou, the butterfly, Alice, the Red King—strolling contentedly through the meanders of an intensely specular and insistently articulative world, experiencing that world both from the inside out and from the outside in, both as if in a dream and as if wide awake.

Works Consulted

Carroll, Lewis. *Through the Looking-Glass and What Alice Found There*. In Martin Gardner, ed. *The Annotated Alice*. Seaton: Bramhall House, 1960. 167-345.

Dällenbach, Lucien. *Le Récit spéculaire: Essai sur la mise en abyme*. Paris: Le Seuil, 1977.

Diamond-Nigh, Lynne. 'Phosphor in Dreamland.' *The Review of Contemporary Fiction* 18.3 (1998): 217-22.

Ducornet, Rikki. *The Fan-Maker's Inquisition*. New York: Henry Holt, 1999.

---. *The Jade Cabinet*. Normal: Dalkey Archive Press, 1993.

---. *Phosphor in Dreamland*. Normal: Dalkey Archive Press, 1995.

Gregory, Sinda and Larry McCaffery. 'At the Heart of Things Darkness and Wild Beauty: An Interview with Rikki Ducornet.' *The Review of Contemporary Fiction* 18.3 (1998): 126-44.

Hancock, Geoff. 'An Interview with Rikki.' *Canadian Fiction Magazine* 44 (1982): 13-32.

Matthews, J. H. 'Rikki Ducornet's Non-Nonsense Almost-Fairy Tales.' *Symposium* 42.4 (1989): 312-27.

Nabokov, Vladimir. *Pale Fire*. New York: Berkley, 1981.

Shakespeare, William. *The Complete Works*. Ed. Alfred Harbage. Baltimore: Penguin, 1969.

Zhuangzi. *Basic Writings*. Trans. Burton Watson. New York: Columbia University Press, 2003.

Our Friend Rikki

ALLEN GUTTMANN

Having attempted once, in an essay entitled 'Rikki Ducornet's Tetrology of the Elements',[1] to map some of the more obvious contours of Rikki's marvelous, full-of-marvels fiction, I have chosen to leave the detailed critique of her fiction and poetry to those better qualified than I to trap the elusive nuances of her language and do justice to the complexity of her vision. Although my wife Doris Bargen and I own three of Rikki's drawings (and an oil painting by Guy Ducornet), I have decided to admire silently rather than to attempt a verbal reduction of Rikki's endlessly intriguing depictions of objects that might be seashells or seeds or female genitals or—perhaps—bits of a lunar landscape. If not the fiction or the poetry and not the drawings, then what <u>do</u> I mean to talk about? Rikki in her role as a friend rather than as a verbal and visual necromancer. Few if any of those who write about and praise Rikki's work can claim to have known her longer than Doris and I have. (I am not so impious as to say we know her better.)

Doris and I met Rikki and Guy at a reception for "international visitors" hosted by Amherst College in 1972. Guy, thoroughly and somewhat aggressively French, taught French (and studied ceramics at the University of Massachusetts, which is also in Amherst). Although Rikki, who was writing and painting rather than teaching, had a Cuban father and a Russian-Jewish mother, she was at the "internationals" reception because she was married to Guy. Doris was invited to the event because she's German (and was destined to become a renowned scholar of Japanese literature). I attended because I was curious about

---

1 *Review of Contemporary Fiction*, 18:3 (Fall 1998): 184-95.

the international newcomers and because I wanted to keep Doris company if Amherst College professors, behaving like Amherst College professors, talked only to one another rather than to the invited guests. I chatted for some time with various "internationals" and then turned to look for Doris. She was standing with and excitedly talking to Rikki and Guy. I joined them and felt an almost instantaneous intellectual and emotional bond. Stronger with Rikki than with Guy, I admit, because I was quite entranced by her dark beauty. She seemed, and still seems, forty years later, to change the dimensions of whatever space she occupies.

We saw each other several times before Rikki and Guy returned to France. Each time we met, I murmured to myself, "These two are people whom I want to see again. What are they like in their 'natural' habitat?" Eventually, my question was answered. During the academic year 1977-1978, I taught at Tübingen and took advantage of relative proximity to visit Rikki and Guy in Le Puy-Notre-Dame, the small town in the Loire Valley where they owned a vineyard and a pottery whose kiln they had constructed. (From the ash of his grape vines Guy made his glazes.) The 700-hundred kilometer drive from Germany took much longer than expected and our arrival was complicated by the sad fact that Guy had not sent us the map of the town as promised. We were not worried about finding the right house because Doris was sure that the village had only eight houses and one of them would surely have a light on because Rikki and Guy were expecting us to arrive after sunset. The village, however, had several hundred houses and all of them were dark. It was nearly midnight when we parked Jean-Jacques' Peugeot in the square in front of the church. Fortunately, the local bistro was brightly lit. It was occupied by a group of serious late-night drinkers. Unfortunately, it was not open to transients (i.e., to the two of us). I banged on the window and was waved away. Undeterred, I banged until the door was opened. I explained to the group (hosted by the mayor) that I was *l'ami américain de Monsieur Guy Ducornet.* Magic words. *Les gens aimables et bourrés* invited us in for a glass of champagne. The occasion for the champagne was to celebrate the liberation of France in July of

1944. Identified now as Guy's <u>American</u> friend, I was more than welcome. Identified as *ma femme,* Doris was discreet about *nationalité.* When everyone, including Doris and me, had had more than enough to drink, one of the celebrants walked slowly downhill and guided us, driving slowly behind him, to *chez Ducornet,* which stood at the edge of the town, adjacent to the vineyard that Rikki and Guy had bought with the help of a small advance for a children's book. Rikki was still awake and greeted us warmly. (Guy was in Paris.)

We were not the only guests. The Ducornets' son, Jean-Yves, destined to be become a very successful Hollywood producer, composer, and arranger, had invited one his Amherst playmates to visit him in Le Puy. Gandon Thurman, brought by Guy from Paris, was good company. Gandon, who was destined to become the Executive Director of New York's Tibet House, was the son of Robert Thurman, the renowned Buddhist scholar; he was the brother of Uma Thurman, the even more renowned film star. Gandon was as prankish as Jean-Yves, not an easy accomplishment. Children accustomed to the company of the Dali Lama are not easily awed. The conversation, in which the children eargerly joined, was lively and full of multilingual jests. Exasperation with the political madness of the Seventies did not lead to malicious imprecation.

The meals, prepared by Rikki, a woman of many parts, were banquets *en plein air.* I still remember the duck *à l'orange* and the thin slices of breaded eggplant that were served on ceramics that she and Guy had created. (I have ceramics from Le Puy, but my breaded aubergine will never be as delicious as Rikki's.) The feast was brought to perfection by red wine made from Guy's grapes. It was the first of our several visits to Le Puy. (Whether or not Gandon returned, I cannot say.)

Between visits to Le Puy-Notre-Dame there were many letters. Rikki's were often enlived by drawings of herself as a bare-breasted flying sphinx or by her comic renditions of whatever it was I that had written to her about. (When I did a history of women's sports, Rikki produced a cartoon, a caricature of female athletes that might have graced the cover of my book and quadrupled my sales.) Quite apart from such artistic embellishment, Rikki's letters were inimitable. In them, she was serious but utterly without solemnity. She managed in her correspondence as in her conversation to be fiercely engaged without the descent into irrationality. Neither in her letters nor in our face-to-face interactions have I ever seen the wildly eccentric behavior that makes so many of her fictional characters—Septimus in *Entering Fire,* the Marquis de Sade in *The Fan-Maker's Inquisition*—so vividly memorable. If she were ever transformed at midnight into someone demonic, I was never there to witness the phenomenon.

In her letters as in the flesh, she was solicitous and affectionate. Doris and I expressed our affection for her, but "I adore you" doesn't resonate as does *"je vous adore"* or, better yet, *"je t'adore."* That such terms of endearment were not mere floscules is testified by the strangely, almost surreally beautiful illustrations Rikki provided for her friend Frédérique's fiction, *L'Orénoque* (1980). To be Rikki's friend is to receive bounty. Did I not note the cherished drawings that hang in our house in Massachusetts? We gladly purchased Guy's oil, *Le Bout du Monde,* and his ceramics, but Rikki's pictures were gifts. The books we sent Rikki were paltry recompense.

Perhaps it's not inappropriate—as an entry into the mind of the writer and visual artist—to quote from one of the many letters she wrote to me and/or to Doris. Not at all linear or narrowly logical, this letter was richly digressive in the way that Sir Thomas Browne's *Urn Burial* is digressive. Rikki began, however, by telling Doris that she had given her father a copy of a book I had written on the nature of modern sports.[2] Mad about <u>games,</u> Gerard DeGré was "planning to use [my book] in his new game theory class (required reading: think of all those pale and quivering masses of Ontario brain food-starved students hastily gobbling up your book, Allen, at the Waterloo bookstore!). . . . Ah Doris! I am a 'faculty brat' and the 'intellectual striving and reckless ambition' you speak of also have driven me up the walls ever since . . . Yet I love the campus and miss it and miss intellectuals so much. SO

---

2 *From Ritual to Record* (New York: Columbia University Press, 1978).

MUCH! We do meet so very few in Le Puy! . . . Sometimes I'm reminded of my high school days during the McCarthy era when I was I still remember being called a 'communist' (not that anyone knew what that meant) because I had been seen READING on too many occasions. (And once I was called a witch.) Amherst and Le Puy are in many ways VERY far apart." Rikki admitted that the small town was not entirely bereft of interesting people. "There is . . . a young Swiss potter who is lovely and her friend. We spend long meals discussing Kenzan, that great Japanese potter/painter/poet (who proves to me at least that one CAN speak in three tongues without being swallowed).

"We miss you so much. Please DO come biking through; this time you'll find us settled and me back on my feet too . . . I do more and more work in the pottery; and this does not interfere with the writing at all but gives strength; clay a strong arm and fire a breath! I've done a whole new series of poems that I'll send to you sometime in not too distant a future, when they have been allowed to cool off! Yes, I do have stories that you haven't seen—many! They are all in the collection *Butcher's Tales* . . . The Elkin really turned me on[3] and I have done some fiction writing. But have stopped for the moment—I got into a novella and decided it was all wrong . . . I've worked harder on it than anything I've ever done; it's caused me the most pain." She described the reaction to her manuscript by her friend, the novelist Robert Coover. (He liked parts, disliked parts.) She then lamented her isolation in Le Puy-Notre-Dame. "I can read [her work in progress] to no-one, can't really talk about it here to anyone. And it is hard to be in a 'vacuum.' Sometimes I feel like tearing the whole thing up . . . Then a little (but deeply rooted voice) squeaks: there is some truth here. Don't kill me!" (The stubborn work in progress was Rikki's brilliant first novel, *The Stain*, published by Chatto & Windus in 1984.)

"I've started the new illustrations for Susan Musgrave's new book, *Kestrel and Leonardo* . . . Leonardo is a mouse (who wears Da Vinci wings) and kestrel is—a kestrel. Half way through the book she eats Leonardo

---

3 Doris, who had written a study of the novelist Stanley Elkin, sent Rikki a copy of Elkin's best book, *The Franchiser* (1976).

UP.

"Yes I know [Günter Grass's] *The Tin Drum.* Read it years ago. I loved it!"[4]

In 1988, when Rikki was awarded a Bunting Fellowship to live and work at Radcliffe, there were opportunities for us to see her in Cambridge and for her to visit us in Leverett, the small town near Amherst to which we had moved. In the midst of the exceptional women at the Bunting Institute, she received (and gloried in) the intellectual companionship that she had missed in provincial France.

Convinced that Rikki could contribute enormously to Amherst College, I arranged for her to become the Copeland Lecturer for the spring of 1993. The terms of the lectureship were almost as generous as those of the Bunting Institute. Rikki needed only to reside in an apartment provided by the College, interact at her pleasure with faculty and students, and give one public lecture. I seized the opportunity to assign *Entering Fire* and *The Fountains of Neptune* in one of my seminars. Rikki came to class to help me teach the books. Or perhaps I came to class to help her teach them. At any rate, the students were thrilled by the books and by the classes. One of the boys asked if[5] he could speak with her again. She took him for a walk in the College's bird sanctuary. That he fell (harmlessly) in love with her . . . *ça va sans dire.*

After Rikki's divorce and remarriage—to Jonathan Cohen—Doris and I visited her in Denver, where she was, for ten years, the university's novelist in residence. The house was full of but not cluttered by *objets d'art*, many of them by Rikki. Although her eyes troubled her, she drew and painted. It occurs to me, as I mention this visit, that Rikki always spoke about her verbal and visual projects, almost always enthusiastically, and yet she always asked about and seemed genuinely interested in my research into the history of sports and Doris's into *The Tale of Genji* and other Japanese classics. At the time of the Denver visit, we were on our way to Japan and Rikki commissioned Doris to acquire for her a scroll or woodblock print of a seashell. That was significant.

---

4 Rikki Ducornet to Doris Bargen and Allen Guttmann, 2/23/79.
5 I cannot think of teenagers as men and women.

The images of Rikki's art came from deep within. Perhaps the seashells (and the seeds, and the genitals) came, like *The Fountains of Neptune*, from *la source créative*.

The last visit, which occurred after Jonathan's death, was to Port Townsend, on Washington's Olympic Peninsula. In this seaside community of writers and artists and *collectionneurs / collectionneuses* Rikki seems entirely at home. Her house is open and airy and—like her home in Denver—filled with but not cluttered by *objets d'art*. (Most of them were Indonesian artworks bought in Denver. I was quite entranced by the Balinese puppets.)

During the visit to Port Townsend, I thought, once again, how strange it was that this still beautiful, powerfully attractive woman who strolled with us on the shore of Puget Sound was capable of perfectly reasonable reflections on the (sorry) state of the nation and thoughtfully critical analyses of surrealistic fiction.

Why do we get along so well? I like to think that Doris and I can be also serious and yet indulge in what Samuel Johnson ponderously referred to as "innocent merriment." In 1968-1969, when my children were small, I taught for a year at the *Ruhr-Universität Bochum* (where I met Doris). My children and I were charmed by the *Mainzelmännchen,* cartoon characters who performed (and still perform) imaginative and frequently surrealistic tricks between the advertisements on German television. A *Mainzelmännchen* might draw a circle on a wall and then spring through it.) Milton Mainzelmann and his sons—there are no female *Mainzelmännchen*—have been a part of our household for more than forty years (during which time none of them has learned English). To provide company for Milton, Rikki acquired a cloth monkey whom she named *Monsieur Le Singe*. Shortly after his arrival, Rikki wrote us. The letter was ostensibly to congratulate me on a *New York Times* review of one of my books, but there was a prelude in which Rikki informed us that *Monsieur Le Singe* had "recovered from his initial shyness (he was <u>so</u> impressed by you all) + is proving to be the congenial fellow I know he is. He doesn't <u>let on</u> but he has a doctorate in meta-music + for a short period entertained a correspondence with Italo Calvino who called him 'my dear spook.' If he was less a dreamer (I shan't say 'lazy') he'd be one of the world's leading postmodernist architects. His plans for the Wiffeldörf stadium are among the most inventive I've seen (+ the 'poet's corner' for Bloomingdale's! A work of <u>such</u> charm!). (Yes! That's <u>his</u>!) P.S. Once again, HOORAY for the boys at the *New York Times*. Bout time they came to their senses!!!"[6]

She was clearly on a roll. It was always lovely to roll with her. *Vive l'amitié.*

---

6 Rikki to Doris Bargen and Allen Guttmann, 10/20/88

Even the Night is Bright with Starlight (Beauty and Perversity in Rikki Ducornet's Fiction)

MARY CAPONEGRO

> *If a book is a place to think, it is a pragmatic place, a place of experiment and discovery, a battleground (Calvino's words) where the orthodoxies—religious, political, neurotic —that interfere with clairvoyance are dismantled and replaced by a new order* (Ducornet, *The Deep Zoo*, 12).

Throughout the extensive oeuvre of Rikki Ducornet, the relation of the good to the beautiful is explored tenaciously and rigorously—as well as with great nuance. Platonic dialogues established and codified this relationship (*Kalos Kagothon*) in antiquity, and Ducornet's contemporary literary works investigate it and problematize it, while through the lyricism of her language consistently delivering "the goods" to the reader, i.e. beauty. Ducornet is never simplistic or didactic—nor schematic—as she illuminates the contours of injustice, oppression, domination, inhibition, as against those of compassion, generosity, curiosity, connection, desire. This form of engagement in her work is far from pious and anything but politically correct, given that in its various forms of risk-taking as it is as controversial as it is beautiful. In fact, to foreground language and lyricism to the degree that Ducornet does within the genre of fiction is itself controversial.

Pervasive in her rich oeuvre is the mythic lure of Eden and the shadow of our banishment from it. Ducornet posits the garden we collectively long for, one reconstituted from its Biblical origins—a garden in which every fruit and flower and creature, though named, would not be owned. Classification would not stunt the essence of experiencing any single fruit or flower's beauty: its fragrance, its feel against fingertip or tongue; it would merely add verbal texture to what is already redolent sensually. This beauty would not be under anyone's jurisdiction to withhold or dispense, but universally available, and thus would resist being packaged as carrot or stick. In fact, controlling beauty—rather than exercising free will or resisting authority—would very likely be her version of the fall. In the words of the ardent amateur botanist, Lamprius, in *Entering Fire*: "only foolish men worship a god who banishes his children from Paradise" (*Entering Fire*, 33). Lamprius is determined to reside there, and to the rancor and disgust of his son Septimus he actively seeks Paradise, although his Eden takes the form of South America: "Eden embraces beauty and danger with equal passion: yellow orchids suspended in the air like clusters of bees but also mygales and souroucoucou, poisons that detonate in the blood; the fragrances of forgetfulness, of paranoia, of Paradise" (*Entering Fire*, 29).

Throughout his sections, a reader is seduced by the verbal and visual richness of his imagery, the allure of his alliteration, the ingenuity of his metaphorizing. Lamprius is bounty, abundance; his language is a garden in full bloom. It is florid and fluid, elegant and slyly humorous. This is seductive virtuoso writing with an ostentation that is gorgeous rather than unctuous: the peacock whose iridescent tail we can't stop gazing at. Each voice Ducornet creates in *Entering Fire* has a unique presence and serves a contrapuntal function within the fugue that her narrative becomes, and Septimus's is of course the most commanding in its manic energy: "Eden! P'pa left us for a sewer the size of a planet. A jungle where everything, even shit, shines in the dark. He raved on, attempting to turn our heads with a sack full of mystical garbage. Thank God I was a born skeptic and sniggered at his lunatic fancies . . ." The extended passage closes with Septimus's absurdist reduction of Darwin: "How I hate that monkey business!" (*Entering Fire*, 17).

Anything reminding Septimus, beast that he is, of his 'ascent' from apes, is repugnant to him, given his own need to reduce the human "other" to the status of vermin. The only woman for whom he feels affection and respect is his mother, Virginie, since she, imprisoned in her static platitudes, is incapable of evolving.

"Perfume is agreeable to the nose . . . The shade is agreeable to those who walk . . . Books . . . are agreeable to the wise . . . The most agreeable coffee comes from Arabia" (*Entering Fire*, 51). The ludicrous monotony of her speech is the inverse of her son's. Her sole outlay of emotion is reserved for the defeat of Hitler.

The linguistic intensity Ducornet assigns to Septimus demonstrates the vile vigor of fascism and its ability to put the hearer in a trance state. We find ourselves both repelled and riveted by the outrageous assertions of this emotionally and morally stunted son, who despite his Oedipal attachment, perceives nearly all connection as miscegenation. We may recall Ducornet's own inspired comparison of Ovid and Darwin in her essay collection, *The Deep Zoo*. The evolutionary, the creative, and the protean are all of a piece in her capacious vision, and the perilous foil of rigidity is ever-ingeniously construed in her fictive universes. An openness to possibility, one might suggest, is a form of beauty.

There is perhaps no writer more acutely observant of the gross distortions of the natural—how it is sclerotized by rigid belief systems, by greed, sadism, imperialism, fascism, narcissism, egotism, and no writer more devoted to the dissemination of beauty. "I rush after beauty," says Akiko in *Netsuke*, though we know she will be thwarted by her nihilistic spouse who worships chaos. "It's something of a habit, a compulsion—" (*Netsuke*, 23) The more compulsive he becomes, however, the more these words of introduction acquire pathos. She had been speaking of her gardening. Not surprisingly, there is a Bosch-inspired triptych of Paradise by Akiko in *Netsuke*, which inspires the psychoanalyst-spouse narrator to reflect on her pursuit of Paradise and his of Hades.

The Fan-Maker who befriends Sade in *The Fan-Maker's Inquisition* has a sign over the doorway of her atelier with the motto: *Here Beauty and Laughter Rule All Day and After*. (That statement could in fact legitimately be placed on every work of Ducornet fiction.) But wherever beauty resides inside her fiction, it seems that reason stands ready to go awry, the rational courted so fervently that it inevitably tips over to become its inverse: "Now, it may well be—surely it is so—that women belong to the human community, as Olympe de Gouges insists that they are capable of reason and deserve to be included in the Declaration of Rights. It is, however, one thing to be capable of reason, another to be reasonable" (*The Fan-Maker's Inquisition*, 107). And in *The Jade Cabinet* we encounter the emphatic statement: "Beauty must and will be subordinate to the demands of logic." (*The Jade Cabinet*, 28)

But lest we be distracted by the rich array of supporting roles, we would do well to return our attention to the family dynamic of *Entering Fire*. The father/son relation between Lamprius and Septimus may remind us of the 19th century writer, Mary Shelley, who, like Ducornet, was preoccupied with the distortions of the natural and the limitations of the rational. Septimus, like Shelly's monster, seeks to destroy those whom his "father" loved in revenge for the father's abandonment of him, leading Lamprius, like Victor Frankenstein, to wish he had destroyed the son. Lamprius is acutely aware of what a simpler, "lower" creature, like a crocodile, would have done to correct filial imbalances, although he would never act out such fantasies. A far more sympathetic character than Shelley's Victor, he does not engage, as Victor does, in a codependent obsessive antagonism. Yet intoxicated as Lamprius is by beauty and eros, his obliviousness passively allows for Jane's and Marta Strada's death.

Shelley's fictive monster was ugly to a human eye, but through his eloquence he persuaded us of his nobler sensibility. Septimus, in contrast, is ugly through and through, spiritually and physically, the more so as his body is excoriated by syphilis. Ducornet allows us to appreciate the latter's vulnerability and insecurity, since he has, in effect, lost a father; it is instructive to put his words beside the monster's. His language supplies a verbal energy that meets the 19th century monster's in degree, but not in kind, for Septimus's linguistic universe is chaotic rather than controlled; it is one that becomes increasingly irrational and vile, manic as opposed to measured—exuding something like Satanic animation. And of course both Shelley's monster and the son of Lamprius become increasingly obsessed as their quests for vengeance proceed, with Septimus "trailing my father's arse like the tail of a comet" (*Entering Fire*, 147). It is through the vantage of moral capaciousness and compassion that Ducornet is able so persuasively to enter and occupy the mind of the manipulator, to lay bare insidiousness and engender pathos. She deploys both the subtle and the hyperbolic as her visionary tools. Seldom do the parodic and the poetic go hand in hand with such skill and efficacy. Her language travels from the rhapsodic to the Rabelaisian.

For all her promulgating of beauty, Ducornet is not naïve. She suggests that those who rush after beauty may be blinded by it. She gives us Lamprius, propagating, heedless of the drastic consequences, indulging his sensual appetites at whatever cost. He neglects to open his son's letters lest their negativity pollute his transcendence. She gives us Akiko, in *Netsuke*, attending to her garden and curating her evocative figurines, essentially oblivious to her husband's deviousness and exploitation of others—until she is obliterated. Lamprius loses those he loves to the clutches of a son who uses phrases like "The vaulting swastika of our hope" (*Entering Fire*, 116), and makes pronouncements such as "What P'pa calls evil is order" (*Entering Fire*, 34). Ducornet endows Septimus with Gogol-like verbal inventiveness as his deranged mind continues its entropy before our eyes and ears: "The wheel of fortune is turning, its axles greased with the bodies of misfits, mulattoes, Muskovy geese, mutton-heads, matricides, magicians, melancholics" (*Entering Fire*, 118).

This frightening, hypnotic hate speech of Septimus Docornet contrasts with Cucla's vibrant and condensed music, meant to represent an Edenic connection to nature before the fall, that is to say when nature was unmediated. Cucla too distorts the conventions of the ratiocinative through creative verbal anarchy: juxtapositions, substitutions, slang, etc., but as a way to liberate rather than to enslave. Her playfulness reanimates language and thinking, reinscribing childhood wonder into that which has undergone hypostasis, and even through the compact, idiomatic playfulness of her language, she is far more sensible and direct than her lover Lamprius, wisely suggesting to him that he should glance at the accumulating letters from his unstable son: "You should read them, lamb. He's your kid, even if he is bonkers" (*Entering Fire,* 104). Cucla as endlessly inventive, versatile, playful, capable, supple. She has a bottomless capacity for learning and adapting. She is an icon of fecundity, and her miscarriage is thus all the more tragic. She is the inverse of static Virginie, the latter a bastion of sobriety and mediocrity. In Cucla's character Ducornet marries levity to integrity.

Marta Strada is the second foil to Virginie, Cucla being the first, and her presence among his lovers further demonstrates that Lamprius isn't interested exclusively in underage women. Marta's maturity and gravity inform each sentence.

> Often people came from the village to look at us. We were horrible to see, stranger than any zoo, our feet and hands black with frostbite and our faces knotted with grief. We begged for anything, anything at all: a scrap of food, of wood, a scarf, a cigarette. We had burned our wooden shoes for warmth and filthy, tattered blankets we wore did little to conceal our sores and our sore skeletons. We were enraged by lice and hunger.
>
> In the summer, a child who had brought us eggs was severely beaten. She had come to see us like a vision of grace in the early evening. The egg she tossed to me exploded in my hand and I put everything into my swollen mouth—yolk and white smashed shell—sweetness like a hive crumbling on my tongue. In the fall, a boy who threw a package of cigarettes over the fence was shot down.
>
> . . . And so we are prodded, ashen, naked and

creaking, into the maw of Death . . . (*Entering Fire*, 157)

In Marta's eloquent gravity, Ducornet creates an alternate inverse of Virginie's folly: the latter's parroted platitudes all the more ludicrous once we arrive at this penultimate page given over to Marta, whose dignity and reserve resonate in the book's wake, holding their own in their historically replete integrity, even though the book gives Septimus the literal "last word." The vileness and pettiness he exhibits as the curtain closes only serves to underscore Marta's incisiveness, giving ballast to the beauty of her words. Her legitimate outrage contrasts to Septimus's narcissistic and sadistic outrage; her compassion is the counterpoint to his self-pity. She deems her lover Lamprius innocent of his son's crimes, while the son will never absolve his father of abandonment. And in closing the novel, the reader understands that Lamprius did indeed fail Septimus. We, like Marta, forgive the father and revile the son, though we do not condone that entry into the tunnel of beauty and eros that blinded Lamprius to his actions' consequences.

Akiko, the blameless, deceived wife of *Netsuke*'s insidious narrator, is similarly held in thrall by beauty: perceiving it as if through a filter that admits no other frequencies, creating it and curating it through her figurines, and using it unconsciously as a refuge from the knowledge of her husband's treachery. That she is an artist at the highest level is not as salient to her husband as her obliviousness, which he diagnoses matter of factly: "My wife has her own practice. She practices innocence, blindness even. And this despite her worldliness, her sophistication" (*Netsuke*, 26). It is not irrelevant that even such a manipulator as *Netsuke*'s narrator ponders what an Eden might have been "before the smack." (*Netsuke*, 47)

Marta's language has an appropriately understated elegance, a complement to Lamprius's, and if we analyze each passage we can appreciate yet further Ducornet's stylistic brilliance and deep ethical commitment. The egg imaged as a hive and placed entire upon the tongue is hauntingly beautiful, preserving the solace of the sensual within this bleak ethos, and transforming one symbol of fertility into another as an antidote to death. "Stranger than any zoo" is a comparison yet more poignant and striking coming as it does from an "insider" who has been coerced into the role of spectacle: a curiosity, an object of disgust in a menagerie. "Our sores and our sore skeletons" is a modest rhetorical flourish appropriate to the context and tone; a polyptoton might seem a meager gesture against historical depravity on this insuperable scale, but literature in Ducornet's responsible, artful hands here strives to honor historical memory and to, against all odds, seed beauty and benignity back into a fallen world. How instructively this tone contrasts with Septimus's crass, black comic perceptions and excoriations, he who reads perversity in all things natural.

Martha Strada mercifully does not end her letter with the image of the "maw of death." She resurrects the memory of how Lamprius "seduced me with stories of the sexual lives of the flowers on a night dizzy with crickets and blazing, blazing with fireflies." This lovely, tender image and especially the repetition of the participle offers infinite solace and implies much about the empowerment of memory. It allows us the consolation to think of other forms of fire than conflagration, and for those familiar with the entirety of Ducornet's oeuvre it might summon to mind the comforting, subtle observation in *Gazelle* that describes Egyptian painted tombs: "even the night is bright with starlight."

Native Range

(After/For Rikki)

ELENI SIKELIANOS

She once climbed up a ladder in tight zebra-striped pants. Take note. I was told this story as a famous writer's dream. Her ass was perfect, rounded and upturned like a button nose. You will surely notice the first syllable of that penultimate word; but will you hear the glottal stop if said by a Texan—*button*—made possible by her epiglottis—have you ever seen a picture of one? The fleshy outbreak in which everything swims. Where mothering takes place, and breaks. One of those flowers that stinks of rotting meat, a carrion call to attract the most perfect pollinator. You've in your arms 15 pounds of mouth/flower that drags like a ripe corpse.

Or Voodoo lily. That's what this stunning lady reminds me of. A witchy long black-velvet tongue stretching forth toward air to talk and talk, and a Byzantium-colored lower yawp to catch every jeweled crumb the world can toss. And toss it does.

She can spin a story tighter than the aforementioned dream pants, to bind you to your own. Stank-story, rich-story, world-story, ripping and stitching at once, whatever's needed. With her dragon arum, snake lily, stink lily, stinky lily, black lily, ragons, dragonwort words.

In Greece, they say the long spadix of the flower has a petite dragon hiding inside its spathe. In the bulbous chamber, inflorescent, the private mating takes place. A *Scarabinid* beetle enters the tube and crawls down the long corridor, blindly palping one of the passageways to Hades, where heaven is found. You dig there with your spade.

She once noticed the break—

A rose snipped off the bush—how it tosses its scent freely toward air, undressing, and its self-scent as quickly begins to fade from this world.

Wearing her dream pants, she put the words back on the rose and offered it to you. As if the sweet smell had regathered to its bloom.

She said, If I say a hen dips snuff, you better look for the can under its wing.

Kismet

IGO WODAN

My enthralment with Mesopotamia was fired by a performance of *The Labyrinth*, held in the catacombs, those wondrous serpentine pathways housing the dead, beneath the streets of the City of Light. Before that evening, my nocturnal imaginings were as tasteless, odourless, and colourless, as distilled water. The hewn-rock tunnels, the countless skulls illuminated from within by myrtle-perfumed candles, Isis-Venus shining her flame of fecund wisdom aloft, all combined to inspire an ecstatic joy expressed with a loud deep purring and a fond kneading of my lady's shoulders (happily she was wearing the pelt of a loathsome blue fox, wretched creature!) as we sat beside a local politician.

My lady had yet to acquire the notoriety of her host, but his presence prevented any admonition of my vocal rapture. Rather, it became *de rigueur* among ladies of elite circles to adorn themselves with silver-and-smoke-striped Mau while attending state events in European capitals. I disdained to be perturbed by this sudden burgeoning of feline accessories, despite having enjoyed my unique and exotic status since departing Alexandria as a kitten in my lady's arms.

My sleeping visions, on the eve of *The Labyrinth*, were an *awakening*: a consummation of my most nebulous longings invoking the potential of dreams. Thereafter, I realised myself to be *removed* from the other descendants of Bastet. Gods have mercy, but I was no longer *ordinary*, content with a saucer and a caress. The notion was pleasurable, naturally, but also painful: I felt intolerably isolated and insensible with inertia—the routine of every evening, when my lady entertained the high-ranking wives of Herr Benefactor's trusted cohorts, and I was encouraged to congregate with the neighbourhood's moggies—listening to plaintive and tuneless mewlings to the moon, or squabbles over the merits of a field mouse (a delicacy but uncommon in urban wastelands) versus the rankness of a sewer rat. Not every such occasion passed peaceably: huge and terrifying specimens who lived by cunning and claw alone made meals of the weakest of us, and one as refined as I was a favourite, albeit elusive, target. So much did I desire the blade Ra used to vanquish Apep, or at least Solomon's Temple!

To return to my dreaming during that visit to Paris: it was not the vision of loveliness that is Venus which ensorcelled me. No, it was the goddess who came before her, not Isis, but earlier still, Inanna of the Tigris and the Euphrates, of the Fertile Crescent, standing astride her two magnificent lionesses clasping her staff of the harvest, Inanna with as many lovers as a cat has whiskers, Inanna with her bronze-sandaled speed and her blood-bathed spear bringing floods of destruction to the bountiful lands, Inanna whose eponym—shrieked as the bleating of a goat before its beheading, or murmured as the last instant of *la petite mort*—is *primal*. Already, before the plans of geo-expansion executed in airstrikes and fortress raids and suicide bombings, the benevolent radiance of her rosette had dimmed; it was the malevolence of Inanna that possessed every hall of power from Washington to Moscow, Brussels to Baghdad to Beijing.

Thus did the cradle of civilisation become a fascination, a daydream to while away the hours while my lady practised her callisthenics, or sat —not always patiently—being primped and preened for a photo-shoot— I was always a pampered attendant at these extravaganzas of glaring lights and bustling stylists and silken-voiced photographers, when not being cajoled myself to model—or rehearsed her speeches insisting on a woman's right to conform to some ideal of beauty, to make a home for her husband and children, to expect national defence of borders and restriction on immigration—those scurrilous gypsies! During this period she caught the eye of Herr Benefactor, fortuitously of course, as much in need of respectability, good breeding, appropriate politics, and glamour as she. How well matched they were, he in deed and she in her patient memorisation of his preferences, his balance sheet, and his party affiliations. How the information age has made us all so *intelligent!*

The morning my lady contrived to give an afternoon radio interview, it was reported a foot soldier posing as a refugee had snuck through Mediterranean boundaries, and thus provided her with a perfect platform to rail against the laxities of European border control and the retaliation of those miserable, profligate Hellenes in letting such a monster loose on the continent. In mellifluous, modulated tones she paraded all her intellectual leanings and trickeries—so deft even I was bedazzled—and wound the interviewer like a piece of pliant copper round her finger with her populist statements cobbled together from the internet threads of various online newspapers. Not only he succumbed; she received a discreet invitation to dinner that very evening from someone she had long admired, and expended the remainder of the day in a flurry of preparation: a carefully selected outfit cinching her waist and popping up her breasts like peaches floating in water, her hair piled high on her head, stiletto heels of crucifying proportions, discreet gold ear-rings, and a whiff of the *parfum* Noli Me Tangere. I consented to my lady fastening a filigree chain around my neck from which a black velvet leash dangled, and we minced from the taxi to the entrance of the hotel, accompanied by a doorman, to where an aide of Herr Benefactor waited to conduct us to his table inside. We dined on plump oysters *au naturel*, quinoa-crumbed sweetbreads dressed with cranberry *jus*, caviar and honey-laced melon, chargrilled lamb testicles wrapped in lemon zest and rosemary, cuttlefish stuffed with goose-liver pate and truffles, pheasant marinated in *barolo*, panna cotta flavoured with anise and mint, caramelised dates, and saffron-scented white chocolate. Over his spiced Nicaraguan cigar and Borderies *eau-de-vie* and her clover-infused *grappa*, they flirted around their ideologies like two chess champions contemplating opening moves. At midnight, when Herr Benefactor intimated a stroll along the banks of the river slicing the metropolis like the veins of a kidney, I promptly regurgitated the ram jewels over his fine wool trousers. Too late, alas, they were each so enamoured of the other that he merely suggested I be excluded from their next rendezvous, to which my lady—fickleness, thy name is woman!—agreed.

~*~

Were cats to be recompensed for the chic and mystery they loan to their owners, I would not waste my earnings on the mundanity of flea collars or the hallucination of catnip, instead I would procure myself an overland passage to the ancient cities of Sippar and Babylon, Umma and Uruk, Ur and Eridu, and feast my senses on the many-splendoured wonders to be unearthed there. For as the cuneiforms reveal, the quotidian to those inhabitants is now the mystical to us—what bibelots of learning await discovery!

~*~

Herr Benefactor is zealous and reasoned in public debate, never failing to impress with a nuanced perspective that still permits a simple journalistic distillation, while in private he tends to the banal. Were the public to know of how unremarkable his daily rituals—an half-hour shit on the toilet while reading the tabloids every morning, the nightly stroll with his Alsation pooch around the park, the weekly visit of his nephew and niece to consume *zwetschgenkuchen* in summer and *schokoladentorte* in winter—his tedious reminders to himself—a yellow post-it note here, a digital chime there, a message from his secretary— his stature would certainly shrink, but he is careful, in this age of the cult of the celebrity, to maintain his larger-than-life persona. He encourages frivolous articles in feminine magazines linking him with this or that actress on a revolving basis, all the while prolonging the myth of the right woman awaiting him to sweep her off her feet, yet in reality it is my lady who has staked her claim to his affections and loyalty. She is prudently biding her time until a formal announcement, perhaps after the coming elections, when instead of being merely entourage, she will take her own prominent position in the party hierarchy and demonstrate how a *rightfully* emancipated female embodies subservient independence.

Herr Benefactor, in orchestrating a campaign to appear sympathetic to all aggrieved participants in the peace process, is planning a journey to my most holy of holies! He is, as he espouses to my lady dutifully agog, intending to meet with like-minded dignitaries in Aleppo, Baghdad, and Kuwait, to *negotiate* the exchange of necessary supplies—one of his companies manufacturers first aid equipment, another bullets—the control of water, the production of fertiliser, and joy of joys, the preservation of artefacts! It is enough to make me swoon. We share a common inspiration, he and I, the ravening of history and the penetration of mystery. He suggests, as he rolls her over and raises her naked haunches, kneading her flanks as we cats do to stimulate a smooth entry, that she accompany the mission as official photographer, and like a cat after coition, she hisses an answer and bites his wrist. I will assist in persuading my lady in the morning; the moon beckons, along with several lusty malkins.

Over a breakfast of poached eggs and salmon, she is not listening and I slink off in disgust, to stare beyond the window pane framing a grey-streaked sky and rain-slicked streets, seeing instead date-palm fringed lakes and the high square-cut stones of a ziggurat temple. If only she were as eager as I—an opportunity too rare to be missed! It is the eve of oblivion in the cradle of civilisation; at any moment, yet another ancient citadel will be blasted to smithereens by missiles, or the headwaters of a river damed above an excavation site, hiding forever the daily discourse of life in Sargon's time, or a library of untold treasures choked to extinction on its own ash. Herr Benefactor is waxing sublime about ceramics, vases of astounding beauty, miraculous tablets which hint at the origins of humanity, all manner of scientific and artful invention, and I sinuate myself around my lady's ankles, purring intensely. He pulls a new model drone from his briefcase and explains how she can visually record any object from 500 metres high and up to two kilometres distant with its remote controls, and I leap on the table and picture myself in a special harness hanging above the shimmering horizon, negus of all I survey. "Miaow," I swipe playfully at Herr Benefactor's elbow. "O conqueror of lands and custodian of antiquities! Hail to your visionary audacity! Let me join your legion!'

My lady nods in non-committal and Herr Benefactor departs for the office, while she returns to contemplation of the daily paper, and in particular, the finance column. The DAX is down, the FTSE is fragile, the CAC is climbing, the NIKKEI is nervous, and the S&P has slumped. She adjusts her portfolio minutely: an increase in defence and military stocks, movement out of tourism and luxury items, a new acquisition of pharma and chemicals shares, and a few currency swaps. How *woefully* profane.

She does, however, owe an international journal her weekly contribution, and pens an article denouncing any society supporting policies other than conservative—which naturally affords her as many targets as allies, since the left is now the right, the right is now the liberal, and the liberal is now the left; corporatism is the new totalitarianism, the shared economy is the new communism; and the effect of pluralism is to render patriarchy again prominent. As expected, this puts her in a very agreeable mood, and Herr Benefactor manages to extract a promise from her to journey with him, at least as far—or so she confides with a sly smile to me—as Vienna.

~*~

Sunday brunch amongst the inner circle in one of the city parks: a smattering of children, who thankfully are occupied with pulling dogs' tails and prodding carp in the pond, or careening along the paths on scooters and bicycles, and I sun myself lying around my lady's neck, safe from infant interference. The conversation has shifted to the most recent skirmishes in Gaza and a general denunciation of military aggression. The wife of a professor sets her tea cup with a *rat-a-tat* clatter on its saucer, and puce-faced, declaims: "The problem was Hitler." Some nods around the table, most faces register slight surprise: in public gatherings of adherents to Mussolini's fascism, Hitler's name is not commonly spoken. "Yes, the problem, I say, was Hitler. He failed." She sips her tea, swallows. "He failed because he didn't exterminate the Jews. Those dirty Israelis, they wouldn't be bombing the poor Palestinians if Hitler had succeeded in ridding the world of them." She adjusts her headscarf in the ringing silence. "We should be sending missiles there!"

A "bang" detonates near the table, the entire company jumps—I dig in my claws—and my lady squeals and slaps at my paws. Her neighbour ducks and someone else falls from a chair. The company is plunged in pandemonium until one of the children, brandishing a toy rifle, runs past the table, screeching: "Enemy fire! Run to the hills." The little terrors disappear along the park paths towards another stand of forest trees.

~*~

My lady has determined I am in need of a companion. I suspect that she plans to spend her time shopping in Vienna and would prefer to leave me at home and the—she thinks—lure of companion is compensation. As she intends subterfuge with Herr Benefactor, so I pretend agreement with her, and in due course, a stunning specimen of virulent gold and pearl white and sleek whiskers arrives. However, my lady is more subtle than I have credited her, for this cat is a native of none other than the destination of my dreams! I imagine us in spirited discussion concerning the evolution of our species, from its first domestication in the Fertile Crescent nine thousand years ago to our elevation as the favourites of Pharaohs—I can trace my lineage back to the eighteenth dynasty—to our long descent via Rome to the status of rat-catchers, even if we are today the most popular domestic animal. The new inhabitant merely arches a golden back, licks a paw, and delicately washes an ear. It is not a propitious start.

I roll out an old map which precipitates a game of 'catch the corner', for the map recoils just as soon as I have smoothed it out, and eventually we are poised at opposite ends of the globe, weight strategically distributed, tails occasionally twitching. "Look!" I jab at the upper reaches of the Euphrates. "King Nebuchadnezzar II's magnificent Hanging Gardens lie buried somewhere there. Herr Benefactor has it in mind to visit the region. The Great Ziggurat at Ur! Where is your spirit of adventure? Are we mere moggies to lie pampered on an alcove cushion while life rushes by?"

My answer is a snap of rolling map and I nimbly twist aside to face a picture of nonchalance kneading that cushion. "Since you are so desperate to discover architecture, pad over to the museum."

"Sssss!" My tail bolt upright like a witch's broomstick, I leap the lounge in a single bound, ricochet off the mantelpiece and swing on the drape-curtain tassel, collapsing a length of fabric on the newcomer, before disappearing via an attic window to the neighbour's garden, where I spend the rest of the afternoon hunting sparrows and contemplating how I will limpet myself to Herr Benefactor's mission.

First, my lady must be convinced that I will pine in her absence, inducing her to pack me in my catbag—without that dullard puss—and thus presenting me with the opportunity to smuggle myself amongst Herr Benefactor's lackeys. Unfortunately, the whole excursion is cancelled when a series of bomb blasts and shootings—how the streets stream with crimson, how high the bodies lie, how the carrion eaters circle—occurs in each of Europe's capital cities; in Cairo in a bazaar filled with young street urchins and family businesses and milling tourists; in Baghdad where the great dome of a mosque implodes and crumbles and all that can be seen in the rubble are white-clothed legs and hundreds of pairs of shoes; in Ankara where the force of the detonation sprays bloodied bits of brains and bodies across rooftops and through windows, while thousands are reported dead and missing in another air raid, in another surge of tanks rumbling over shifting frontiers, in the long lines of human misery trudging in one direction while the weapons of war pour freely along the other.

The cat companion foisted on me laps daintily from a saucer of milk, licks its fur in proper place, admires itself in the hallway mirror, and stalks across to the fireplace. "You are so tiresome. All this murder and mayhem you persist in rehashing, it's *unnerving*. Can you not relish your good fortune to be born here and now, away from the grime and muck? You are no feline of distinction, but simply a bourgeois house-cat! Accept your place in the scheme of things."

And that was the nub of the matter. Having been quickened with the toxin of chimaera in the instant of Inanna's appearance, I subsisted no longer as a creature of comfort, driven by instinct, but had metamorphosed to one of meditation, inspired by noble purpose and esoteric ambition. In the household which had always cherished and nourished me, before this elegant and supremely indifferent creature chosen for me, I had no choice but to stifle my dreams and gag my passion. What I could not express with my intellect, I did so copiously with the only means available: I coughed up hairballs in the hallway, sprayed my scent in bedrooms, and scratched the furniture.

Banished to the attic—and my window of escape—I curled up and slept, fancying myself as the comrade of an anthropology professor, or a scholar of palaeontology, or even the trusted confidante of the new breed of entrepreneur who envisions conquering space and time. There shone my moirai: to accompany a seeker after the arcane, the enigmatic, the transcendental! To become the feline of a Don Quixote! To dance as a cat of adventure: how swiftly would I—like Puss in Boots! —fearlessly discard the familiar and plunder the unknown. Better a hero's demise than the tedium of a townhouse! I had wearied of my plebeian existence, longing for the scintillating exchanges between philosophers and artists, explorers and scientists, those for whom every day heralded the possibility of new wonders. Instead I was nothing other than *domesticated.*

~*~

Sharing the alcove of the bay window overlooking the street, some weeks later, I sought to excite an element of enthusiasm in my permanent guest. "Are humans not admirable for their creativity, for their awareness of the future and the past? Once we cats partook of the divine, now we busy ourselves only with the next mouse, next meal, next treat, or the scent of a bête noire or a beloved marking his or her passage—a cuneiform of perfume—through our ceremonial territory. Perhaps," I miaowed softly, "we should appreciate this being in the instant? It is a constant flow, we lose consciousness of ourselves and instead find the consciousness of the everlasting. I am a mote of awareness, yet not of myself, only of that which is nameless, a sensation common to us all. I know you feel this luminescence, even if only for the briefest flicker!"

My eloquence was rewarded with a cuff across my nose. I hissed my dissatisfaction and leapt from the alcove to the floor, padding quickly to the attic, and butting open the window to the circumscribed freedom of the neighbourhood. The air was chill, dusk was beginning to fall, and I ran along gutters, across rooftops, vaulted from branch to branch until I found myself at the very edge of the zone I considered my own. Below me, in a small park and scattered over benches and fallen monuments, several of my species clustered. I crouched along the branch with my claws raked in the bark, waiting, watching, hoping for a scrap of conversation concerning other than the lowest tier of Maslow's Pyramid. So intent was I on listening, I failed to note the silent approach of another, until a rush of air twitched my whiskers and a lean dark shape sailed overhead, testicles hanging low enough to clip my ears before the tom somersaulted mid-air and landed before me. I sprang up and spat.

"Borderline behaviour." The tom was a tortoiseshell, tiger-markings of black and gold; a thick ruff encircled its neck, making it seem monstrous. Recovering my composure, I slunk backwards, flattening my ears but unable to still the flick of my tail; this was not the place to indulge in a tiff. "Better," he nodded, settling to a crouch. "You're from across the other side of the park. What brings you here?"

"How do you know where I live?"

He blinked slowly. His eyes were a deep, mesmerising green, like the chips of jade studding my lady's pewter plates. "Educated guess. You didn't prance across from this side of town."

"No." I eased myself up, sitting on my haunches, ready to drop to a lower branch. "I don't think I've seen your clowder here before."

The tom growled, though lightly. "That's not *my* clowder. That bunch down there is just the usual collection of strays and strutters, queens and opportunists. If I have to endure a debate on the virtues of tinned tripe versus truffle treats one more time, I'll castrate myself."

I licked a paw and brushed my ear, considering. The size of his endowment—two swollen black walnuts—suggested his threat would lead to a lingering lapse unto death; either gross exaggeration, or else—dared I even think it?—did incandescent knowledge burn within him that he could imagine his own mortality? Could he possibly aspire to experience life beyond the petty realms of our daily pleasures and troubles, ache for the glory of the world as it could be, rather than the pedestrian it was?

"What *is* your preferred debate?"

"Follow me." He bounded across a branch to a great spreading tree and I followed, up through the limbs of the oak, but as soon as I had almost reached him, he leapt again, gliding a breath-taking distance to another tree, where he turned and, watching me, deliberately sprayed, his demeanour an unspoken challenge. Without thinking I hurled myself after him but he had already sprung away to another perch, this time the roof of the park's folly. I chased him along the park perimeter and through suburbs hitherto unexplored, his scent always marking his route even if his outline was obscured, until at last, after the moon had risen, he stopped at a broad chimney. Before us spread the river, gleaming an oily, silver-scarred black, and the city, slate rooftops shining in the moonlight, the rustles and hoots of nocturnal animals filling the air around us. The church bells chimed midnight.

From that moment until dawn I listened enraptured to his story, how he had journeyed countless seas—the Far East, the Pacific, the Americas—skulking in the hulls of vessels and surviving on rodents, travelled Europe hidden in the freight carriages of the Trans-Siberian, huddled in the ruins of a mosque in Libya, played guide in the catacombs of Pompeii beneath the Grand Teatro, watched the unearthing of a temple in Giza—that of Egypt's Napoleon, Tuthmose III —and o wonder! O joy! He had, in truck and boat, by bicycle and on horseback, trekked from the Persian Gulf to the Mediterranean coast via Ar Raqqah. What a magnificent creature! What dauntlessness!

When the first aubadal rays stroked our fur, he nudged a loose brick in the chimney and with his paw teased out a small red packet from a recess. "Here. If you would learn to be bold, take this home, and when we next meet, bring it filled with salt, or sugar, or some other common substance." I took the packet between my teeth, rubbed my face against his in farewell, and with my tail flag-staff proud in the air, loped home. If only Herr Benefactor could have spoken, I would have woken him from slumber and regaled him with the tales of my new friend, so alike in spirit did they seem.

Each time we met, Uridim encouraged me to more daring physical feats, challenged me with puzzles and philosophical conundrums, and described for me vast horizons beyond my imagining. After that first sharing, he never spoke again of his own circumstances, instead drew from me the picture of my dreary home-life, questioning me about my lady, Herr Benefactor, their appointments, even the meetings of the party faithful. If ever I seemed hesitant, he would change the subject, arousing me with some event out of history of which I had never heard, until the conversation returned to the quotidian, and without thinking, I would mention the household schedule for the week. And always, the parting task, which progressed from bringing him items of a trivial nature—once he asked for nail clippings—to returning home with objects of interest—a belt of candles shaped like small logs which I placed in the fireplace, bottle caps strung together on a chain, red ribbons as a present for my lazy companion—nothing extraordinary, but charged somehow with a significance fashioned by our association, as though each action, each discussion, was collectively of an impact greater than its individual import.

My improved temperament did not pass unnoticed, and once again my lady allowed me to accompany her and Herr Benefactor to events, and of course, I rubbed the nose of my house guest in such preferential treatment. The festive season and the election were mere days away, and both households brimmed with the comings and goings of flunkeys and family, as well as preparation for a grand ball to which various personages had been invited. Owing to security concerns my lady offered to host it, since our dwelling was generally anonymous to the paparazzi and more suitable to the placing of surveillance and repulsion forces.

The day before, I stole an ungutted fish from the pantry where it awaited the tender ministrations of a chef, and brought it as a gift to Uridim, who of late seemed gaunt and lacking in vitality. We shared it together in the lee side of the chimney, away from the swirling wind and snow.

"You should sleep indoors." I licked my paws and wiped my whiskers, breathing steaming clouds of fish around us.

"I should. Perhaps before the next full moon." He dragged a bundle towards us and prodded away the covering. "Here is a gift for you."

It was the oddest assemblage of leather and studs, laces and rings of steel. "What is it?"

"Don't you know? A battle-cat's armour!"

"Armour? Battle? Are you planning a crusade?"

"Yes. But you need to practice wearing body protection first. After that, weapons training!"

I miaowed ecstatically, envisioning myself on a military campaign to protect buried treasures from marauding invaders. With a concerted, coordinated effort, we dressed me in the singular outfit: black scales of interlacing leather, surprisingly heavy—the internal padding stitched inside each scale, according to Uridim—with a row of gleaming spikes along the spine, and the underside hooked together. Around my neck, secured with elastic, was a small plastic box. "It opens as a frill of blades when you shake yourself, so avoid doing that." Uridim sat on his haunches, looking pleased, and inexplicably, relieved. "So. It's late, and the snow falls steadier. Practice moving around in it. But keep out of sight of your household until we've had our first session. Until tomorrow. Return when the moon has risen."

He ran along the pitched roof and disappeared.

I had no difficulty in avoiding my lady and Herr Benefactor, but could not resist the opportunity to shock my otherwise indifferent companion, who on coming face-to-face with me in the hallway before breakfast, shrieked like a barnyard fowl and shot up the staircase, remaining in hiding for the rest of the day. I commanded the entire attic floor to use for my own devices, and practised prowling and pouncing, springing and somersaulting, bolting over furniture and furnishings at delirious speed. I could not wait for midnight to arrive. Eventually however, the smells and sounds of the festivities downstairs made me realise the demands of my body and I succumbed to an overpowering hunger. I crept down the stairs and slunk through rooms, under curtains and behind lounges and cabinets, until I was at the entrance to the reception room in which a convivial crowd had gathered. A string quartet occupied a corner and I manoeuvred myself to pass behind them. The doors to the dining room and kitchen stood directly opposite. My lady had placed the chaise longue before the fireplace and I had almost crept underneath it when a loud snarl backed me hastily away. A cream-and-gold paw swung wildly at my face and I jumped, in full view of the company, and tumbled against the poker stand and the fireplace shield, sending iron pieces clattering and clanging to the floor. Heat blasted me and singed my whiskers.

"You wretched beast!" My erstwhile companion hissed at me dreadfully. "What is that ridiculous costume?"

Around us, long folds of dress fabric and trousered legs swished away. I caught sight of myself in the mirror and arched and spat at the reflection—a cross-between an armadillo and a porcupine. Somewhere, a woman screamed and the string concerto stilled.

"Good God. What's happened to your cat?" Murmurs arose all around, as my lady stood clutching a hand to her throat. A burly man burst through the dining room doors, yelling, "Stand back. Keep calm."

A loud buzzing vibrated through me, starting at my neck, echoing through the suit of armour. Without conscious volition, I danced towards the fire, terrible heat scorching my fur. I saw in the flames Inanna stretching out her arms, the promise of infinite bounty and wisdom in one hand and the scourge of unending plague and disaster in the other.

"Stop it! Get it away from the fire." The large man lunged at me as the buzzing rose to a hideous trill, piercing my brain and my last thought: *Inanna, the coriolis storm of destruction cleansing the earth. What harmony might our dreams have wrought, and now we feast on ashes and dust.*

"... and in breaking news, a bomb blast in Zurich appears to have claimed the lives of a number of senior officials from Europe, the Middle East, China, and the US. So far no group has claimed responsibility for the attack..."

Publishing Rikki

STEVEN MOORE

I had the honor of being Rikki Ducornet's publisher during the first half of the 1990s, when she went from a cult author published mostly by small presses to a nationally recognized one published by the major New York publishers.

In 1991 she sent a packet to us at Dalkey Archive Press seeking a U.S. publisher for her second novel *The Fountains of Neptune*, which had been published two years earlier in Canada. Along with a copy of it, she enclosed the manuscript of *The Jade Cabinet*, along with the latest *Ontario Review* containing a selection from it. I was impressed by *The Fountains of Neptune*, but I really loved *The Jade Cabinet*. After getting the boss's OK, I told Rikki that we would like to publish both right away, so she extricated herself from Ontario Review Press (whose Joyce Carol Oates wanted to publish the new novel) and we brought out *Fountains* in 1992, and *The Jade Cabinet* in the spring of 1993. By then we were already talking about publishing her other works: first an expanded edition of her 1980 short-story collection *The Butcher's Tales*, which we brought out in spring of 1994, and then a corrected reprint of her 1984 novel *The Stain* in the fall of 1995.

Earlier in 1995 we also published her new novel *Phosphor in Dreamland*. That summer, Rikki told us she would be out west and the idea of doing a mini reading tour to promote it came up. By that point I really hated being around Dalkey's publisher and, eager for any excuse to get away from the office, I volunteered to fly from Illinois out to California. Once there, I rented a car and met Rikki for the first time at her son Jean-Yves's place in Oxnard, outside of L.A. I drove her to a daytime reading at Chapman University in Orange (at Mark Axelrod's invitation), and maybe one at Dutton's in Brentwood, other L.A. suburbs. Then we drove north to San Francisco. I believe Rikki gave a reading at Black Oak Books in Berkeley, and also at some performance space in San Francisco, where she shared the bill with Dale Peck. (He read from his novel *Martin and John*, which we both found whiny and annoying.)

During the early 1990s she occasionally contributed to our journal, the *Review of Contemporary Fiction*, and at my request she did the cover art for our translation of René Crevel's 1933 surrealist novel *Putting My Foot in It*. By 1996 she had caught the eye of the New York publishing world, and the last project I worked on with Rikki was typing up the manuscript of *The Word "Desire"*, which Henry Holt published in the fall of 1997. (Rikki showed her appreciation by dedicating one of its stories to me.) By then I had quit Dalkey and moved back to Denver, where she then lived, and we saw each other occasionally over the next few years. I once invited her to do a reading at the Borders bookstore where I worked, and also interviewed her for a local arts magazine called the *Bloomsbury Review* (January/February 1998). In 2001 I moved to Michigan, but we've kept in touch ever since, and I've read each new work of hers upon publication with deepening admiration.

Like many editors, I need only read the first few pages of a work to tell if it's something I want to publish, and *The Fountains of Neptune* quickly seduced me. The sensibility was cultured but unorthodox, the form achronological but cohesive, and the content an intriguing mix of science, psychoanalysis, myth, and fairy tale. But it was the author's quicksilver way with words that did it: after a few more pages I was intoxicated by the colorful, imagistic diction, the Rabelaisian raunch, and the rum-fueled fancy displayed by the denizens of the Ghost Port Bar as they swap increasingly phantasmagoric sea tales. She had me (at page 15) at her description of the sea as "a green-eyed witch; she speaks in tongues," which seemed to describe la Ducornet as well.

For all the whimsy and wordplay, there was also a toughness of mind on display, a blazing intellect stoked by wide reading, a deep contempt for conservative thinking and their repressive institutions, a pro-sex swagger, and an uncompromising allegiance to the unconventional, the heterodox, the subversive. My kind of book, my kind of author.

There was even more whimsy and wordplay in *The Jade Cabinet*, appropriately so in a novel featuring Lewis Carroll. This may be my favorite novel of hers. It is a paean to English eccentricity, but also a parable about substantiality vs. ethereality, of commerce vs. aesthetics. Above all, it is an investigation into the mysteries of language, everything from hieroglyphics to muteness. The villain of the piece is a cartoonishly vulgar Victorian industrialist, and the whole thing reads like Dickens's *Hard Times* reimagined by Jorge Luis Borges.

This is the first book of Rikki's that I edited, though "copyedited" would be more accurate, for I did little more than correct a few typos, maybe suggest a few word changes. Unlike some editors who feel a manuscript is unpublishable until they work their magic on it, I take a hands-off attitude toward writers who know exactly what they're doing, as Rikki clearly did. It was fun to work with the graphic elements —handwritten sentences and hand-drawn sketches and diagrams—and Ducornet enlisted the help of her friend Rosamond Purcell to supply the artwork for the cover and endsheets.

I can't remember whether it was my idea or Rikki's suggestion to bring out next an expanded edition of her early short-story collection, *The Butcher's Tales*, which Toronto's Aya Press had published back in 1980 and which Rikki had sent me. Here in miniature were all the qualities I appreciated in her novels, along with excursions into surrealism and science fiction. I deliberately placed at the end an early story that concluded with the lines, "Sleepers awaking, our grey flesh tingling beneath the warm tongues of sister suns, the old dreams stirred; our blood flowed fast now, darkening, already inventing a new language for Desire." That struck me as an appropriately sensuous description of Rikki's whole fictional project: inventing a new language for desire. Most of Rikki's novels have historical settings, set in times and places when "desire"—not "love" but capital-D *Desire*—was regarded as disruptive and irreligious, a threat to decent society. Rikki respects it for the life-affirming force of nature it is, and in her work finds new, more positive ways to speak of it. We called our edition *The Complete Butcher's Tales* because it also included all the stories she had written since 1980, and once again Rosamond Purcell supplied the outré cover art and endsheet illustrations. I remember that the conventional-housewife publicity coordinator at Borders wouldn't allow me to display it for Rikki's reading because she found the cover obscene.

Shortly after *The Complete Butcher's Tales* came out in the spring of 1994, Rikki sent me the manuscript of her next novel, *Phosphor in Dreamland*, handwritten on legal-sized paper. Previously she had hired typists to prepare her works for publishers, but I volunteered to type this one myself on my newish Apple word-processor, figuring I could copyedit it as I went along. Perhaps because of this hands-on involvement, *Phosphor* remains one of my favorite Ducornet novels. I'm not a quick typist, so the procedure allowed me to savor every word as I went along, to attune myself to her cadences, to trace the twists and turns of her syntax. (Cadence was especially important to her; Rikki rejected a few of my diction suggestions because of rhythm). There were even more graphic elements than in *The Jade Cabinet*, including a portfolio of drawings we decided to include as an appendix (not something every publisher would allow). I designed the book's interior, and it was my idea to use a tiny seashell for section dividers.

My snail's pace also allowed me to marvel at her manipulation of tone: though the novel is as airy and sunny as its Caribbean setting, it deals with oppression, environmental degradation, religious fanaticism, and madness. The balance between light and dark elements resembles *The Jade Cabinet* in this regard—Ducornet's subsequent novels tip much more to the dark—as does its antiquarianism and natural history excursions. I noted the seamless shifts between the 17th century and the present, and how she used the modern natural history museum as both setting and form—the novel imitates a tour of an exotic museum—and I followed the slowly developing love story between the docent narrator and the artist Polly. (The *Wunderkammer*, or cabinet of wonders, is another model for the novel's form.) I watched how she cleverly worked her interest in Swift into the novel, and I recognized in her puritanical "Clean Sweepers" an allusion to the Promise Keepers, a boys-only evangelical Christian group making fools of themselves at that time in Colorado, where Rikki was living. I would have appreciated these things had I simply read the novel, but typing it was like looking over Rikki's shoulder as she composed the work, a Pierre Menard feeling of participating in its creation.

My years at Dalkey Archive were depressing and frustrating, but Rikki and a few other writers kept me sane and entertained. For that reason, I am as grateful to her as she is to me (as she has graciously said) for publishing her works during that crucial period in her brilliant career.

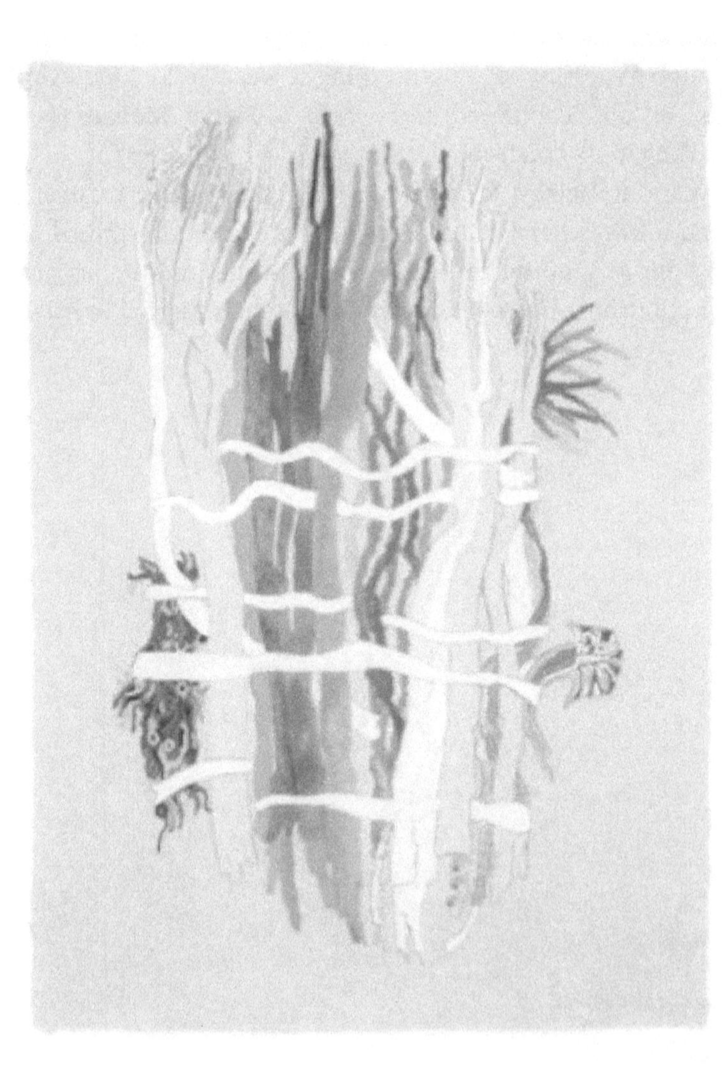

All the Waters Everywhere — Forever and After

RICCO BARBELS

Neither the most insightful of essayists, nor the wittiest of raconteurs, in fact, pedestrian or plain would be adjectives too extravagant in praise to accord these attempts at either. No, if flashes resembling brilliance (that of iron pyrites) occur, it is when seized by the scruff and thrust inside the perspective of a narrator possessed of the conviction of imparting *singular significance*. The following, sadly or happily, depending on the preference for one and not the other, falls within the former.

Reader! Imagine floating, in water salted or sweet, without the sinking that commences in heels and gradually drags the body down, via legs, through hips and torso, to a vertical position with only the tip of the nose showing until water obscures it and the whole is entirely submerged.

A trick to the art of lounging on liquid surfaces exists.

Breathe deeply, so deeply that not only the diaphragm expands, but the belly as well, in fact, the better the bubble of air within the body swells the better the effect, and while doing so, lean against the water as if in the arms of a lover, let the head sink backwards on the neck thus raising the chin, gently contract the iliopsoas to allow the feet to drift skywards, toes pointing upright like a row of pebbles in the water.

Allow the arms to stretch perpendicularly away, feel how the water propels the whole to the surface, how it caresses, how the body is made buoyant and the water cradles and cushions. Pillow the head with the arms and inhale shallow breaths using only the stomach while quietly snoozing away an afternoon flat on the back, the mind ballooning with aether as the stomach balloons with air.

It is not necessarily the most entrancing subject, the idea of someone sleeping more than half a life-time through both world wars and awakening to discover loss in all its legion forms. An easy hook to catch a reader, perhaps, but as misleading a precis of *The Fountains of Neptune* as asserting that Moby Dick is about a big whale: "*. . . For here, millions of mixed shades and shadows, drowned dreams, somnambulisms, reveries; all that we call lives and souls, lie dreaming . . .*"[1]

The first three untitled pages of Part One, although a frame of reference suggesting the entirety of themes rippling through the book, hint at the dazzling array of the fanciful and the ferocious, or, borrowing the title of a book of essays in which Ducornet makes explicit her preoccupations, *The Monstrous and The Marvelous,* that are to be found between the pages of *The Fountains of Neptune:*

> . . . the world would perish because the accumulating traumas of human history were poisoning the human soul, just as morphine saturates the lungs and lunar caustic collects in deposits of metallic silver beneath the skin . . . nothing is stranger than reality; the reality of a life spent dreaming.[2]
>
> . . . Once [the] gardens were allegories . . . Water, both real and metaphorical, is in evidence, everywhere . . . an aquatic maze of deep and shallow basins. . . is still talked about in the village because it fostered promiscuity.[3]
>
> . . . "We forget," she said, "that other mental states exist . . . thought is a process which has evolved over the ages from anterior states. Just as our finger-bones still resemble those of the lizard, so at

---

1 Herman Melville, *Moby Dick* (*The Fountains of Neptune* epigraph)
2 Rikki Ducornet, *The Fountains of Neptune*, Dalkey Archive Press, Illinois, 1993, p. 11.
3 *Ibid.*, p. 12.

depths deeper than dreaming our thoughts may echo the lobster's."

. . . "Our dreams, *Fröschlein*," K said, her mood deepening, "are islands. Floating worlds. But just as certain poisons pass through the protective membrane of the brain, so Trauma infects our dreams, transforming those islands of Paradise into infernal regions . . ."[4]

Although careful, the reader may not be prepared for what is to swirl through awareness, even if primed for the leitmotifs that dance, like light and dark dancing on the surfaces of myriad forms of water and dreams, through the story, describing—unlike the convention of a depart-port-A-intending-to-travel-to-port-B-and-while-weathering-storm-at-place-C-be-blown-off-course-before-finally-triumphing-via-place-Z-over-misfortunes-and-arriving-soundly-home-the-same-but-different-at-point-A-plot—a journey through childhood to adulthood and an exploration of losing the chart to navigate both and the finding of it in the twilight years of a life. Like the ocean itself, composed of varying pressures and zones: the abyssal through to the pelagic, *The Fountains of Neptune* has a multitude of layers and tones, requesting the reader to sink like a stone or rise like foam, from the depths of melancholia to the highs of the lively language that illuminate a comic genius at delighted work:

> "The New Hebrewdees or some such. A mere girl
> I was, no bigger than the Pope's nose, I learned
> all I know from the cook, one Madame Pittance,
> a cut-the-gills-and-don't-slouch sort of person,
> proud of her culminary talents—as well as she
> had a right to be—who instructed me in the arts
> of cookery and related matters: herbaldry,
> marketing, pickles, and what have you. A stout

---

4 *Ibid.*, p. 13.

> woman, this was, not to say obese, and when at fifty she succumbed to auricular ataxia—and it was I who found her headfast in the vinegar barrel and never have I, Heaven help us, seen such various veins (how she must have suffered yet gave no wind of it), I was dramatically propulsed from scullery to kitchery. I hired a miniature Parisienne, old as my shoes but nevertheless up to snuff, to scull in my stead."[5]

The voice of Rose: the ballast in the life of Nini (Nicolas), orphaned at two in a small French coastal village and succoured by surrogates Rose and Victor—affectionately named Totor—who are the keepers of the secret dwelling in Nini's past, and between them they represent the mundane and the magical, but on rotating planes, because Rose' cooking is prestidigitation, and yet the stuff of the stomach, the everyday, the material existence keeping Nini's feet planted firmly on mother Earth, and Rose is a pillar of the community, a devout Catholic, the purveyor of churchly gossip and canonical aphorisms, while Totor is an old sea wolf, devoted servant to Thalassa, singer of shanties and believer in the power of story, who treads lightly on the land because he has the legs of a sailor, and who fails to teach Nini how to fish but instils a reverence for the sorcery of the sea:

> "Did I tell you the time I saw the Vouivre? . . She's amphibious too. She haunts the limpid eyes of the world, Nicolas: oceans, lakes, pools, ponds, and rivers . . . She is enchantment—a warm-blooded aquatic animal. Crab and girl, serpent and siren—see that froth there . . . see that foam . . . She talks to the fish, knows all the oysters by name . . . Makes her bed on the sand beneath the water; just lays down and the snails' conversations put her to sleep . . . If you look

5 *Ibid.*, p. 18.

> well and hard, Nicolas, you may—if you are lucky
> (and I believe you are)—see her, see her *just once,*
> for she can't be seen twice, else you pay for your
> curiosity with blindness or your life."[6]

Totor initiates Nini in the Heavenly Mystery and Hellish Nightmare of the Ghost Port Bar, with its collection of crackling, carnevalesque characters who play a part, banal or brutal, in the descent of Nini to the death of innocence and his retreat to conscious unconsciousness:

The Cod: "a foul tempered hyperbolic . . . used to sitting on horns.";[7]

The Cod's Wife: "tuned" by a gang of three: The Marquis, and twins Gilles and Gillebis (Goat and Twice Goat, or Goat and Brown Goat—goats are associated with satyrs, who belong to Dionysus, for their unflagging obeisance at the altar of lust);

Charlie Dee: the chimpanzee, the beloved child substitute of the Cod's wife, although his "relations with the Cod's wife are rumoured 'seditious' by Rose"[8] according to after-sermon small talk, and whose manner and name suggest kinship in the tradition of Darwin's theory;

Aristide Marquis: the mimic, the modern day Marcel Marceau, whose "'ancestors were traders in gold and ivory and wax . . . [and] have become scavengers . . .without dreams, tending fires of thorn, fires of dung . . . [taken into] Slavery.'";[9] his name translates from the Ancient Greek as 'the best type'; and

Toujours-Là: always there, with his mesmerising tales and his baleful commentary and his readiness to pierce Nini with the double-edged sword of knowledge, dark and corrupting: "'Now you know what women are, Nini. But you ain't seen the worst. Blue Beard's closet is *fathomless.*'"[10] Toujours-Là "is powerful, too, magical, a man of keys. Keys to the past, to the Land of the Dead, to the mystery of parents departed—but not at rest. His knowledge of the story behind all stories is the tantalizing prize he holds up in the half-light again and again and

6 *Ibid.*, pp. 20-1
7 *Ibid.*, p. 23.
8 *Ibid.*, p. 24.
9 *Ibid.*, pp. 38-9.
10 *Ibid.*, p. 88.

always just beyond my reach."[11]

If each of these characters builds upon and precipitates Nini's decline to madness, by protecting him from the reality of his history, or spurring his efforts to uncover it, or simply dancing as puppets on the strings of the master marionettist who parts the curtains to reveal the glimpses enticing Nini ever closer to his irrevocable plunge: "I had been haunting an underworld . . . I thought of myself as fallen . . . The Cod's wife was a fallen woman; undoubtedly, so was my mother. But the more I thought about it, the further back that feeling of falling seemed to reach . . . I knew the underworld had always been with me . . . a sort of all-encompassing fog . . . that only the truth could cause . . . to lift;"[12] they also regale Nini with some of the most memorable, magical, immersive stories ever penned since Alice tumbled down a rabbit hole, and in richly inventive, lyrical language that tickles the cockles as it teases the humerus. These stories fire the heart of the novel, for these are fountains of joy, fountains of desire, fountains of reverie, fountains of allusion and allegory and the mystery and fantasy that leaves and forever eludes once we have tasted of the fruit of the Tree of Knowledge of Good and Evil and surrendered to the squalid reality of a world devouring itself, a world in which no benevolent divinity has ever existed and malevolence appears to reign supreme; if the reader yearns for a restoration to the wonder of childhood, the ecstasy of Keats on First Looking into Chapman's Homer, the delight of diving in unfettered imagination and rediscovering untainted curiosity, this then, is the current that eddies through the *The Fountains of Neptune* and sustains it even as Nini is sucked within the maelstrom and lost in the mere of his dreaming.

With typical irreverence, Gilles and Gillesbis discuss the fate of Bottlenose (not a porpoise, but nosed like one), who represents the delusion of pursuing the material:

> "Everybody goes crazy sooner or later," says
> Gilles. "Just look at – "

---

11 *Ibid.*, p. 93.
12 *Ibid.*, pp. 97-8

"Bottlenose!"
"He had a nose for fishes . . . and so he thought
he had a nose for – "
"Riches!"
"He was crazy for adventure – "
"Farted higher than his arse!"
"He had this obsession. Should have been
smelling – "
"Fish!"
"Not the fumes of – "
"Fancy!"
"Bottle and Jeanne d'Arc – both crazier than – "
"Bedbugs!"
"He was always a brooder – "
"Hatching castles in the sky!"
"He dreamed of a skull – "
"Filled to the brim – "
"With pearls!"
"So Bottlenose went cir – "
"Cum – "
"Ambulating! Me and my twin brother here, we
ain't – "
"Dreamers!"
"We ain't poets!"
"We ain't pre – "
"Sumptuous!"
"And [whoever's] in Heaven – "
"Feeling charitable,"
"And if in Hell – "
"Too occupied – "
"Begging for mercy – "
"To care!"[13]

---

13 *Ibid.*, pp. 70-4.

These snippets of conversation reverberate and ricochet in macabre combinations when Nicolas retreats in coma at the end of Part 1, after Toujours-Là has seduced him to seek the terrible, destructive, knowledge of his murky past and Nini gazes at the reflective[14] surface of water—glimpses a face, the face of Totor's Vouivre—and struck with divine insight, recognises the face of his mother Odille (The Black Swan: narcissistic, egotistic, and concupiscent), and falls in the water to become "the prisoner of that dream [he] was dreaming when, no bigger than a fish, [he] swam Odile's salty womb beneath her darkly brooding heart."[15]

For all the stifling efforts of practical but prosaic Rose to prevent his discovery of the ancient treachery, and Totor's quiescent and accomplice-after-the fact avoidance of truth, the persistent endeavours of Toujours-Là to wrest the scales from Nini's eyes succeed, and it is Aristide, the best among them, the alchemist who spins the straw of words to the gold of stories who drags Nini from the water, drowned in a coma. Where, amongst this company of adults, each well-meaning but ignorant according to their individual interpretation of the world, is the beacon to illuminate Nini's passage back from a uterine dreaming?

*

The character of Dr Venus Kaiserstiege, counterbalance to those who have betrayed Nini, is briefly introduced in the opening pages of *The Fountains of Neptune*: she is the psychotherapist to whom the sleeping Nini is entrusted in the spring of 1914, who writes a case book entitled *The Fountains of Neptune* concerning Nicolas:

> The Sandman . . . lives in coma . . . all that I do to
> rouse him (the bells, the cries, the clapping
> hands) only serves to animate his dreams. The

---

14 Informed by her readings of Bachelard, reflective here signifies not only a mirror-like quality, but the introspection of reverie (see the eponymous essay in *The Deep Zoo*, Coffee House Press, Minneapolis, 2015, in which she discusses Bachelard's interpretations of literature and elements).
15 *Ibid.*, p. 113.

> waking world is that optical clarity he denies; he has veiled life's ice and fire in the preferable nebulosity of dreams.[16]
> Nicolas . . . is the survivor of a triality and the witness to his family's tragedy. His answer is coma. One could not find a more poignant example of the Ego forsaking Itself.[17]

It is not until Part 2 that Dr Kaiserstiege emerges as having been instrumental in Nicolas awakening from his coma. She is steeped in the science of Freud, having studied under him, and has developed her own unorthodox therapeutic treatment involving the use of water and harmonised surroundings, not, perhaps, appreciated by "an international bourgeoisie and *petite noblesse* suffering from minor *maux*"[18]; of whom she despairs of healing, particularly in the face of encroaching and welcomed conflict:

> K was visited with the terrible certitude that her patients were at the spa not so much to mend their bodies but to kill time. It horrified her to think that what had been conceived as an island of love and light was nothing more than a genteel amusement park.
> . . . "My little universe of water and quiet pale beside the jubilant, bombastic promise of war. When the dreadful news arrives it will be received with enthusiasm. What is to become of us if we embrace Evil as eagerly as we embrace entertainment?"[19]

The voice of sensibility, echoed throughout Ducornet's oeuvre, is lost in the wilderness as war is announced, and Dr Kaiserstiege's sanitorium

---

16 *Ibid.*, pp. 11-2.
17 *Ibid.*, p. 13.
18 *Ibid.*, p. 122.
19 *Ibid.*, p. 125.

becomes a refuge for slumbering patients, is transformed to a cabinet of living curiosities filled with "'people, *people*, Nicolas, in all their glorious singularity!'"[20] Their wondrous origins and stories (the cobbler, the lovers, the eelman, and others) briefly entwine with the unravelling of that of Nicolas, but they, like so many, are extinguished in the Great Unspeakable of the second world war, and Nini survives by a small stroke of blind fortune, to awaken in a future where Dr Kaiserstiege's "ideal domain" has fallen in ruins: "the paths were overgrown with weeds and the fountains gutted with leaves. As I recall, I told her I thought her garden was a paradise."[21] To which Dr Kaiserstiege, demonstrating why hope springs eternal, why Ducornet's work, even while encompassing the macabre, the mad, the foolish and the frail, recognises that evil exists but can never dominate given the presence of minds at once curious, playful, eager to think and imagine and unafraid of scrutiny, replies: "'I have always known that Paradise is an impossibility. More impossible even than meeting up with a unicorn, or reading an opera written by a whale. This said: I have always behaved *as if it were possible*. And the only thing worth fighting for.'"[22]

Here, in Part 2, Ducornet infuses *The Fountains of Neptune* with the experience of living in a French village, her vast and impressive reading, and the fascination with battle games and rules, battle figures and their creation, and battle scenery, that so preoccupied her father. As Dr Kaiserstiege acts as midwife to Nicolas' second birthing, soothing the emergence from the dreaming state to one of wakefulness, Nini is introduced, much as Ducornet's own father opened the world of books to her, to "K's favourites; Kafka and Lao Tse, Bachelard and Perrault, Melville and Freud"[23] and Nini's voice, in struggling to find expression, is its own bestial *kunstkammer*, mimicking sounds found in *The Jade Cabinet, Phosphor in Dreamland,* or *The Complete Butcher's Tales.*

In seeking to create associations with Nicolas' dreams, memories, and his waking reality, to quicken language with symbols in his mind,

---

20 *Ibid.*, p. 127.
21 *Ibid.*
22 *Ibid.*, p. 128.
23 *The Fountains of Neptune*, pp. 131-2.

Dr Kaiserstiege assembles for him an array of signs Ducornet has imbibed herself, as an impressionable girl in Egypt, in Cuba, as a teenager and adult exploring natural history, as a young woman in Algiers and France, through her affinity with Carroll and Borges:

> The printed images were so colourful they seemed ready to ignite: a tiger, a hammer; a firefly, a flaming torch; a windmill, a Buddha; a lighthouse, a mermaid . . . a handsome devil, his pronged tail coiled about one leg like a snake, a robin with a beetle in its beak; a scorpion, and a bucket; a bee[24], and a bottle; a wheelbarrow . . . a corkscrew, a church bell; a cooking pot, a helmet; a Gila monster and a barometer; an apron and an apple . . . an eagle, a sphinx, a turkey.[25]

As Nicolas gradually recovers his ability to exist in a world catapulted from his past to an unimaginable future, in which his memories are the repository of what once existed, just as Dr Kaiserstiege's notes and drawings, the architecture of her healing Paradise, are the testament to its vanished glory, he is introduced to the superstitious and small-minded villagers who have inherited Paradis sur Loire:

> "Paradis," she said, "is a village inhabited by women who have lost their men repeatedly to war . . . Their lives are like their knitting: introspective, yet mindless; fussy exacting, repetitive, and pale—tinted by the cheaper

---

24 One of Ducornet's primary totems, sensitising her to Eden: "I was infected with the venom of language in early childhood when, sitting in a room flooded with sunlight, I opened an alphabet book. B was a Brobdingnagian tiger-striped bumblebee, hovering over a crimson blossom, its stinger intact. This image was of such potency that my entire face—eyes, nose, and lips—was seized by a phantom stinging, and my ears by a hallucinatory buzzing." Rikki Ducornet, *The Monstrous and The Marvelous*, City Lights Books, San Francisco, 1999, p. 1.

25 *The Fountains of Neptune*, pp. 132-3.

dye. . . their only comfort is the hairdresser where they exchange the nutshells of their lives. And if God is notoriously absent, they are his ambassadors nonetheless, and call me a heathen because I once took to court a local sorceress who, on the pretext of banishing demons, had starved a man to death. he was suffering from an ulcer.

. . . The ugliest among them . . . Figuebique is the most powerful woman here . . . and at the time of the trial she sided with the witch . . . her father was the village's only doctor, and I threatened him from the start. His practice relied upon purges (he was of the Old School) and, when they came into vogue, eccentric uses of antibiotics and a smattering of fractured psychoanalytical vocabulary he had learned with the intention of impressing me."[26]

These are the same villagers peopling *The Stain*, set in the 1880s, appearing a century later in *The Fountains of Neptune* with as little recourse to science and learning to inform their values and beliefs. Ducornet lived years in Le Puy-Notre-Dame, "a small, impoverished village in the Val de Loire, among vineyard workers, mushroom growers, and extremely right-wing people . . . really run by nuns . . . The landscape is unchanged even now, and even the little grocery store, with its silk thread and brown soap and old ladies gossiping . . ."[27]

These villagers, as Nicolas discovers, are part of the pattern that rejected the colossal sensuality of his mother, the same infinite famishment possessing the mother of Elizabeth in *Gazelle*: as a woman, Odille deserves nothing other than death, while Lamprius, in *Entering Fire*, imbued with a similar zest and being male, is permitted the

---

26 *Ibid.*, pp. 135-6.
27 Interview with Steven Moore, October 1997, first published in *The Bloomsbury Review*, January 1988, pp. 11-2.

realisation of his sins and the effects of his actions on his vile son, Septimus. Speaking of her experiences in Algeria, Ducornet notes "it was so difficult simply to be a woman in Algeria . . . impossible to simply walk alone, it was much too dangerous . . . young women committed suicide in massive numbers . . ."[28] Neither Odille, nor her lovers, are given the redemption reserved for Lamprius. The key figures in Nicolas' previous existence are visited by Dr Kaiserstiege during the years of Nicolas dreaming; when he finally awakes, she relates to him, in the recreated voice of Toujours-Là, of the fascination Odille exerted, and how, as perverse justification of the malicious intent inspired in others, her fascination must somehow have been consciously, morbidly purposed. Toujours-Là "feared and loved and hated [Odille]"[29], just as the villagers fear and hate the unknown. The origins of Toujours-Là's hate are pondered by Dr Kaiserstiege, and as in *Entering Fire*, where the "monstrous mother" of Septimus has moulded her son in the ways of evil, Nicolas reveals, mimicking Toujours-Là in a recollection confided to his younger self Olivier animated as a companion created by reverie during Dr Kaiserstiege's visit to the US, it is Toujours-Là's mother that has shaped his visceral mistrust of women:

> "She was bloated on bile and all our little
> world . . . She taught me thish important thing—
> that the essence of the universe is ignorance . . .
> If there ish a God sh-she's as my mother was—
> stumbling blindly through a dark room and
> thrashing out in anger, indifferent to suffering,
> the enemy of dreams . . ."[30]

In a subsequent book, *Netsuke*, Ducornet will further pursue the profound effect of parent on child with the character of the psychoanalyst damaged and betrayed during childhood by his mother.

While Dr Kaiserstiege is absent, Nicolas embarks on a recreation of

---

28 Interview with Carolyn Kuebler and Randall Heath, first published in *Rain Taxi*, Vol. 1, No. 1, January 1996, pp. 14-6.
29 *The Fountains of Neptune*, p. 192.
30 *Ibid.*, pp. 198-202.

Paradise, aptly named The Kingdom of d'Elir, in which the geography, nature, history, and culture of the entire world is reimagined and constructed with chalk, sand, coloured paper, cardboard, glue, paint, string, whatever materials Nicolas can find; the spa becomes the cabinet housing Nicolas as a curiosity, a museum that is home to the wonder of Nicolas; the detailed topography described and the manner of its initial creation (and eventual destruction) a sly nod to the Heavenly City in Ducornet's *The Genius*[31]. The Kingdom of d'Elir, peopled with apes—"gnomed gorillas"—is the scene of myriad wars between Nicolas and Olivier fought for territory, merchandise, religion, heaven and earth, galaxies; of battle movements; of invented rules, dice, symbols for disaster and munificence. It is where Nicolas retreats to assimilate Olivier as himself: "The Kingdom has become my world, but only when he is near. Without him it is a mockery, a shambles of a world: paint, dust, and shadow . . ."[32] even as he acknowledges that it is the "affection and science" of Dr Kaiserstiege that has provided him with the path back to his conscious self.

As is Elizabeth's father in *Gazelle*, Nicolas (and Olivier) are bestowed with Gerard DeGré's expertise in game theory[33], and Ducornet gives the title of her father's game-playing demesne its double entendre: "his own country was called the Kingdom of Elir—in French, Le Royaume d'Elir—the kingdom of the elect. But if you think about it, d'Elir also means "delirium" [French *délire*]"[34], madness fingered also by the self-righteous pseudo-pious character of Figuebique, who, accompanied by an army of village women, equally deluded and insane as the lunatic enemy they imagine dwells within Dr Kaiserstiege's spa, appear with the sole ambition of destruction, on the eve that Nicolas has recreated for his repose the body of his mother reprised as a room:

> "*Allons, Mesdames! Après moi!*" . . . I have felt

---

31 *The Complete Butcher's Tales*, Dalkey Archive Press, 1994, pp. 113-6.
32 *The Fountains of Neptune*, p. 188.
33 Gerard L. DeGré, *The Social Compulsions of Ideas: Towards a Sociological Analysis of Knowledge*, Transaction Publishers, 1985.
34 Interview with Steven Moore, October 1997, first published in *The Bloomsbury Review*, January 1998, pp. 11-2.

Figuebique's incomprehension and dislike from the start, but I am not in the least prepared for what follows.

. . . The fumes of pesticide, ammonia, and black soap seep under the door, followed by a spill of sudsy water . . . A troika splinters near my door. I hear a hammering, a mind-splitting *C-RACK!* as an island is ripped from the body of the sea, a continent shorn of its mountains, the Ottoman Empire chucked down the stairs. Hags ascend the attic to swamp Shangri-La, to pulverize the battle royals and royal regattas of Rangoon.

. . . "Forward, ladies! No, let's clean up this birdhouse!"

For the rest of that interminable night I can hear their shouts of triumph, the clatter of their pails, their mops and brooms—as those vandals engulf, cast down, and raze my valleys of diamonds, my peninsulas of precious stones, my gardens of Paradise, my beloved Kingdom of d'Elir.[35]

In place of Nicolas' Kingdom, Dr Kaiserstiege directs his attention to the production of *The Fountains of Neptune*, a book and neither collection, recreation, nor diminution, and although she shares his lament for the Kingdom's lost beauty, and the necessity for its creation, she identifies its limitations: "*an isolated object too small, too illusory for its own inventor to enter.*"[36] Nicolas remains, after her death, with the final remnant of a *kunstkammer*, that other object that reduces: the memory of a "fetal monster . . . it still inhabits the keeping medium of my mind."[37]

---

35 *The Fountains of Neptune*, pp. 207-9.
36 *Ibid.*, p. 217.
37 *Ibid.*, p. 220.

Life with Eros

ROBERT COOVER

Rikki, a mere mortal but with immortal gifts, was seduced by the mischievous Eros at an early age, and, though often dismayed by him, she has remained devoted to that tender but terrible deity ever since. He has been her inspiration, her scourge, her teacher, her clown. We met fifty years ago during my first year as a college prof, Rikki the young wife of a teacher of languages and daughter of a games-playing colleague. She was best-known at the time for her sensuous line drawings, Eros now guiding her hand as he already guided her understanding. It is a skill she has never abandoned, and one by which I myself have often profited. But Eros, while teaching her the gestures of desire, also taught her the *word* "desire," and out of that word has flowed an enchanted lifetime of imaginative writing, and it is this that has sealed her fame. If sometimes nightmarishly violent and cruel, in the manner of her whimsically cruel guide, her writing is also full of an aching love, whether she is writing of slime soup, sea shells, shit, or shoes. I love the sensual world, I love the body, she has said, the mutable, the fragile, the mortal body. It has been as though she were trying with all her heart to keep a dying world alive, searching for beauty even in its bleakest corners—and then, when found (or not), with Eros' help and for her own amusement, to write vividly and lovingly about it.

Class of '64

RIKKI DUCORNET

I remember sitting on campus with some other women and wondering who would be the great female masters we could turn to, because the women's movement hadn't hit yet. (Artist) Judy Chicago hadn't done her thing. I was interested in eroticism at the time and I remember being told that my work was very feminine, and that seemed like such a put-down.

But other than that, it seemed that there was so much room for women to be intellectual beings and sexual beings and imaginary beings, and that was special.

The most powerful memories I have are of Heinrich Blücher, who was Hannah Arendt's husband, and the way his class engaged in political and philosophical issues. The connection between political and psychic life was always very clear in his class. He gave these great Common Course lectures; he wasn't afraid to discuss politics passionately. Unfortunately, it's still true in America that if you discuss politics passionately, you raise eyebrows.

From *The Bardian*, May 1998, "Celebrate Fifty Years of Women at Bard"

The Jade Cabinet: *Rikki Ducornet's* Cabinet de Curiosités *and the Ethics of Reading*

MICHELLE RYAN-SAUTOUR

The world is a translation of the divine, and its manifestation. To write a text is to propose a reading of the world and to reveal its potencies. Writing is reading and reading a way back to the initial impulse. Both are acts of revelation.

Rikki Ducornet —'The Deep Zoo'

Entering the world of the *The Jade Cabinet* is indeed an experience of the potentialities of revelation, as each aspect of the novel carries the reader into unforeseen imaginary territories and points to what lies beyond its pages. It is a novel about "air", and brings to a close Ducornet's tetralogy, which includes three other works based on the four elements: *The Stain* (1984—Earth), *Entering Fire* (1986—Fire), and *The Fountains of Neptune* (1989—Water). It is about the air of the lightness of thought and dreams, but also about disappearances, absences and silent speech. The central figure is Etheria, the daughter of two eccentric *savants*, Margaret and Angus Sphery, and she has been rendered speechless by Angus's obsession with the origins of language. Long coveted by Radulph Tubbs, she eventually marries the rich capitalist when she reaches adulthood and then magically vanishes. Her story is told by her sister, Memory, whose narrative includes quotations from Radulph Tubbs's own memoirs, and is filled with curious figures such as the historical Mr. Dodgson (Lewis Carroll), a destructive hunger artist, a mad architect, and a servant who doubles as a magician.

As suggested by the title, the novel functions in the mode of the cabinet of curiosities. Also known as *Wunderkammer* or *Cabinets de Curiositiés*, such cabinets were particularly popular in pre-Renaissance and Renaissance Europe, and were often composed of objects from natural history, works of art, pieces gathered from archaeological excavations, and pictures of human anomalies. They are considered to be precursors of today's museums and, as one of Ducornet's preferred motifs, are mirrored in *The Jade Cabinet.* The novel's structure, like such cabinets, relies upon the juxtaposition of ideas and speculative figures to reveal the capacity for a thing to be at once itself and more than itself. This novel indeed moves beyond the frame of fiction to function as a museum of ideas. The novel serves as a metafictional prism that opens up thought on collections, memory, narrative, reading, and the forces of language.

Ducornet's *cabinet* indeed challenges the reader, as the forces exerted by the novel seek to break down barriers, penetrate beyond preconceived ideas, and put on display shifting, often infinitely receding spaces of discovery. In her afterword to the novel, 'Waking to Eden,' she speaks in terms of "*Vanitas*" and "*Archetypa,*" foregrounding the "descriptive" and "painterly" (158) dimension of the characters and the text. Such terms suggest a strong visual element. Yet Ducornet does not only propose a vision of physical space, but also that of a particular type of dream, much in the spirit of the French theorist Gaston Bachelard in his reflections on the four elements and "the poetics of space."[1] Ducornet's novel proceeds in a spirit of interrogation and investigation through dreams, and reveals a desire to deploy the forces of language. Behind the surface narrative of *cabinets* one is given the impression of the energy of the purring tiger Ducornet describes in her essay 'The Deep Zoo', or even the buzzing bee/"B," the "Brobdingnagian Tiger-striped bumble-bee, hovering over a crimson

---

1 Ducornet writes extensively of Bachelard's ideas in 'The Deep Zoo' and speaks of Bachelard's influence on the tetralogy in an interview with Sinda Gregory and Larry McCaffery: "Bachelard's great philosophical reveries on literature were in fact the inspiration behind the idea of the entire tetralogy—but not *Entering Fire* specifically. Only when I began *The Fountains of Neptune* did I recognize Bachelard's part in the decision I had made to investigate the elements. I returned to *L'Eau et les Rêves* and decided to convey all possible waters through the language, mood, and music of the novel: salt and fresh, swift and still, calm and treacherous, sexual, glacial" (132).

blossom, its stinger distinct" Ducornet describes in her awakening to the potencies of the alphabet (Afterword to *The Jade Cabinet* 155). This is a world of piercing stings, of jade phalluses and rape, a world of violence associated with reveries, as Ducornet shows that one does not preclude the other; the "monstrous" and the "marvelous" are intertwined.

The paratexts to the novel point to the ideas that riddle its pages. Ducornet dedicates the novel to Rosamond Wolff Purcell, who "brings grace to everything she sees." In an interview, she has spoken of how Purcell shares with her the memory of "formaldehyde", a reference to Ducornet's experience of the collection of strange things "floating in jars" in a biology lab at Bard College where she grew up (Interview with Gregory and McCaffery 128). In her essay 'The Impossible Genius', Ducornet speaks of Peter the Great of Russia's *kunstkammer* and her fascination with the collected anomalies such as those gathered by Frederick Ruysch, a Dutch anatomist fascinated by "aberrations of the human form" (*Monstrous and the Marvelous* 27). Such collections fascinate the eye, and the *kunstkammer* and *wunderkammer* haunt Ducornet's essays and fiction, often in association with an ethics of perception. In 'Optical Terror' for example, Ducornet speaks of the how the influx of curiosities in pre-Enlightenment Europe "had a profoundly unsettling effect upon pedestrian and pious minds persuaded that the finite world was created reasonably, to the measure of man and for his salvation" (*Monstrous and the Marvelous* 7). Here she speaks of physical anomalies in collections, but her interest extends well beyond the body to include collections of strange objects in natural museums (*Monstrous and the Marvelous* 8).

The aesthetics of collected anomalies draws her to the work of Purcell, whose art also appears on the cover of *The Jade Cabinet*. According to Ducornet, Purcell's art seeks to propose "museums of the mind" (*Monstrous and the Marvelous* 73), and her aesthetics of the collection allows objects to open up to primal forces in a manner similar to the power Ducornet sees in language. Through photography, Purcell has "metamorphosed the world into emblems: moth wing, fetal monkey, skeletons and skins are all reduced to precious signs, powers and planets. These creatures posing in their glass houses are gods and masters. Eden belongs to them" (Ducornet, *Monstrous and the Marvelous* 72). According to Purcell, collection jars when placed in light, open "up into rooms" and "extend outward" (quoted in Ducornet, *Monstrous and the Marvelous* 73). Ducornet indeed explains how Purcell's work rethinks the aesthetics of collection:

> By 'systematizing' junk of all kinds—antique bars of soap, fractured machines, bones, beaks, books devoured by worms or fire or made into nests by rats, toys rusted nearly to oblivion, partially digested pins—Rosamond also creates bogus collections, marvelous museums of the mind. Disrupting the closed systems of public or private collections (of naturalia—including anomalies—and artificialia) and reorganizing them, she elaborates novel ways of ordering, articulating and dreaming the world. (*Monstrous and the Marvelous* 73)

There is a definite edge to Purcell's practices, which challenge the politics of ownership and reflect upon the pursuit of forbidden knowledge. Her work ultimately creates a liminal space of performance where the fictional blends with the real, giving way to a space of dream (Ducornet, *Monstrous and the Marvelous* 31).

The title of *The Jade Cabinet* emphasizes Ducornet's shared fascination with Purcell's investigation of the ethics of collection, and the novel proposes a semi-fictional frame in which a storyline serves to thread together a seemingly incongruent array of characters and places. The functioning theme that ties this "collection" together is memory, particularly the imperfections of memory in its re-imagining of time. The question of remembering is the organizing principle of any cabinet of curiosities. The narrator's name, Memory, highlights this in a metafictional manner, while also bringing the question of remembering to bear upon the status of fiction. Her words cast shadows upon the levels of truth in the story to come:

> *Memory*, wrote Mr. Beattie, *presents us with thoughts of what is past accompanied with a persuasion that they were once real.* The ambiguity so delighted my father that with my mother's permission I was named *Memory*—a curious coincidence considering this memoir which has seized the lion's part of my relic years. I write from the new century about the old, my purpose to reanimate planets that have long ceased to spin." (9)

Ducornet takes the trope of the unreliable narrator and conveys upon it a speculative dimension, casting Memory in the light of dream and imperfect perception. The reader is immediately introduced to a liminal space occupied by liminal characters, indeed a museum of memories of beings to be explored by the reader, as suggested by Memory: "There are those who say that the memory is like a collector's cabinet where souvenirs are tucked away as moths or tiny shells intact" (15).

In addition to acting as a structural principle, the cabinet of curiosities takes many literal shapes in the story, the most obvious of which is Angus Sphery's wondrous study:

> Father's study was an especial place. He had a library of lepidoptera pinned in rosewood boxes that are now lost—thanks to a certain odious creature (for the moment in the wings). In early childhood I believed Father when he said that these boxed creatures were books with stories written on their very bodies." (16)

Memory describes this space as an "enchanted playroom", a place of wonder, as opposed to the world of Radulph Tubbs. Tubbs's own remarkable "jade cabinet" is the central cabinet in the novel, and it also appears at first to enchant, but then evolves towards the invasion and ultimate contamination of the world of the Sphery family, with its "fabulous collection of jade" (26):

> As I have said, Tubbs's inheritance included a spectacular collection of archaic jade that caused much excitement at the High Table; indeed, for some time, Oxford gossip concerned itself with little else. Soon after the ebony cabinet and its precious contents were delivered to Tubbs's home on Bear Lane, Angus Sphery asked if he might see them. Tubbs sent a carriage off at once to fetch our father.
>
> The cabinet was Ming and of sober elegance, and the jade of such rare perfection that as he fingered them our father trembled. (29)

Its pieces are implicitly traded for Etheria, Memory's older sister, when she becomes the wife of Radulph Tubbs. This Jade Cabinet, initially associated with the imagination (Etheria revels in its marvels), veers towards monstrosity when Etheria is raped by Tubbs with a jade phallus from the collection, an act that leads to her disappearance "like a puff of smoke." (56). A double edge of wonder and violence indeed persists throughout the novel, such as in the freak show in which the hunger artist/Hungerkünstler draws her viewers to simultaneously marvel and shudder. This show, a sort of collection of human and animal curiosities, indicates the central dynamic of cabinets, which is to juxtapose and foster effects through abrupt dissimilarities: "INCONGRUITIES, MYSTERIES (66)": "They saw a lizard-man wearing nothing but a silver codpiece and a luxurious pair of mutton chops; a horned pig, its horn and hooves stained crimson; a woman who claimed four supernumerary nipples and who, for the price of an auxiliary ticket promised to remove her blouse" (67).

The notion of the cabinet of curiosities pervades the narrative on the story level, while also acting as a powerful metaphor interlaced with storytelling; thus the parallel between memory and the cabinet. Yet, as Memory observes, the act of remembering moves beyond the static quality of the collector's cabinet: "As I write this it occurs to me that for each performance of the mind our souvenirs reconstruct themselves. The memory is like an act of magic" (15). It is this sense of magical performance that infuses Ducornet's fictional "cabinet" with its ethical relevance, as this collection of characters and places comes to live and mutate in the reader's imagination.

Speaking is intertwined with storytelling as a conceptual thread, and the central idea of air is openly associated with the act of speech in the epigraph to the novel, a quotation by James Beattie from *Elements of Moral Science* (1790):

> Human voice is air sent out from the lungs, and
> by the windpipe conveyed through the aperture
> of the larynx, where the breath operates upon
> the membranous lips of that aperture, for as to
> produce distinct and audible sound in a way
> resembling that in which the lips of the reed of a
> hautboy produce musical sound when one blows
> into them" (7).

There are also startling juxtapositions of speech as opposed to muteness throughout the text: "Etheria grew up speechless and yet for all that tremendously clever" (12). Memory and her sister Etheria are placed in metafictional complementarity with each other, with one being the voice of the narrative, and the other being the absent presence that haunts the novel. Etheria's silence heightens an awareness of the unstable language of the visible world: "Etheria knew that the visible world was little more than an infinite game of castles in Spain built in the air with the same building blocks over and over again" (13). Her speechlessness is also contrasted with Memory's loquacity in a dynamic pairing that can only deepen speculation about language. As their names suggest, one is the voice, and the other, air, with Etheria ultimately disappearing while Memory remains on to draw the contours of Etheria's gradual disappearance through storytelling: "As it was, we were loving friends, accomplices, never rivals. I was her chief interpreter, which made up for other insufficiencies" (14). Etheria, in her absence, is the silence of language, perhaps a form of the "mute speech" or *parole muette* Jacques Rancière has referred to in his 1998 book of that title. Together, Memory and Etheria represent the very action of literature, as silence, ellipsis and gaps work alongside words to create an aesthetic effect.

The presence of Lewis Carroll in the overtly historical figure of Dodgson in the novel adds more nuances to the reflection about language. He is a singular figure, one of many in the collection framed by the novel, and his presence suggests meanings that extend well beyond the context of the novel, which is Victorian England in an age of expanding industrialization. He appears as the figure of play with language that underlies the narrative, and is also depicted as a figure of freedom and innocence associated with childhood. He gives gifts to the girls and engages them in whimsical word games, evident in their discussions of oversized vegetables at the Fruit Fair in the beginning of the novel:

> Margaret Sphery: 'Now see what you've done! He's quite green with grief!'
>
> Myself: 'Poor thing! He did *so* dream of being elected to Parliament.'
>
> Dodgson: 'Yet I've told him one hundred times if I told him once: there are enough pumpkinheads as it is!'
>
> Pumpkinhead! We delighted in such words. Threadneedle Street. Ned Nettlebed. A game called 'Hazard.' Jokes such as:
>
> Q. What is the *fastest* cut of beef?
> A. The brisket! (21, italics in original)

Dodgson is associated with a delight, wonder, and creative play. The novel foregrounds the influence of Carroll's nonsense:

> We returned home clutching sweets in screws of
> paper, happy but exhausted, our nostrils rimmed
> with dust. The following day Mr. Dodgson sent us
> a wonderful drawing of oysters munching hay in
> stalls and 'resting up,' he wrote under, 'for the
> race. Next year we'll stay for the race, but as it
> takes them a *very* long time to run (they haven't
> any feet you know), *this* year's race is always *next*
> year's race anyhow. So you see, my darlings, you
> haven't missed a thing.' And he included a
> receipt which 'has been proven to cure 'olds,
> weasels, hopping cough, the bumps, chicken
> rocks, the vague hills and *growth*.' (22, italics in
> original)

Memory's joyful portrayal of Dodgson also challenges commonly held notions and doubts about Dodgson's relationship to young girls. In a 1998 interview with Ducornet, Sinda Gregory comments on the "politically incorrect" nature of Ducornet's fictional Dodgson, and Ducornet explains her need to move beyond received ideas: "I researched Carroll very carefully, and there is nothing in any of the loving reminiscences of the women who were his child friends to imply that he was *voyeur* or abusive in any way. In fact, several insist upon the joy it was to kick off their boots and run around naked!" (137). Ducornet actually sees Carroll as being essentially a little girl himself:

> If everyone knows how much Carroll loved little
> girls, not everyone knows that he loved them so
> much he signed his first published poems *Louisa
> Carolina.* Perhaps, as is my conviction, he *was* a
> little girl disguised by fate as a cautious don with
> a sweet, sad face and flyaway hair—a stutterer,
> deaf in one ear, who idolized Euclid and talked to
> himself." (Ducornet, *Monstrous and Marvelous* 59)

His character, in both his historical and fictional identity, connects with the concept of freedom of perception that moves through the book, with the breaking down of boundaries and a celebration of the power of wonder, as evident in Memory's comment about naked play:

> By the by: I feel it is fitting that I say here what an utter delight it was to run about in Dodgson's cosy rooms unfettered by buttons and braces; to try on all manner of odd tatters, to sit, enlaced by Etheria or plaiting the cloud of her hair before an imaginary seascape, whilst Dodgson told stories about the trials and tribulations of shellfish and sea turtles; how—this I remember well—an eagle enamoured of an eel sent her a new box of croquet balls which she took for a case of Moroccan oranges. The story ended tragically (25).

Freedom ultimately comes from the ability to exist in "constant mutation" a process Ducornet associates with the modes of nonsense (Gregory and McCaffery 138). As such, nonsense "ridicules pompous, vain, and obsessive behavior" (Gregory and McCaffery 138).

It is certainly for this reason that Dodgson is placed in opposition to Radulph Tubbs. Tubbs epitomizes boundaries of the mind, and suffers from a closed imagination associated with the industry and factories of the Victorian age: "Radulph Tubbs was the grandson of a catsmeatman and a corkcutter, yet the smoke from the factories he inherited from his father—a daring, determined rascal who 'single-handed grasped his life by the bootstraps of his will'—is breathed by Englishmen and Englishwomen of all ages everywhere" (23). Dodgson on the contrary represents a freedom of the mind, a creative spirit at play with language and mutable worlds. His energy feeds the imagination, while that of Tubbs teems with capitalist annihilation and closure. According to Memory and Etheria, Tubbs has the "imagination of an oyster" (37). For example, as the figure of rationalization and intellectual control,

Tubbs orchestrates the destruction of the gardens in which Etheria thrives, thus contributing to her ultimate disappearance. His capitalist impulses also indirectly destroy Margaret Sphery, as she falls victim to illness, presumably cholera, after a visit to one of Tubbs's factories. She evolves towards a state of madness, and here is presented through the eyes of Tubbs:

> Just then a thunderous crash resounded from the hall where a weighty collection of mounted Amazonian butterflies had been unwittingly torn from its nail by Margaret Sphery, who appeared panting and unassisted, her red eyes beaming forth from their purple sockets, her mouth screwed into a concentrated blister. Trembling on her feet she held on to picture frames and furniture as the housemaid stood too shocked to put down her platter of curry to assist her mistress. When Margaret Sphery abandoned her moorings and plunged headlong into the room, Etheria and her sister leapt up to catch her. But the madwoman flayed her long, silvery arms to chase them off and, perambulating like a bewitched windmill, approached the table, gasping for breath. (60)

Under the influence of Tubbs, the world closes down, and is reduced to a space where madness proliferates.[2]

Given his predilection for tyranny, it would be tempting to propose a feminist reading of Tubbs. Memory comments on his "almost caricatural virility" (63), and one even senses narrative traces of the fairy tale, and forms of patriarchy such as those found in 'Beauty and the Beast.' Angus Sphery indeed virtually sells his daughter to the beast (Tubbs) for jade, much like the merchant in certain versions of 'Beauty

---

2 There is a repetition of tyrannical figures throughout the tetralogy.

and the Beast.'[3] Aspects of 'Bluebeard' also appear, as New Age looms forth as a sort of Bluebeard's castle: "Tubbs's house of routines and ubiquitous servants and sudden, dark eroticism imposed a solitude of an entirely different order" (49). There is discussion of keys to the garden and the jade cabinet (49), where Etheria's curiosity is punished by the act of rape. The dark roots of the fairy tale, elements of fantasy, and traces of nonsense are interlaced with reflections on power and abuse of power in the novel. Ducornet indeed also sees in the nonsense of Carroll a link between tyranny and language: "To a very great extent *Alice* is all about the irrational use of language by tyrants. Humpty Dumpty is a terrifying figure, for example, insisting that words have no intrinsic meaning" (Gregory and McCaffery 138). A reflection on certain forms of masculine despotism appears to hang over the entire novel.

Yet Ducornet's aesthetics seek not to propose clear criticism, but rather to open the reader's mind for reflection. Tubbs undergoes a transformation, ultimately seeking forgiveness for his actions, and living the final years of his life in the company of Memory. Fragments from his own memoirs are scattered throughout Memory's narrative, in a provocative, and often troubling, foregrounding of the oppressor's voice, as he literally gives his words to Memory: "'I thought,' said he, 'that your order-loving and gentle eye might find some sense of truth in all this and even, perhaps, the manifold potentialities of my own soul'"(153). He is thus set forth in a rich complexity as tyrant, pederast, rapist, and reformed patriarch, another oddity in this *cabinet*, as he mutates before the reader's eyes. The self-reflexive quality of his writing indicates a developing consciousness of masculine abuse of power:

> If I choose to tell my story it is because with age I
> have come to consider that all men are one man;
> that my story might have been yours, and yours
> mine. Are we not all ruled by the same
> treacherous emotions, the same pitiable

---

3 One is reminded here, for example, of the merchant father in Angela Carter's version of 'Beauty and the Beast' in 'The Tiger's Bride'.

> vanities, the same blindness? Have we not all
> ruled our wives, our concubines, our children
> with tyranny more or less disguised; do we not
> live our lives with the laborious futilities, the
> devastating shortsightedness of moles? (45)

Ducornet's characters, despite their archetypal quality, are indeed more complex than they at first appear. They are set forth as clusters of ideas cloaked in human form, yet they are also portrayed enigmatically, in a manner that allows for gradual transformation and defies easy interpretation.

The character of the *Hungerkünstler*, for example, appears as a female figure of consuming appetite. She is perhaps the literal incarnation of Ducornet's 'Death Cunt of Deep Hell.' In her essay of the same title, Ducornet explains how the concept is developed in Pasolini's adaptation of Sade's *120 Days of Sodom*: "Pasolini's storytellers introduce the idea of the Death Cunt, a gnostical perception of the female body as seduction, a lethal detour of the spirit leading to enslavement: the cunt as snare, prison, and coffin" (Ducornet, *Monstrous and the Marvelous* 82). The *Hungerkünstler* embodies the destructive female energy of the "death cunt," and literally eats her way through this cabinet of curious figures, whirling in a wave of devastation through the lives of Angus Sphery, then Tubbs, and finally Baconfield, and ultimately attempting to murder Etheria. As an artist of hunger, she is the figure of desire gone awry; she devours men and food. She is painted into the story as a sort of primal, fierce, monstrous force:

> She stood blazing in the firelight, shrunken and
> swollen in turn, mistress of one million shades, the
> innumerable phantom moths of shadow which
> inhabited the air she breathed. She was very small,
> under five feet, and she was standing stiffly in a dress
> of white brocade, once sumptuous, now threadbare
> and soiled. She looked impoverished, yet her peculiar
> eyes expressed a fixity of purpose, and the faint smile

> which informed her face was coloured by a bitter irony
> so black it caused Etheria to shudder. (68)

Like Tubbs in the early stages of the novel, she wreaks havoc on the Sphery family. Under her influence, Angus Sphery disappears into madness:

> 'And she . . .' he mused, 'speaks a unique tongue,
> inspired, evidently, by divine intuition—for
> where could such an impoverished child pick up
> Chaledean? Zend? Patilavi? Parsi? I . . . I thought
> I caught something of *Old Chinese!*' he whispered
> with awe. Turning about he took his leave of
> them muttering:
> '*I must* return to her tent!' Away Angus
> Sphery stumbled, and his face was that of a man
> lost in an opium dream. (69, Italics in original)

Sphery appears as the *savant fou*, of the novel, as he sees the Eden of language in the *Hungerkünstler's* disjointed discourse. She heightens Angus's disappointment in Memory's practice of earthly "unnatural speech," and the reader is led to gradually understand how Memory's narrative points to an infinitely receding Eden: "But ever true to his vision of Eden, it saddened Father that I was learning what he called 'unnatural speech'" (13).

The notions of language and power indeed plague the characters and objects in this rattling cabinet. "The fever of language had claimed them all" (70) are the words that begin chapter 9, and there is an accumulation of reflections that cannot be pieced together to form a coherent speculative puzzle, but rather, in the spirit of the "cabinet," allow incongruent concepts to rub against one another in explosive ways. The reader is invited to piece together the playful word games of Carroll, reflections on the power of the hieroglyphs of Egypt, the metafictional asides of Memory about her narrative, the *en abyme* memoirs of Tubbs, brief fragments of Etheria's notes and diaries in both

Memory and Tubbs's writings, and Radulph Tubbs burning of one of Dodgson's manuscripts, presumably the manuscript of his "Alice" book. Language is indeed depicted in the novel as being complex, and fleeting, and associated with violence. Etheria animates the silent spaces that surround such violence in the narrative, whether it be the anger of her parents' exchange upon her father leaving her in a field so as to experience the language of nature, or the abuse of Radulph Tubbs. Through the narratives of Memory and Tubbs, she ultimately finds magic as a form of silent expression, and makes herself disappear.

Numerous ideas about language are collected here. The *Hungerkünstler*'s ravings appear as a nonsense language pushed to tyrannical extremes, and Angus Sphery loses himself in the "hum" of primal language:

> 'If I could discover the origins of language . . . I would know the origins of mankind. Mankind and . . . his myths! Simultaneously! The roots of the imagination and . . . *all its fruits!* The sciences, yes, and the arts. Because . . . Language is the Imagination! Language is Memory! And the brain . . .' he pondered, 'the brain is like a gigantic hive . . . it *hums!* It hums the music of the spheres. (69)

His reflections extend to force of language, suggesting that hieroglyphs, for example, are figures of "magical potency" that can allow "the thing signified to spring into being,"(36), or even the reverse in the case of Etheria, as observed by Memory: "Deep down I knew I should never again see Etheria, for if, as our father Angus Sphery believed, there exists a Divine Tongue capable of bringing all things into being, *the opposite is also true.* Etheria had found the Word, surely a silent one, that had caused her to vanish forever from the life of Radulph Tubbs" (153-154). In addition, Baconfield, the proponent of reason and order in the beginning of the novel evolves into a shaman-like figure who, in emerging alive from the underground tunnels of the pyramids, "reads" nature's language around him:

> He intuited a constancy in the disorder of the air
> and in the ebb and flow of village life: the
> braying of donkeys, the moaning of camels, the
> clouds of bats and mosquitoes that every night
> engulfed a minaret of mud, the shrill games of
> restless children and squabbling of wives, the
> migrations of the vermin that infested his own
> face, the random patterns of the flat beans and
> congealing butter in his bowl, the scuttlings of
> scorpions in the cracks and shadows of his walls,
> the frequencies and intonations of the cries of
> pigeons flocking together in their square towers
> or circling the tiny hamlet and its
> Brobdingnagian palms which, at this season,
> were laden with dates as smooth and as yellow
> as amber beads. (112)

Baconfield epitomizes the disruption of not only order, but also disorder, upsetting the binary until the reader hardly knows what to think. The novel indeed indicates a veering into madness associated with language on many levels, but this madness is not of pure psychological value, but is also the madness and disorder of nonsense, with its own forms of disjunctive logic.

The reader navigates this vertiginous space of fictional curiosities to create a "cabinet of the mind," with its rough juxtapositions of characters and ideas (Egyptian pyramids, Lewis Carroll and nonsense, Jade Cabinets, Eden . . .). The reading of *The Jade Cabinet* recalls the reading patterns proposed by *Alice in Wonderland*, in that the narrative laces the characters and story elements together with bumpy transitions and juxtapositions, and sense and logic coexist uneasily with nonsense and disorder. Like in Carroll's world, the reader is led to leap from riddle to concept to character type, and is invited into a fictional universe of mutable ideas that are engaging, but also fleeting and ultimately impalpable according to the ordinary rules of logic. Such are the ethics of Ducornet's imaginative cabinet of the mind. In her collection of seemingly incongruent characters and ideas, one is also reminded of the dynamics of the Surrealist collage, a collage of surprising effects, and piercing violence, leading the reader to "be beed", according to Ducornet's words, that is to "be stung into a reverie of acute wakefulness and watchfulness; to be struck alive with wonder" (77).

In Ducornet's writing we are therefore caught between word and world, and invited into the intensity of the relationship between the two. In 'The Deep Zoo' Ducornet explains how "ideas and language deserve our chronic, our acute attention. After all, a book is above all a place to think, and the lightness of thoughtfulness our way of approaching the truth." This is the truth of "dream," such as that Ducornet celebrates in the work of Ben Marcus (*Monstrous* 73), a truth that moves beyond current thought, and challenges the traditional collection to propose a fictional "cabinet" whose aesthetics are saturated with ethics:

> We must take care that our books do not resemble those 17th century wonder-rooms or 19th century parlors with their meaningless jumbles of stuffed bears, kayaks, giant lobsters and assorted stools. In other words, just as the museum of Natural History has contributed to, perhaps enabled our practical knowledge of the phenomenal world—and do not forget that the development of the museum coincides with the exclusion of Christian orthodoxy from the process of scientific inquiry—so must the books we write be free of those restraints that impede aesthetic invention; so must they be enabled by the rigors of intellectual coherence ('The Deep Zoo').

Ducornet thus calls for "an eager access to memory, revery and the unconscious—its powers, beauties, terrors and, perhaps above all, its rule-breaking conventions" ('The Deep Zoo'). *The Jade Cabinet* demonstrates such an investigative ethics, similar to that what Ducornet perceives in the work of Purcell. Ducornet's cabinet of ideas indeed seeks to challenge closed thinking and avoid smooth conceptual clarity. It attempts to probe the recesses of knowledge, to reveal what we do not know about language and the world, to "move from the street —the place of received ideas—into the forest—the place of the unknown" ('The Deep Zoo'). The "air" of this last element in the tetralogy can thus be found in the act of becoming lighter through thought, in the release from "received ideas and gravity-bound redundancies" ('The Deep Zoo'), as if freedom, like that of Etheria, can be found in a communion with the hidden recesses and silences of language and its powers, and in the revelation of the "wild beauty at the heart of things" (Ducornet in interview with Gregory and McCaffery 143).

Works Cited:
Carroll, Lewis. *The Annotated Alice*. Ed. Gardner, Martin. New York: W.W. Norton and Norton, 2000.
Ducornet, Rikki. 'The Deep Zoo.' *Fantastic Metropolis*. December 22, 2004. http://www.fantasticmetropolis.com/i/the-deep-zoo/. Retrieved 23 July 2012
---. Interview by Sinda Gregory and Larry McCaffery. 'At the Heart of Things Darkness and Wild Beauty: An Interview with Rikki Ducornet.' *The Review of Contemporary Fiction* 18:3. 1998. 126-144.
---. *The Jade Cabinet*. Normal, Illinois: Dalkey Archive Press, 1993.
---. *The Monstrous and the Marvelous*. San Francisco: City Lights Books, 1999.
Rancière, Jacques. *Mute Speech*. 1998. Trans. James Swenson. New York: Columbia University Press, 2011.

Ducornet in Dreamland: An Interview[*]

CAROLYN KUEBLER & RANDALL HEATH

Rikki Ducornet's work resonates with a fiery collision of highbrow intellect and scatological indulgence, yet always it is the ideas that matter. The destruction of nature, the traumatization of the child, the shackling of the transcendent, imaginary vision, are all detailed through a fascinating array of characters and situations. She has written a tetralogy of novels based on the four elements—Earth, Air, Water, Fire—and has published six books of poetry, two children's books, and a collection of short stories. Also a visual artist, Rikki Ducornet has illustrated books by Jorge Luis Borges and Robert Coover and exhibited her drawings and prints throughout the world. *Phosphor in Dreamland*, her most recent novel, portrays through a series of letters, footnotes, poems, and narratives, the history of the imaginary Caribbean island of Birdland. As hilarious as it is tragic, the novel presents, in the form of an ecological fable, a chilling tableau of extinction and the possibility of regeneration as we follow the life of Phosphor, a club-footed inventor poet.

We met Rikki Ducornet in her home in Denver where she treated us to hours of conversation punctuated with eggplant pizza, wine, and mango sherbet. She brought out her stereoscope and its accompanying pictures, and showed us artwork on her walls, some of it her own, some of it the photographic collages of Rosamund Wolff Purcell. We began our interview talking about Rosamund Purcell, whose artwork has been featured on the covers and endpapers of many of Rikki's books.

---

[*] From *Rain Taxi Review of Books*, Vol. 1, No. 1, Winter 1996. RT = *Rain Taxi*.

RT: How did you come to work with Rosamund Purcell?

RD: I met Rosie at the Bunting Institute. I had just come from France where I was working on a series of imaginary archeologies in clay, Tlönic objects, thinking of Borges's Tlön. When I arrived at the Bunting there was a show of Rosamund Purcell's, a whole exhibit of imaginary objects of natural history. It was stunning and I felt a profound sense of kinship. I was so impressed I left the Bunting dreaming of the things I had seen. That evening I passed in front of the Brattle Street Theatre where they were showing the films of the Brothers Quay—I had never heard of the Brothers Quay—but it was snowing so I went in and I saw four films that absolutely knocked my socks off. I sat through them three times. Then I walked back to the Bunting and left a note in Rosie's box saying, You don't know me, I've just arrived, and I would like to meet you and invite you to see the films of the Brothers Quay. In the morning I found a little note that said *Yes*, let's meet tonight. So we went and we saw the films, and when they were finished Rosie said, Can we see them again? After we watched them again she said, All right you've given me a real treat I want to give you a treat—have you ever had sushi? And I had never had sushi, so we had some very Quayesque sushi for dinner. That's how our friendship began.

RT: You both create worlds and images where natural history meets the imagination in bizarre, sometimes beautiful configurations. I've noticed that museums, especially museums of natural history, often show up in your books. The narrator in *Phosphor* visits a museum that gathers fragments from the island's history; a museum which was created as much out of terror of these objects as from delight in their beauty. There's a lot of tension there: while the museums are sort of deathly depositories of things that have been obliterated, they're also places of intrigue, of fascination with the magic in these objects.

RD: Yes, there is some tension there, and that is rooted in autobiography. My first confrontation with such things was on the Bard campus where I grew up. I was playing hide-and-seek one day and I ran into an open room which turned out to be the biology lab—a real *Wunderkammer* filled with a collection of fetuses, monsters, all kinds of things in jars. And actually when Rosie and I met we discovered that for both of us formaldehyde has an interesting and soothing odor because of childhood experiences in such places; we both have been inspired and haunted by them. Anyway, I immediately forgot about hide-and-seek and spent a couple of hours in there just captivated by what I saw. I saw a human fetus for the first time, a two-headed cat, wonderful things. As a child I loved such places and I dreamed of working for the museum of natural history, creating dioramas. There was an innocence to that fascination for a very long time, until I went to France and went to the museum of natural history near Austerlitz, a museum which has been there since the 1850s or '60s and has not been touched. On the downstairs floor they have an incredible display of what they call "compared anatomy." It starts with Siamese twins—I wrote about them in *Entering Fire*—but when I followed that entire display and saw things like baby orangutans literally crucified with all their guts showing, or the bladders of every animal floating in keeping medium, or kidneys, just one row of kidneys: an elephant's kidney, a giraffe's kidney, and so on; or the testicles of twenty different animals and the penis of an elephant sliced like salami, it suddenly occurred to me how horrible this science was, and how much it said about Western science and our crazy separation from the physical world, including our own bodies. As if one could really understand something that way, and not have to spend any time or energy admiring a chimpanzee in a tree, but instead kill it and dissect it, put its pieces in jars. That led to a horrific recognition that species had begun to vanish as soon as world museums wanted such things, and for that matter the *Wunderkammer* started that: princes wanting marvels for their collections.

RT: This collecting, preserving instinct is embodied in characters like Tubbs, Fantasma, and Fogginius who seem intent on obliterating the creatures in the natural world and preserving them for themselves.

RD: That's right. They exemplify an attempt to seize time in order to have control over the mutable world. I'm really interested in that existential problem. The terror of change is also the terror of death, the terror of being human for that matter, terror of freedom, all those things. Such terror is very dangerous. The world is mutable, you cannot seize and hold it, and if you attempt to the attempt will prove disastrous.

RT: Which describes Fogginius's experience in the jungle, when suddenly he can't stand any more of the wildness, the rampant growth and decay there. Which as I see it is also a fear of the feminine.

RD: Yes, the fear of the cunt, fear of hidden places, fear of the unknown but also fear of birth and death. As you know, it's a typical obsession for psychotic people to see toothed vaginas everywhere. It's very strange to me, because when I was working on *Phosphor* and then asked to do a lecture series on Swift, I realized that there were all these connections. Like Phosphor, Swift was also absolutely terrified of woman, woman exemplified death for him. Swift wrote poems about mortality, the horror of beauty dissolving. Did you know that in Swift's day, women used white lead as makeup and literally fell apart because of it; I mean their skin actually rotted, their teeth fell out, their hair fell out. They were killing themselves because of the lead, and the more they deteriorated the more lead they used.

RT: So, there was a big metaphor in those poems that was actually lived.

RD: Oh you bet. There's a real connection in Swift's mind between the vulva and the coffin.

RT: To embrace the feminine is to embrace death. Where does that come from? Is that a uniquely male experience?

RD: No, I don't think it is at all. My own reading of it is that it is fear of the other, it's fear of the stranger, fear of the unknown and the unknowable. And the other is always in some way unknowable, especially the other sex, or another "race." It's part of the same phenomenon of fearing a world that cannot be known and seized once and for all, but is in constant mutation. Which is also why peoples' marriages break up: the inability to accept that the other changes.

RT: Then doesn't that make the whole concept of marriage impossible?

RD: Not if people really have accepted, or have learned to accept the other's autonomy. The same thing is true for child-raising; you have to recognize from the start that though this is someone who needs you physically, literally needs you in order to *survive*, the child is spiritually an autonomous being. That has to be respected.

RT: Many of your books focus on a child growing up through traumatic experience. Some are foundlings, some are so abused; they're raped and beaten but they emerge, they move on. Charlotte learns to paint, she ends up being whole again. Phosphor, too. Fogginius beats him and stuffs him in a box but he comes out of it to be a liberated, self-possessed character as well.

RD: I think it's an immense problem that children are denied psychic autonomy and denied their perceptions, denied their capacity to fully imagine. I think dreaming and imagining is what is behind a truly free and creative human being. I was reading Bachelard recently, his *Poetics of Space*, and he talks about the potency of those spaces in which we daydreamed as children and how those dreams that take us back to the deepest places within ourselves are often dreams of those spaces in which we daydreamed as children. I'm interested in exploring that, too. I feel that all infants are born into the world for delight, to be free, that they are all potentially luminous beings, and that this potential or capacity is in some way or other stolen from them, kicked out of them. So many people's childhoods are fractured. There was a lot of violence in the village where I was living in France, violence against children everywhere, *it was in the street*, and that is also why I write about it so much. How we drive our children mad. And religion is part of it, all those evil justifications for parental authority backed by the church.

RT: That brings up the problem of orthodoxy as a force to control people's lives. In *Phosphor* the Inquisition is the force that silences the poet. The authorities confiscate the erotic, artistic images, but at the same time keep them for themselves to be viewed in secrecy. You often show the hypocritical, destructive powers of orthodoxy, and I'm wondering, what is your definition of orthodoxy?

RD: Inhibiting the other to be, to deny the other's autonomy, to create a world in which being is not becoming, but simply at the service of an idea. And the fear of individuals taking their own lives into their own hands, making their own decisions, dreaming, or, as [Subcomandante] Marcos says, waking from those dreams, stepping out to find others who share the same dreams, which means transforming the world.

RT: Which means going in different directions.

RD: And those directions are, if they're profoundly individualistic directions, liberating, libertarian, in the true sense of individual responsibility. With our market system, individuals are definitely in the way, because there's a kind of vision of a great machine, a machine animated by greed and total control, in which people are no longer perceived as human but as something that will feed into this machine, their lives are being defined in terms of utility, in terms of labor, and the same thing goes for landscapes. The natural world can be reduced to raw materials that have no intrinsic value. Orthodoxies have a tendency to deny intrinsic value, the spirit, the soul, and they're very frightening, they take such strange forms. I thought about this a lot in Algeria because it was so difficult simply to be a woman in Algeria. I became "the other" when I lived there. It was impossible to simply walk alone, it was much too dangerous. The kind of confinement that I was reduced to affected me enormously, and forced me to think about what it meant to all the women around me.

RT: Who never experienced anything else . . .

RD: Or those who had, only to be snatched away from school at puberty. In the city in which I lived young women committed suicide in massive numbers and yet that wasn't enough to convince their parents that they were doing something wrong. But I'm interested in the problem of power, also psychoanalytically, as it touches upon individuals. I'm interested in orthodoxy within family life, or repression within family life, and how that reflects the greater world, the social world. There's a very real connection there: if there is tyranny in the family it's reflected in the greater tyranny of society, and vice versa. I think it's no accident that our society seems about to self-destruct: the rage within the family is really a reflection of the rage within the community, the rage at a national level of the dispossessed of culture, and many in our country are *profoundly dispossessed of culture.*

RT: I also consider your works very feminist because women are equally strong, equally creative and destructive as men, but I wonder about feminism, how it too can become an orthodoxy, something dangerous.

RD: Yes, I think any orthodoxy is dangerous, feminism too. I came back to the states at one point, around 1976, at the height of feminist anger in this country, and a lot of women were giving up their boy babies for adoption. That was terrifying, and I don't think it lasted very long but that's what orthodoxy does: people stop thinking, stop thinking as individuals, and start functioning as an idea, *somebody else's* idea.

RT: Feminism is difficult to claim, there's no one definition for it, for one thing, but in trying to find one definition for it you end up putting a lot of people off.

RD: There can't be one definition. I think as a true feminist one is interested in everyone's liberty, the liberty of children, the liberty of men. And I think it should become a global vision so that as a feminist one isn't only concerned with women's issues but also with seeing the broader problem, which is political, ethical, ecological. I once got into a conflict at a writers' conference for having written about Cûcla, because I'm not an Amazonian Indian. There's this idea of appropriation of voice. I responded that to write from another culture or with a voice which is not one's own with responsibility is a generous act, a loving act. There's a lot of disagreement with that but somebody attacked me in a strange way by saying that cultures have a right to be what they are and that one should not question them, so that if clitorectomy is an institution in a specific culture, or the binding of feet, then that should be accepted by those on the outside. The implication was, well, if the greater society believes in this then it's right, which is horrendous, you know, and this curiously came from someone who considered herself a feminist. I think the issue is human liberty.

RT: I imagine the fact that Cûcla was very young, being a girl at the time of her love affair with Lamprias, was sort of a problem too.

RD: It's strange, you know, that hasn't come up. I thought it would. But in her culture, you know, she's a woman. And she instigates the love affair, she follows Lamprias around.

RT: I found it troubling, yet I also found myself questioning my own assumptions. I felt ambivalent toward the situation, which is part of what I like about the books, that there's no answer, they don't pretend to have answers. You present the issues without dictating what's right and wrong. In some ways I think orthodoxy is about only providing answers and not . . .

RD: . . . and not asking questions.

RT: One thing that's rarely mentioned is the humor in your writing. So much of it is absolutely hilarious. There's this blend of the real bawdy with the serious and weighty, the horrifying. I thought of Boccaccio and the lusty nuns.

RD: Well I love the bawdy, I love the world. So it comes out more Rabelais than it comes out Sade. What I really wanted to explore with *Phosphor* was the idea of sensual love. The other books are more about power and exploring the problem of abusive sexuality rather than looking at the Tantric notion of sexuality as liberating, transcendent.

RT: As with Extravaganza. Until she comes into her own, sexually, she's just a pretty, little, mute thing. Her parents characterize her as unsensual, as incapable of dreaming, yet it was just that she was untried. She hadn't emerged. But the character of Lamprias, who is a very sensual, exploring character, at the same time causes his family so much pain. He's absent both as a husband and a father which (not necessarily directly) creates this Septimus character, who is a horrible, bitter, angry character. So Lamprias seems to use up the people around him. He's a hero and at the same time he's troublesome.

RD: Well, that was something that I wanted to explore, too, I think. The dilemma of a sensuous man of that time getting involved with an utter nitwit like Virginie, which happened often because so many women were nitwits, they were fabricated nitwits. They spoke the gospel and learned by rote all these little phrases. Some of Virginie's phrases came from an actual book which was given to girls at the time, the *Manuel d'exercices*. I was intrigued with the idea, too, of the artist's dilemma, which is often about creating beauty but being isolated from family or isolated from the world in some way. So that's somewhat Lamprias's dilemma; he's created one of the world's most beautiful things, this hybrid orchid, and has followed his dream, and in so many ways he's an inspiring figure, and yet he leaves his son behind in the hands of his monstrous mother, so he also is responsible for tremendous havoc. He could be seen by some women as exploitative and yet I think he's kind of an innocent, and that he is a real life-giving force. I was really quite in love with him when I was writing this book, and I was trying to get across how someone could be like that, someone who loves women, who fucks women, and also worships them somehow, which also isn't politically correct, but is very sincere and life-giving too. He bungles without intending to and then is sensitive enough to recognize where things went wrong, which he ultimately does.

RT: You also place women in the promiscuous, sensual roles, like Odille, who was entirely vilified, who was murdered, in fact, by society. Was she sort of a Lamprias character who, being a woman, was entirely forbidden to be this way?

RD: Yes! That's a great connection. Odille was also a victim of some kind, a victim of her beauty, a victim of her need, of her lust for life.

RT: So she acted upon it and it destroyed her. But her sexuality was her only power, it was all she had.

RD: Yes, and to be a powerful woman then, too, was a dangerous thing,

RT: I'm also curious about Alicia Ombos, the woman whose work shows up in the footnotes of *Phosphor*. She seems to represent an academic language that's both enlightening but also ludicrous, and I was wondering where that came from.

RD: A lot of that came out of my work on Swift. I wanted to find a kind of heightened language to write about him, it seemed like the only way. It's such an extraordinarily grotesque world portrayed by Swift so I stole a lot from my own notes.

RT: I thought that voice might be one of yours.

RD: It was, but then I did play with it so that it's further heightened and contained, and even more baroque than it was originally.

RT: I loved Ombos's line about Swift's imagination, how it pierces to deflate. Ombos seemed to have a real issue with Swift, like she was making an argument against him and for life.

RD: Well, for the sensual world. I found the connections between Phosphor and Swift so odd. Of course it makes sense that when I was investigating Swift I would be drawn to the very things that I was drawn to about Phosphor's personality, that those connections would be there.

RT: You were drawn to Swift, but at the same time didn't you find him very troubling?

RD: Swift? Yes, his is a scary vision. From what one knows about his life he never really could love, and that's another issue that interests me a lot.

RT: There are characters in your books who can never love, so fame and power replace that, but it usually ends up being a destructive use of power. Yahoo Clay completely resents everybody else because he is incapable of love. And yet *Phosphor* was very much a love story; love was what gave Phosphor his poetic voice and woke Extravaganza from her coma.

RD: Yes! Because I think it is what nurses the soul, what awakens the soul and without it one walks around numb, the living dead; it's a tremendous existential problem. I'm teaching Beckett, and also Bowles *Sheltering Sky*, which is such an extraordinary book, and Kafka; so much of the work is about that, the incapacity to love.

RT: Which is maybe an extension of being a cog in a faulty system of beliefs; being, like you said, dispossessed of culture. What do you think is the place of the arts in our culture? Where should they exist?

RD: I think the arts should exist everywhere. I think everyone should be doing it in one way or another; it is *par excellence* what enables us to function fully, and I think we are meant to be imagining beings, I think it is part of our makeup and I think we suffer terribly when we are unable to do that. There is so much need, too, for spaces, free spaces that are not only beautiful but quiet where one can truly think and dream, spaces where the imagination takes root. They're fewer and fewer. In the city very often there is some truck that's beeping or somebody's radio is on. On my worst days I feel there is this effort to make sure no one is imagining. We're supposed to be out buying not thinking.

RT: The media barrage sort of disrupts our dreams and replaces them with other, implanted dreams. You mention dreams often. How do they inform your own work?

RD: I find dreams essential and informing in all kinds of ways. One is simply that I look to my dreams to know what I'm really feeling about things, or to understand a complex situation. The subconscious picks up all sorts of things and the dream is a way of revealing them, a kind of window. But I'm very much a lucid dreamer so I write my dreams down very often, and I do a lot of dreaming as I'm writing. Many books have either been precipitated by dreams, or characters have revealed themselves, plot twists have made themselves clear in dreams.

RT: So is there some level of truth in the subconscious that comes out in dreams but otherwise you might not see?

RD: Oh definitely I think so. I had an amazing dream the other night actually, so interesting in terms, of what I left behind when I left Europe, and what I have been given since I have been here. I was in Paris, in the brocanteur antique sellers' quarter at dusk, and one place intrigued me. I had to go downstairs to get into it, and down in this cellar room was an amazing box. It contained an old game of cubes with lithographic colored plates covering the surfaces. The gilt on the outside was very old, it was coming off in my fingers. There was a glass cover and beneath it a *commedia dell'arte* image, an etching that was very old and worn. There were gilded letters behind the glass. At first I thought they were Hebrew letters, that it was some kind of cabalistic text, but then I looked again and they were Norman peasant words, a species of lexicon. Looking at that object I was tremendously moved, and I thought yes, one could write a book just looking at this box. Then the scene shifted to Mexico, because Mexico is what has replaced Europe for me in some odd way, or is beginning to. I was swimming in a sacrificial pool and my lover reassured me it was safe, and he also reached into the pool and he brought out a beautiful Mayan head of clay in absolutely perfect condition. It had a wild expression on its face —an expression of sexual delirium. The dream informed my whole day because for one thing I have been writing a story about France, a story about a marché, someone who grows vegetables, and even though it had nothing to do with the story specifically it fired up my mind and made France come alive again for me, the magic of all those old spaces that truly fed me there. Also I've become so interested in the Mayan culture which I hadn't realized was as complex and rich and gorgeous as the great cultures of Heian Japan and Song Dynasty China.

RT: Did much of *Phosphor* come out of dreams? The structure of it is so different from your other novels, being written as a history with letters on either side and woven into it, forming several stories at once. The narrator is in this growing love with Polly, the naturalist, and he's also really in love with Krishnamurti in some way, saying *I want to tell you about this, you must come visit!* I'm wondering how that came about. The characters are very imaginative.

RD: It just happened that way. It's hard to talk about because it involves a personal correspondence that I had with the man I'm living with now, who wrote me these wonderful Krishnamurti letters. In fact, the first one I received I didn't realize was from him; I received a few letters before realizing that Krishnamurti did not exist. I got these strange letters from Australia and I never checked the stamps! But I loved the voice of Krishnamurti and I imagined him and I was very disappointed when I realized he was imaginary. I said what, no more letters from Krishnamurti? And my lover said, Oh I'm sure there'll be more letters, and of course there have been more letters; so the novel came in a way out of that wonderful experience, much to my surprise. I didn't expect that to happen and it just turned out to be a very appealing vehicle for the book. I actually write all my letters by hand, and my novels, too. It's amazing the number of things I write by hand. When I did a review for the *LA Times*, I said, you know, I write by hand and the editor there said Fine, just fax it to me.

RT: Are you working on a novel now?

RD: I'm working on a book of short stories; it's the first time I've done this, actually. *The Butcher's Tales* were very tiny, some of them only one page, while these are much more classic, they're fifteen, twenty pages long. I'm loving it.

RT: All of your books contain a range of the very beautiful and ethereal, and the horrific, grotesque, and scatological. It's a really important balance, I think, and I find a lot of writing these days, or art, just focusing on the grotesque and not enough on the beautiful or the transcendent. It's all being mired in a certain sense of the ugly.

RD: There is a cult of the ugly and I think it's based on a tremendous misunderstanding: that because the ugly is the lowest common denominator it must be democratic. It's a horrendously dangerous way to view democracy. Aesthetics are also a part of human liberation. The aesthetic life. And I like to think that we are moral beings, and that this is important, something to be safeguarded. But we're living in a very amoral political system, which is based on exploitation, so that lack of value or concern for quality in life is filtering through to everything, including the artists.

RT: I found the end of *The Fountains of Neptune*, where Nicolas is completely immersed in his own world, to be one of the most inspiring, yet desperate scenes in all your books. What comes out of his energy, and his isolation, is this absolutely amazing world that he has created, and yet of course at the end it all gets destroyed by the angry housewives. It seems that no matter how hopeful some of these stories may be, somebody always comes and ruins everything. As in *Phosphor* when at the end the narrator is looking through the museum and he finds the funnel that they used to pour lime down the poet's throat. It's just horrifying.

RD: I've lived in so many places where horrendous things have happened; Chile, Algeria, and Egypt's another one right now, so it's not only a question of ideas that I know, intellectually, are wrong but viscerally, too. I often wonder about people I once knew, have they survived the terror? And it could happen here, I'm very conscious of the fact that fascism could happen here, and it is happening here, it's just not quite as evident, except in the prisons, and in the cities too, in subtle ways, and ways not so subtle . . .

RT: I feel this way and I sense somewhat in your books, too, that there's an inevitability of that progression toward destruction, in the same way that Phosphor's island has been destroyed, and the way World War II destroyed the village in *The Fountains of Neptune.* That's very troubling to me because it seems like that's just the way things go and what we're left with is a few fragments in a museum.

RD: Yes, well I know, it's an apocalyptic vision. At the same time, though, I get very excited by, for example, what's happening in Chiapas, because I also have this hope that something like that could be the seed of change. There are always others to pick up the lamp. There are always those who refuse the easy lies, the ways of death. The true poets of becoming, the true lovers of imagining, of erotic life, of liberty.

A Sentence for Rikki

LAIRD HUNT

While it would be tempting to land, butterfly style, on how beautifully and at what generous length, Rikki Ducornet read to us from Herodotus, during her visit to the University of Denver some years ago, and how incisively she commented on the so-called "father of history", who is also sometimes called the "father of lies"—which is to say his historical observations and concoctions make a perfect platform from which to launch a meaningful intervention on fiction, what Rikki had come to DU, where she herself had taught for many years, to do for us—I would rather plunge, hawk-style, out of the skies of my memory of that afternoon and onto the remarks she made in and around the edges of her consideration of Herodotus, about the extreme importance of virtual reality and the role it was going to play in the coming years in shaping the collective and individual imagination, and it must be said here that most of us present were thinking "virtual reality, really, that thing from the early aughts that made everyone lurch around with a headset on then feel sick and that we've now more or less forgotten?" and yet it was virtual reality, *really*, that Rikki spoke about at some real length, four or even five years before the recent Oculus Rift breakthrough and the second wave of virtual and augmented reality that we are experiencing now and that has tech magazine after tech magazine talking about how *everything* is about to change, and so as I rise again, back into the upper reaches of memory, claws covered in fur or feathers, I find myself marveling not just at Rikki's fiction (which is fierce and brilliant) or her essays (same) or her poetry (same) or her visual art (same) or her person (same) but at her ability to see years forward through the wreckage even of bungled shopping-mall-hosted technology to a future that I have no doubt, none whatsoever, that even now she is far, far ahead of.

The Word and the Flesh

TAMMY DASTI

Of all the world's numerous religions, Christianity has heavily influenced the arts, and of all the types of Christianity that have existed, none has been as powerful or as divisive as the Roman Catholic Church. Few other religious institutions have been such a powerful influence on western culture and history, and even fewer evoke such strong emotions within parishioners, both positive and negative. Those who remain within the folds of the church are eager to share stories about how their faith has helped to guide them throughout their lives, while those who have left are just as eager to point out how the church is out of touch, useless and possibly even dangerous in modern times. There have been numerous writers who have dismissed the importance of organized religion, including Sigmund Freud and the Marquis de Sade, to name but two.

Rikki Ducornet follows de Sade's example in dismissing the usefulness of the institution of the Church in her 1984 novel *The Stain*. Unlike de Sade, however, she replaces it with a more practical, useful religion based on the lessons learned from nature. The image of the Catholic church in Ducornet's novel is that of a rampantly corrupt institution that is totally out of touch with lives and the needs of its parishioners, while at the same time attempting to exact total control over the population through fear, misinformation, and intimidation. The image of God the Father is notable only by His complete absence from within the walls of the church. The God of Nature, by contrast, rules not by fear and intimidation, but through subtle signs and practical, life-affirming information. In *The Stain*, God is not absent entirely, as He is in de Sade, rather, He dwells in the details of Nature, not the church.

A student of the writings of the Marquis de Sade (whom she casts as a major character in her 1999 novel, *The Fan-Maker's Inquisition*), Ducornet has certainly been influenced by his opinions on religion and religious institutions. De Sade's writings are filled with characters who, while appearing to be pious in public, participate in countless sexual and immoral acts in private. In addition, de Sade uses his writings as a means of expounding his atheistic views of society, the world and the universe. De Sade (in character) writes: "[above] all, beware of religion, nothing is more apt to lure you astray than religion's baneful institutions" (*Juliette*, 19). For example, de Sade (in character) writes that the existence of God is a "fantasy" and that

> [...] God has its origins in nothing but the mind's limitations. Knowing not to whom or what the universe about is to be attributed, helpless before the utter impossibility of explaining the inscrutable mysteries of Nature, above her we have gratuitously installed a Being invested with the power of producing all the effects of whose causes we are profoundly ignorant. (*Juliette*, 29)

For de Sade, God is simply not needed, since Nature and the natural law is independent from religious dogma. He goes on to write:

> God nor religion [...] runs the universe [....] [Since] the universe runs itself, and the eternal laws inherent in Nature suffice, without any first cause or prime mover, to produce all that is and all that we know; the perpetual movement of matter explains everything: why need we supply a motor to that which is ever in motion? [....] We need not fret if we find nothing to substitute for

> chimeras, and above all let us never accept as cause for what we do not comprehend something else we comprehend even less. (*Juliette*, 43)

Like de Sade, Ducornet also holds the physical world as being of the highest importance, and she once said: "I love the sensual world, I love the body, and I love the physical, natural world", (Gregory and McCaffery) and that *The Stain* "is about the Christian idea of sin—the world and the body seen as satanic vessels" (Gregory and McCaffery), a facet of Catholic dogma which is direct contrast to her personal views. The idea of the body as sinful, a thing to be tamed and controlled, however, is fundamental to: "the Catholic tradition, you grow up being taught that the flesh is bad. The world, the flesh and the devil, those are your enemies" (Riley, 148).

This concept of the flesh as evil is personified by Edma, who constantly represses not only her own body, but also the bodies and physical needs of those around her. Edma frequently links physical pain and suffering to religious devotion and expression, first seen when she forces Emile and Charlotte into daily prayer on their "knees upon the unforgiving linoleum of the kitchen floor—daily torture for Emile, a seasonal sufferer of gout" (14). Edma does not stint on her own pain either, as shown in the scene where she takes Charlotte to church prior to the meeting between the Mother Superior from St. Gemmes School, and the Exorcist. After settling Charlotte in a chair and telling her to pray for the recovery of her voice,

> [...] Edma fell to her knees and made her way from the chapel down into the transept's north arm, down the north aisle and across the naive into the south aisle, the transept's south arm, the ambulatory and the aspe, and on into the axial chapels—[...] in a harrowing ritual that lasted well over two hours and left her panting for breath and her knees badly bruised. (67)

For her pilgrimage to Lourdes, Edma goes even further, crawling around the entire compound, being

> [...] satisfied only when her knees began to bleed [....] [....] [...] she knew from her pain that she, at least, was worthy of salvation.
>
> 'I'm bleeding for you, Lord,' she needled [....]
>
> Each day Edma traced the same itinerary until the flesh of her knees was mashed to jelly. By the time she was ready to go home, she could only stand with the help of a cane she had bought from one of the numerous souvenir shops. (94)

Edma also refuses to eat on her fourteen hour train ride to Lourdes even though she "packed a voluminous luncheon-basket" she is "unable to eat in public, before strangers, as if mastication was as much a sin as fornication" (92). Indeed, any type of bodily function is repugnant to Edma, who even poisons the domestic animals of the neighbours "which she despised for fornicating and defecating in public, in the street, without shame" (40). Edma's continual physical and verbal abuse of Charlotte, evident throughout the novel, is only suspended when Charlotte completely represses her own physical desires by refusing food and by frequent bouts of vomiting. Charlotte's tendency to vomit results in "unqualified sympathy from her Aunt Edma" who praises the child's illness and lack of appetite by exclaiming: "Imagine! The angel lives on water and air! The little nun" (52). This is, indeed, the only time in the entire novel when Edma praises Charlotte for anything. Even when Charlotte enters the Catholic school of St. Gemmes, Edma is more pleased with the fact that the child is "off [her] hands at last" (105) than with Charlotte's finally receiving a formal education.

While Edma's extreme repression of the flesh could be dismissed as religious fanaticism, her views on the connection between physical torture and divine grace are mirrored by Mother Superior from St. Gemmes school who sets out to meet Charlotte, not because the child is seen as especially devoted to Christ, but because Charlotte's "devastating [...] act of violence upon [her] mortal husk" (65) catches her attention. The Mother Superior "believed that it was only the punished bodies which received visits from God" (60) and so is convinced that "this child, dramatically marked from birth—who had *eaten glass*—was a rare clay body destined for Purification in the Fiery kiln of Beatitude" (60). Mother Superior is thrilled by Charlotte's act of self-mutilation, as she is convinced that it is the act of a future martyr, and the Mother Superior is "interested in Martyrdom professionally" (60) and she encourages Charlotte to emulate the physical suffering of other, "contemporary" (65) martyrs, whose feats of physical torture and self-denial are recounted to the child as examples of perfect piety. Indeed, Charlotte is told that if she is not judged "to be worthy to shine with" these modern martyrs by God, then Charlotte will be "excluded" from heaven and "God's Divine Grace: Excluded forever" (65) since Mother Superior believes "that the price of Redemption [is] Disgrace" (61). Mother Superior is thrilled to have found Charlotte, and feels certain that attending St. Gemmes will cause the child's spirit to "shine forth, illuminating God's Glory, the Glory of St. Gemmes and, above all, the Glory of the Mother Superior. Hallelujah! she sang within herself . . . What a prize! What a prize!" (65).

The repetition of the phrase "what a prize" creates the impression that Mother Superior sees Charlotte more as a prized calf at the county fair than a spiritual being in need of guidance. Indeed, Charlotte's spiritual needs and questions are completely ignored by both Edma and Mother Superior, both of whom are intent on using Charlotte for their own ends and whose treatment of the child is hardly virtuous. Indeed, de Sade (in character) pointed out that "the virtuous sentiment . . . is a low, base impulse that stinks of commerce: *I give onto you in order that I may obtain from you in exchange . . .*" (*Juliette*, 144). Edma's only concern is to keep the child from embarrassing her in front of the neighbours, while at the same time exacting pity from them for raising her orphaned grand-niece, while the Mother Superior wants to turn Charlotte into a holy martyr in order to elevate her own standing within the church. Neither has any concern for Charlotte herself, as she is just an instrument of their desires, a means to an end, rather than a young soul in need of guidance. Clearly, if Charlotte wants any kind of spiritual guidance in this world, she must look beyond the walls of the Catholic Church.

The appearance of virtue and duty, the appearance of piety, the appearance of devotion to God are all that matters for many of the characters in *The Stain*. Edma for example, decides that she will save the thick scabs from her knees after she returns from Lourdes as proof that "she, at least, was worthy of salvation" (94), while Mother Superior is only interested in how Charlotte's eventual horrific death as a martyr will glorify the Mother Superior by making her look better in the eyes of the Church Fathers. Edma even dislikes her local parish priest since "God knows a man who is satisfied with ill-fitting dentures cannot be trusted as a spiritual leader" (20). Appearance, however, can be deceiving and while it is clear that neither Mother Superior nor Edma are as pious as they might appear to be, Ducornet underscores the deceptiveness of appearance in one critical scene. During the first meeting between the Exorcist and the Mother Superior, the Exorcist attempts to impress the nun by incorporating several Latin quote into his conversation. For example, "*Ingentio formae damna rependo meae*" (75) and "*In toto corde meo exquisiui te . . .*" (78). The Mother Superior cannot resist adding her own Latin quote, and chimes in with "*Ignitum elquium tuum vehemnter*" (75). Since most readers are unfamiliar with Latin, and are likely to be more interested in the rather intense erotic game that the Exorcist is playing with the Mother Superior under the table anyway, these Latin quotes are most likely to be skimmed over by the vast majority. Even the narrator adds a quote at the end of the chapter, "*Dominus vobiscum. Ite, Missa, est!*" (80), a line that the reader would assume is a comment on the preceding chapter. However, once these seemingly learned quotes are translated into English, it becomes clear that none of them actually make any kind of sense at all. Rather, they are a literary hodgepodge of Latin words that are strung together in a way that appears to have meaning, but actually doesn't. For example,

"*Ingentio formae damna rependo meae*" (75) actually translates into: "Cleverly form condemnation to ransom meae". While "*In toto corde meo exquisiui te . . .*" (78) translates to: "Upon all together corde meo sought after you". Indeed, some words, such as "meae" and "corde meo" are not Latin at all. The Mother Superior's quote: "*Ignitum elquium tuum vehemnter*" (75) is no better, and means "unknown eloquent your violently." Even the narrator's Latin quote translates into so much nonsense: "Master you. Go, Holy Mass is!" The reader simply assumes that the characters and the narrator understand the meaning behind the Latin, not realizing that they are in fact, gibberish. In direct contrast to the important sounding, meaningless Latin is the quote from the opening of the novel, a quote that appears before the novel begins. Ducornet credits the quote as coming from "Jesus, the First Book of Jesu (from *Changing Concepts of the Bible* by Werner Wolff)" (6); however, the quote itself appears to be nothing but gibberish. It reads in part: "œaaa ooo zezophazazzaieozaza eee iii zaieozoakhoe" (6). When an interviewer commented on the nonsensical quality of this quote, Ducornet corrected her, saying that this nonsense "is a Gnostic mantra. Its intention is to empower the navigating soul as it passes the planets—all guarded by demons—on its way back 'home'" (Gregory and McCaffery). If one thinks of reading a novel as taking a mental journey, then the phonetic spelling of a mantra to guide the reader on their journey through the world of the novel is certainly appropriate.

Clearly, Ducornet is playing with the reader's preconceived notions regarding not only religion, but the writer's craft itself. The lay reader (as most are, since so few people understand Latin) assumes that the characters are using quotes and a language with which they are familiar, and certainly the reader would assume that the writer would also have inserted Latin quotes into a novel in order to serve a purpose. Indeed, the Latin quotes do serve Ducornet's purpose, but not the one assumed by the reader. The Latin appears to have meaning which it actually lacks, while the quote that appears to have no meaning, in fact, has a meaning. The same is true for the church itself, since the Mother Superior, Edma and even the Exorcist's belief in the Devil lends the

Church an appearance of credibility and purpose which it clearly does not actually have. None of these characters are interested in saving anyone's soul, not even Charlotte, and are only interested in using the authority of the church for their own purposes. Clearly, this is an atheistic view of the church, any church, regardless of denomination, as a decaying and corrupted institution which does not care at all about the people that it is supposed to serve; an institution that has long since outlived its usefulness.

Sigmund Freud, an avowed atheist like de Sade, referred to religion as "the universal obsessional neurosis of humanity" (*Future*, 76) he nevertheless also acknowledged that "religious ideas have exercised the very strongest influence upon mankind" (51). However, while de Sade encourages the complete rejection of religion as useless, Freud admits that "countless people find their one consolation in the doctrines of religion, and only with their help can they endure life" (*Future*, 61). Ducornet must have been keenly aware of how many people do rely on God in order to get through life, since, despite her criticism of the Catholic church, the image of God is not absent from *The Stain*. Again flouting reader expectations, Ducornet takes great pains to include images of a God who does not dwell within the walls of the church, but instead can be found in the natural, physical world. God may not be in his stone house, but that does not mean that He does not exist entirely.

According to Sigmund Freud, the purpose of any religion or culturally based moral system is threefold: "they must exorcise the terrors of nature, they must reconcile one to the cruelty of fate, particularly as shown in death, and they must make amends for the sufferings and privations that the communal life of culture has imposed on man" (*Future*, 30). Freud also adds "that the two main points in the modern educational programme are the retardation of sexual development and the early application of religious influence" (82). Throughout *The Stain*, Ducornet shows the Catholic church as failing Charlotte in each of these areas, save the last one, while the God of the physical and natural world fulfills these purposes. It is the God of nature who supports Charlotte and teaches her practical lessons that allow her to live and even thrive, while the church leaves her feeling frightened and alone.

As mentioned previously, both Edma and the Mother Superior repress the needs of the physical body as a means of becoming closer to God, since "it was only the punished bodies which received visits from God" (60) and the "world, the flesh and the devil" (Riley, 148) are the ultimate enemies of mankind. Flesh and the natural desires of flesh hold a special terror for them, as shown by Edma's fury with her neighbours' animals for "fornicating and defecating in public . . . without shame" (40) and Edma's praise of Charlotte's rejection of food (52). Rather than using religious teachings to exorcise the terrors of nature, Edma uses her own "unremitting hatred for the imperfect universe" (14) and the animals around them to inspire fear in the child and to frighten Charlotte into submission. The natural world is uncontrolled and dangerous, and even the garden is fraught with danger:

> Aunt Edma's yard, like a medieval forest, afforded little pleasure and much to fear. The charming, furry rabbits, munching comfortably in their greenwire hutches, were lascivious creatures given over entirely to the dubious delights of fornication. It was impressed upon Charlotte that the rabbits were diseased, that at any moment their ears would fall off, and that this malady was highly communicable. Charlotte . . . must not go near the chickens either, for fear they fly into her face and peck out her eyes, mistaking them for grubs. (34)

None of the animals around her are safe, and even Charlotte's stain is in the image of a dancing rabbit, one of the diseased, lascivious creatures that Charlotte must avoid at all costs. Indeed, the hare is seen as a symbol of the Devil (16) and is viewed by Edma as the mark of the sin of "licentiousness", a sin committed by Charlotte's mother which has been branded on the child.

The stain of the hare also becomes a social stigma which prevents Charlotte from attending school (35), and which Charlotte interprets as "a mark that God Himself had laid upon her to set her apart from the cruel, snot-nosed creatures who went to school" (36). While Edma is furious at the stain's existence, it is Charlotte's interpretation of its meaning that comes closest to Freud's concept of religion making "amends for the sufferings and privations that the communal life of culture has imposed on man" (*Future*, 30). Rather, Charlotte's religious interpretation justifies her exclusion and rejection of communal society, rather than making up for being a part of it.

While Edma impresses fear of the natural world upon Charlotte, Mother Superior impresses upon Charlotte fear of the afterlife by telling her that she will be "excluded forever" from God's Divine Grace (65) and therefore cast into Hell if Charlotte is not worthy of becoming a martyr. The acceptance of death is not merely a means to the end of becoming a martyr; rather it is portrayed as the ultimate state of perfection. In other words, Charlotte must be perfect in order to become a martyr, which causes the child to come to the conclusion that "to be as perfect as an egg, perfect people must be dead" (34). Rather than using religion to accept the inevitability of death, again as per Freud's suggestion, Mother Superior uses it to glorify and celebrate the possibility of a horrifically painful death to match Christ's sufferings. In the end, there is no aspect of the world which does not contain an element of fear. One really can't win for losing, so it is unsurprising that when Charlotte writes to the "Priories of the Convent of the Thorny Agony" (151) to ask to become a nun, that she begins her letter: "Dear Mother Marked by evil since birth, I have lived in horror of life and dream only of Salvation" (152). It is only towards the end of the novel does Charlotte realize "she had always been afraid, that it was above all fear, not faith, that was driving her on" (167).

The physical world of flesh and death, however one might try to repress it, will not be denied, and the result of religious rejection of that fleshy world climaxes in Charlotte's terrifying vision of God's pyramid temple constructed from "pieces of red meat, sewn together with thick, black thread, and that the whole thing stank of rotten chicken offal" (51). This nightmare edifice is the true "House of God" (51) a world of flesh, death and decay that cannot be denied. While the God of Nature presents His dark face as a counteraction to the attempts to repress him, both Charlotte and the reader have already seen his kinder side. The God of Nature first appears as Charlotte uses Emile's seed catalogues and the Bible as reading text books; Charlotte chooses to pray to "the Lord God, the God of the Tulip and the Tomato, the God of the Strawberry and the Scarlet Gem" (40). Charlotte also uses nature to illustrate lessons from the Bible, by using pastel crayons to draw "faces on the smooth pebbles . . . of the garden path" (38) these "pebble-people" become Biblical figures in Charlotte's games. God-the-Father is one of Emile's pails, who nevertheless punishes the wicked with as much severity as the Old Testament God, as shown when "God-the-Father" punishes the pebble Joseph by "dropping Joseph down the well —a punishment so severe that Charlotte was riddled with guilt for days" (39). Charlotte moves this severe God-the-Pail back into the shed, and covers "Him with rags so that he could no longer be witness to what she was doing. Yet, even when blinded and banished to a sunless corner, He continued to exert a weird influence. Whenever she thought of Him, a monstrous wing would blot out the sky" (39). The influence of the Old Testament God is "weird" to Charlotte's natural pebble-people, He is a "monstrous" figure whose capricious wrath is something to be feared and avoided at all costs. Rather than alleviating the fears of Charlotte and her pebble-people, this Old Testament God adds to them, just as the figure of God as taught by Mother Superior and Edma adds to Charlotte's "horror" of life and the world around her. Charlotte's attempt to reconcile these two images of God clearly demonstrates how one image is incompatible with the other. The God of the Old Testament is a monster who blots out the sky, while the God of the Tulip and the Tomato quietly answers Charlotte's prayers and provides all that the garden plants require to survive and thrive. The decaying pyramid of meat is, while an integral part of the God of Nature, is but one side of a much larger message.

Every religion needs a holy spokesperson from whom the parishioner can receive the divine word, and the same is true for the God of Nature, whose human spokesman on earth is Archange Poupine. Unlike Edma and the Mother Superior, Poupine not only accepts the natural world as it is, he revels in it by choosing to live within the woods rather than in the town. Poupine stands in direct contrast to Edma and the Mother Superior in that unlike either of them, he tells Charlotte "all he knew (and was there anything he did not know?) about life, love the seasons and dogs" (96). It is Poupine who tells Charlotte that her bleeding is not a kind of stigmata, as she believes, but means that she "can have babies" (170). This is the only instance where the Catholic church fulfills one of Freud's principles, namely "the retardation of sexual development" (82). Indeed, despite her rigorous education by the nuns at St. Gemmes, no one has told any of the girls anything about their approaching puberty. Therefore, when Charlotte begins her first menstruation cycle, she is at first horrified and then decides that it must be a kind of stigmata. It is only the "sensible" Poupine who realizes that such information is "damn . . . important" (173) and is willing to explain the reality of the situation to Charlotte. Even more specifically, he answers Charlotte's questions about her parents, while Edma "won't tell [her] anything" (98) about either of them.

Unlike the townsfolk, Poupine is unafraid of the gold coloured she-wolf that has been seen around town. He tells Charlotte:

> Wolves aren't like men [....] It's just famine that
> makes them cruel and that's the truth. [....] The
> roots of all things whisper together in the earth.
> The wolves know far more about the world (Oh,
> they know things!) than most people—living
> among the roots as they do. (97)

While the townsfolk, including Edma, see the wolf as a sign of evil, Poupine understands its ways and is unafraid of the animal. Even after the wolf attacks him, kills his dog and rips off Poupine's ear, he wisely harbours the animal no ill will, saying that the loss "doesn't matter" because he can "still hear the deer singing" (172). After all, it is only men who are cruel without reason, while the wolf only becomes cruel when it's starving.

Poupine knows "all the names of the wild flowers in the woods, roadsides and meadows" (98) and which plants of the forest can help heal Charlotte's broken arm "everything in these woods is a medicine or a mystery" (172) he tells her. The mysteries of the woods don't frighten Poupine, who recognizes the gold hare and the sulphur-coloured she-wolf for what they are; images of the God of Nature, they act as His messengers, His agents for change. It's a gold-coloured hare that Charlotte's father kills while his wife is in labour and it's this hare that stamps its image onto Charlotte's face (11); it's the sulphur-coloured wolf who humbles Poupine by ripping off his ear, thereby causing him to give up liquor (172); it's the gold hare who causes Charlotte to leap from the train and escape into the woods (168); and it's the hide of a yellow wolf that the Exorcist uses to disguise himself, thereby attempting to masquerade as a messenger of the God of Nature in order to justify his own madness and murders (186). Unlike the gilded gold of the church, the gold colour of the hare and wolf are natural gifts given to them by the God of Nature that marks them as His messengers, but only to people like Poupine, who are not fooled by appearance and who have the eyes to see these agents of change for what they really are. It is Poupine's practical lessons that ultimately save Charlotte, and the townsfolk from the Exorcist's murderous rampage. Charlotte tells Poupine: "You gave me the eyes, Archange, to see . . . to see how mad he was. Always" (189). It is the God of the Tulip and the Tomato who gives Charlotte the eyes to see what the Exorcist is, and the knowledge to survive without fear within the wilderness. Indeed, it is God of the Natural world as voiced by Poupine that allows Charlotte to at last become her own person, a creature free of fear and the physical suffering demanded by the Catholic church. It is only in the woods, away from the church, that Charlotte is able to find spiritual salvation.

While both de Sade and Freud completely reject the idea that there is a God of any sort, Ducornet clearly doesn't entirely agree with them. While her depiction of organized religion and Catholic dogma in *The Stain* is of a decaying institution more concerned with appearance and inspiring fear in the populace than with actual spiritual salvation, the idea of a Divine Being, however, is not totally absent, He is to be found in the natural world rather than within the walls of a church. The God of Nature is one who loves the physical world, who speaks to His followers through subtle signs and the wisdom of the body a deeply personal God who is more powerful and wise than the Old Testament creation. For a writer who follows in the footsteps of an avowed atheist like de Sade, it's an usually spiritual message and one that is not expected within the context of a novel like *The Stain*, again Ducornet flouts our expectations and presuppositions about her work, which makes her such a powerful and interesting novelist.

Works Cited

De Sade, Marquis. *Juliette*. Trans. Austryn Wainhouse. New York: Grove Press, 1968.
Ducornet, Rikki. *The Stain*. London: Dalkey Archive Press, 1995.
Freud, Sigmund., *The Future of an Illusion*. Trans. W. D. Robson-Scott, London: Hogarth Press, 1928.
Gregory, Sinda, McCaffery, Larry. 'A Conversation with Rikki Ducornet.' *Dalkey Archive Press. The Review of Contemporary Fiction*, Fall 1998, Vol. 18.3. Web. May 15, 2009.
Riley, Michael. *Conversations with Anne Rice*. New York: Ballantine, 1996.

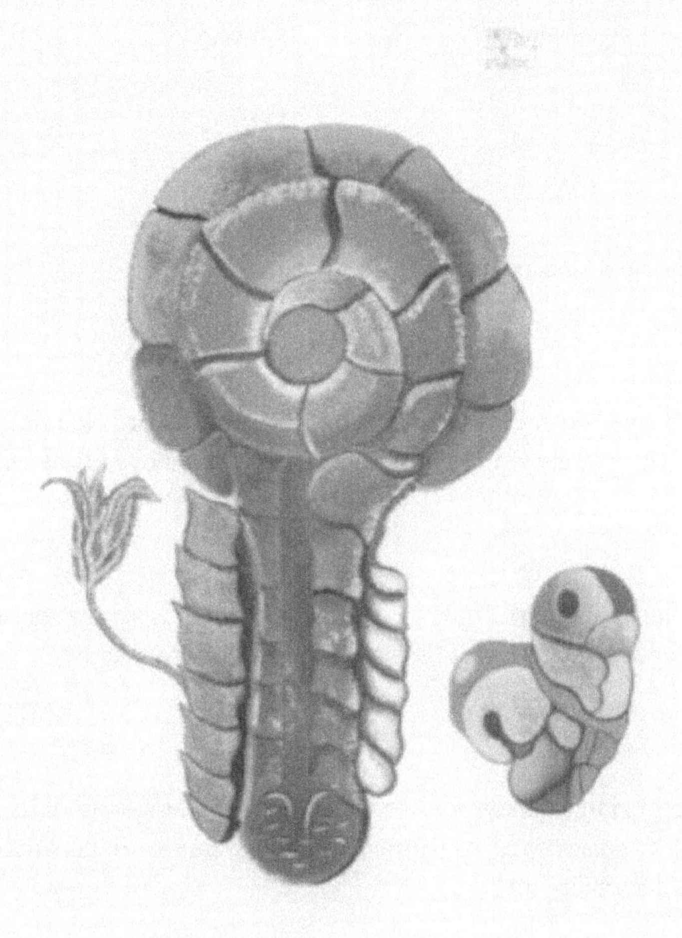

On Measurement

LILY HOANG

SPRING

Chinese New Year begins in the spring.

*

When I lived in Indiana, we neither sprung forward nor fell back. We stayed completely stationary while other states moved time without us.

*

Some music scholars argue that Vivaldi's *Four Seasons* are sonnets. Some go so far as to say Vivaldi himself composed those poems.

*

The Gregorian calendar was proposed by Pope Gregory XIII in 1582. The New Year was moved to winter, and leap years were calculated to the fourth decimal point.

*

Spring is an awakening. All that has been dormant wakes, as though Charming has pumped life through these limp bodies. Buds push their way through sleeping branches like birds know to begin their migration north when the days commence their elongation.

*

The scanning of music against a metronome that counts downbeats.
    There is no downbeat in words, just a series of accents that imitate an unwavering tick.

*

The pendulum clock was invented in 1656, and time learned some consistency.

*

Leap years are divisible by four.

*

The academic year begins in the fall when no other calendars begin there.

*

The stars say the year begins in the spring, with Aries.

*

Time, by Papal decree.

*

With only a pedestrian understanding of animals, I didn't know a ram is

a male goat.
  The way its horns spiral.

*

I have two apps on my phone for horoscopes. I check the Internet, too, to see if stars can be interpreted the same way. I find the most optimistic one and hold it close.

*

Celestial time.

*

I look to fate to determine my day.

*

Lunar time.

*

Any five consecutive months—excluding February and all its wackiness—contain 153 days.

*

Time must be taught. It's confusing.

*

There is no variable for time in physics.

*

Although its math is precise, time has the texture of magic.

*

Greece didn't accept the Gregorian calendar for centuries, but in 1923, the state relented.

*

Without a leap, it is called the common year.

*

Time standardized for trains and later for the bombs of the Great War.

*

Before, you boarded a train in London and arrived in Paris without synchronicity. It could be any time at all.

*

I played the second movement of "Winter" my sophomore year of high school. An articulation of loneliness, sound compressed and released my desolation.

*

Largo is defined as a direction. Its slow movement, 40-60 beats per minute.

*

The human heart pounds softly against the ribs at 60-100 beats per minute.

*

Andante versus largo.

*

But in his score, Vivaldi marked the second movement of "Winter" andante, which is 76-108 BPM.

*

Time by rotation: of the moon like uniform cogs.

*

Winter used to be faster.

*

Under the Julian calendar, a year lasted 365.25 days. According to the Gregorian calendar, the year was only 365.2425 days long, reducing the year by ten minutes, forty-eight seconds.

*

Up to 68 beats per minute faster: a whole heartbeat's worth of time.

*

The Common Era or Current Era or Christian Era: time measured through religion.

*

Time neglects to honor Eastern traditions.

*

Composed around 1720, time had accepted the Gregorian calendar, but *The Four Seasons* revolts, stands in the past, untaught.

SUMMER

In Port Townsend, reclined in a park overlooking the farmer's market and behind it the ocean, Rikki Ducornet and I eat salmon burgers. She says, "I don't like this boyfriend of yours."

"No one does," I say. And, "But I'm in love."

"Do you really want him in this book?"

There's so much green here: the grass, the trees, the whole Pacific opening into Rikki's serious eyes.

And of course she was right about everything, which becomes this revision.

FALL

According to the stars, August ushered in my house of true love.

If I was single, I must meet the man of my dreams in these next two months. It was a command, or, a threat.

If I was in a relationship, it will be true.

*

According to the fortune-teller in Brooklyn, I need to be patient.

Selah tells me to wait.

*

The academic year is already boiling deadlines, and I determine that all of my focus needs to center on my breaking relationship.

I constantly go looking for love, searching for men to fix and mend, like rags can become ball gowns, and there are only cotillions and proms and gay bars left for dancing.

I look to tarot for guidance. I turn to a Magic 8 Ball to tell me if Harold loves me, if he ever did. "Reply hazy. Try again," it says, and I do. "Better not tell you now." I shake my phone, ask, "Does he love me? Yes or no," and a pop-up says, "Out of energy. For premium—" and I press no. I will try to remember to remind myself to try again in an hour, but I will forget about the whole thing until tomorrow when I will begin the whole ritual anew.

*

In August, I found out that Harold was an infidel.

So I put my relationship on pause to tryst with another man.

*

Before bed, I check my horoscopes again and compare my day against fate's predictions. If there were another Lily, this is how her day would have gone: she would have been patient with the old man, despite his insults; she would have visions of great authority, but she would be wary of sharing them with those she does not trust; she would meet her true love. Whereas my day was quiet and full of typing. There was no excitement, nothing monumental or even special. Another Lily had a magnificent day, though, and she may not even realize it, because to her, it's just a day like any other—because she doesn't get to see just how spectacular her life is from my eyes.

*

The fortune-teller in Brooklyn sold me a crystal for ten dollars. She told me to exfoliate it with sea salt and put it in a window to absorb the sun. "Like we need vitamin D," she said.

*

I went to a New Age boutique to buy the hematite Selah told me would protect me. The stone was cradled in copper wiring. I bought a simple silver chain to hold it around my neck.

Thinking it might fix us, I left it in Houston on Harold's back porch.

Months later, I will find it in his bike bag and assume he was planning on giving it to another girl—the *other* girl.

*

I am being patient. I wait.

*

After an interview that I grand-slammed out of the stadium, I went to a fortune-teller in Old Vegas. She used an angel deck and flipped over the cards very quickly. She spoke of God's fate.

I didn't get the job she promised me, and the sun sits low in every desert climate.

*

Months later, when Dorothy helps me clean my room, I find the crystal buried in a tote bag. I throw it away because it is just another piece of packrat junk.

*

Last spring, I donated twenty dollars at a graduate student fundraiser to have my cards read. My student said, "Stagnation."

He flipped over another card, consulted the miniature book that accompanied the deck, said, "Yikes, stagnation again."

Three cards later, "Lily, stagnation."

Earlier this week, when I submitted my tenure box, I said, "I haven't smiled like this in a long time."

*

When I was little, my mother drove me all the way to Houston to go to the fortune-teller. The dark room smelled of jasmine tea and jasmine incense, and I held a cup filled with sticks in my little hands.

*

Today, my horoscope is inapplicable. Nothing about it portends to the day I imagine myself having. I close the app and try another.

*

Wanting control over my own fate, I re-write the *I Ching* to fit my life. When I read from this book, the coins have been lost and the sticks have been burned. I replace them with a pair of Dungeons and Dragons dice.

If a number greater than sixty-four is rolled, I say, "Try again. This time, really think about your question." I say, "Your concentration was divided."

I turn to the correct page and say, "Listen carefully."

WINTER

To ward off a winter of depression, I bought hundreds of dollars of yarn and knit cowls for all my friends. Knitting, I felt manic and desperate and then finally calm. My fingers looped yarn, and something solidified, quickened into something else.

*

I am in Iowa on my final day. I have spent four weeks here teaching a fiction workshop on magic. There is barely any snow left on the ground, and the sun has not yet risen. This afternoon will be warmer, and I will already be gone.

*

On my first day here, I didn't think I could last for the whole four weeks. I felt weak, and winter bore down on me with all her gloss, and even my muscles felt brittle, delicate, breakable. It was just weather, but what remains in my memory of that moment was its stalactite isolation. I began unpacking my very large suitcase and made the bed.

*

Cornell College had supplied me with an old Victorian house, gabled and ivied, as if straight from a fairy tale. The wood below my socked feet groaned at every step, and ghosts are only imagined in stories.

*

On the first day of class, as an ice-breaker, I had my students play Light as a Feather, Stiff as a Board. "It's a game little girls play at sleepover," I said. Then, "I never actually played it as a kid because I didn't really have any friends, but yeah." I upbraided myself for being unnecessarily honest and self-deprecating and vulnerable and pandering. It was still just the first day of class and already I had stripped myself and outside snowflake ballerinas spun and they spun.

In small groups, the students huddled around a student lying down on the ground, perfectly stationary. Using just two fingers per hand to lift, they chanted, "Light as a feather, stiff as a board," and I walked around and saw nothing was happening and so I said, "You have to believe it. You're not believing," and the students chanted, "Light as a feather, stiff as a board," and still nothing was happening. This was no surprise to me. I have done this exercise, which I stole from a friend's workshop, a handful of times and it never works. It shouldn't work, and so I said, "Come on, guys, you have to at least try," and the students chanted, "Light as a—" and a girl began to lift off the ground. Her classmates' fingers barely touched her. She was simply rising. And then I looked over and another group was standing and their girl was floating nearly waist high.

The students re-arranged the tables and returned to their seats.

*

I call a thing magic if I cannot immediately understand the process by which it is made, like electricity and felt, happily ever after and swamp coolers in the desert.

*

"How did that work?" I asked. "That's not supposed to work."

The students' faces were bright, celebratory, like they had just defied something great, and they had.

"I mean, physics tells us that you can't lift a whole adult person off the ground using a couple fingers and some chanting." The heater kicked on, and its low buzz invigorated me. "It's not possible!"

I had an entire lecture planned about why the exercise hadn't worked: about how we're too skeptical as adults to believe in magic; about how we put all our faith in science, which not too long ago was also a form of magic; about how we're cynical and that's sad; about how we can no longer access childhood wonder.

Except that it worked.

J— raised his hand and politely waited to be called on. "Fairies," he said. "It's the fairies here."

*

Still without sun, the sky begins to lighten. This is my favorite time of day, just the watching. As if using vision for the first time, these colors absolve everything. In a few hours, I will leave here and I want to say I'll leave here changed, but I haven't. I haven't learned or grown or matured. But at least I made it to the end.

*

I taught fairy tales and myth and magical realism; students wrote stories of the travail of foxes, the housing of damaged souls, eternal return. Workshops were too polite to be useful, and I had forgotten how courteous Midwesterners are raised to be.

They praised without critique, and speaking, I became a monster.

*

Row 1 (rs): kfb, *p1, sl1 pw pwif - repeat from * to the last 3 st, then p1, k2tog

Row 2: sl1 pw wyif, *p1, k1 - repeat from * to the last stitch, then sl1 pw wyif

Row 3: kfb, knit to the last 2 st, then k2tog

Row 4: sl1 pw wyif, purl to the last st, then sl1 pw wyif

Repeat until piece measures 4".

*

I took pills to keep me alert, to push aside sleep to finish my critiques in time for workshop. I put little hearts next to beautiful passages, and across their pages, I drew squares around my marginalia.

I read my endnotes verbatim because I have never had confidence to speak without talking points.

I said, "Once is an accident, twice is a coincidence, three times is a pattern."

I said, "If there's a rifle over the fire place in the first act, it needs to fired by the third act."

My students wrote down every aphorism.

*

I took a guess and pronounced it incorrectly. It took her two tries to guess "cowl." "Oh," the lady at the yarn store said, and I said, "Oh," and felt incredible shame.

*

A loneliness that might as well shove you into the snow and leave you there, broken.

*

The wind, its savagery and wrath.

*

The lady at the yarn store invited me to the knitting group there. "We have some wine and sit around the fire and order pizza." The pizza was gourmet, and I felt banished.

*

My ambivalent desires.

*

I want to hold time in my fists, I want to remember.

*

What is tense—that slippery beast—I purl and then unpurl, counting stitches in multiples of four.

*

On *The Autobiography of Red*, a student said, "This book was a waste of my time," and it was first time I felt violence against a student.

*

My students sewing books as coffins of memory.

*

The weekends here make me desperate. Alone with myself, its jarring solitude and quiet. The dimming of noises, I am only my knitting bones.

*

Nights of pushing heat, I removed my clothes and sweat. My house was dry and it felt like summer in here, but outside, winter continued to bloom.

The thermostat was set to eighty, and no one seemed to be able to fix it.

I unbutton my coat—because it is balmy in here.

*

I unstitch the real, and out tumbles magic.

*

We read *The Bible* and *The Odyssey*, the Brothers Grimm and Ovid.

*

I've made my bed every morning: it's the little things.

This morning, I pulled the sheets from the bed and coiled them in the corner.

Suddenly, things felt incomplete.

*

We read Homer, Calvino, Carson.

*

Some night I fell asleep with every light on. I couldn't reach the lights: I was crawling around with exhaustion.

*

Winter, deep in my bones.

*

Watching the Iowa sunrise, the pink sky: it is captivating.

Rethinking Rikki Ducornet as a Rascuache *Latina Writer*

RAYMOND L. WILLIAMS

Having published an impressive body of work widely recognized as "American fiction", having been raised in the United States before moving to France, where she lived in a small village as a foreign resident for two decades, Rikki Ducornet has been identified as an "American" writer. As a professional academic who reads, teaches and writes primarily about Latin American literature, I find reading Ducornet special in many ways, but I often find myself thinking of her as "Latin American" rather than strictly "American" writer. I am not the only reader to see Ducornet in this light: the informed critic and scholar of modern American fiction, Larry McCaffery, has connected this writer both with "Latin American fabulism" and "magical realism".[1]

To begin with, Ducornet has always been a Borgesian writer for me. Her language, her tendency to create highly elaborate dreamworlds, and her wildly free exercising of the right of invention in general all associate her with the Argentine master. As children, Borges dreamed of infinite libraries and Ducornet dreamt of libraries that were aquariums. Like Borges (as well as Gabriel García Márquez, Salman Rushdie and Carlos Fuentes, to name a few), Ducornet understands that writing fiction involves a rewriting of other texts. Borges's story 'Pierre Ménard, author of the Quixote' was a play on this matter. For Latin American writers such as García Márquez and Fuentes, Borges's stories, such as 'The Secret Miracle', 'The Library of Babel', and 'The Aleph',

---

1 Sinda Gregory and Larry McCaffery, 'A Conversation with Rikki Ducornet by Sinda Gregory and Larry McCaffery', *Review of Contemporary Fiction*, Vol. 18, No. 3, Fall 1998: 1-14.

represented a reaffirmation of the right of invention in a Latin American region that, before Borges, was bound by very traditional (realist-naturalist) aesthetic norms. Consequently, Borges's fiction has been a revolution and a liberation for several generations of writers who because of cultural tradition, have felt bound to realism and the need to write fiction exclusively to denounce the social ills of Latin America.

Borges's impact has resonated beyond the most immediate scenarios of the respective Latin American writers of the 1940s and 1950s who felt stifled. His metafictional musings and linguistic tours de force were translated and widely read in English and other languages in the 1960s. John Barth, Nabokov, and Calvino were Borges's cohorts in creating a self-reflective and cerebral type of fiction that not only entertained, but also invited readers to reflect upon language and literature themselves. The situation of literary culture in the United States has probably changed almost as much in North America as it has in Latin America. Nevertheless, still today, in the second decade of the twenty-first century, the presence of Borges is palpable in both North American and Latin American writing. Rikki Ducornet's fascination with Borges is not a matter known only to academic specialists: she has illustrated a volume of Borges's writing, and the back cover of her novel *Phosphor in Dreamland* declares boldly that the novel "can be described as Jonathan Swift meets Angela Carter via Jorge Luis Borges."

Borges and Ducornet, unlike García Márquez and Fuentes, make a playful farce out of rewriting history. For Fuentes and García Márquez, Latin American historiography has betrayed and failed the citizens of the Americas. Thus, for the latter, an important role for the fiction writer is to recoup what is more real than classical historiography, the supposed truth of history. Borges and Ducornet obviously are very interested in history too, but they tend to eschew the very concept of truth in writing. These two writers are far too fascinated with the possibilities of perverting history and historiography to engage in historical projects such as those of García Márquez and Fuentes.

Perhaps the strongest alliance between Borges and Ducornet is to be found in their attitudes toward language and their uses of it. Ducornet's language itself is often arresting, and the two writers' simultaneously stunning and subtle uses of language suggest more than a coincidence in style. Ducornet's language involves playful twists—a sideshow for the reader consisting of phrases such as "gelid grasp" and "saturnine spouse" used in *The Stain*. However, just when the unsuspecting reader might believe that Ducornet cultivates only the precious and the Borgesian, she drops a phrase such as "dog turds" (from *The Stain*) or "It seemed to them that the entire cosmos reeked of mildew, stagnant pooks, the shit of fish, the saliva of snakes and the sulfurous flatulence of saints" (from *Phosphor*). Her indulgence with language in *Phosphor in Dreamland* occasionally pushes the limits of linguistic tour de force and the celebration of the word. Borges explored similar boundaries and limits. In the end, Ducornet's language has much of Borges's erudition and self-consciousness, but little of his prudishness.

In *The Stain* Ducornet explores a sordid and essentially un-Borgesian world, a world of the *rascuache*. This word, *rascuache*, is a Mexican colloquialism and is used in Mexico and the U.S. Southwest to describe a cultural item of inferior quality and proletarian origin. Some examples of *rascuache* culture are Pachuco fashion of the 1940s in Los Angeles and the Mexican working-class humor, style and dress of Cantinflas. As Alfredo Mirandé points out, *rascuache* sensibility has become a critical component of Chicano art and its most prevalent use is negative, slapdash, and shallow.[2] Tomás Ibarra Frausto has added that one is never *rascuache*, for it is always someone else, someone of lower status, who is judged to be outside the demarcators of approved taste and decorum.[3] Some of this writing of Ducornet, like some Chicano art that is *rascuache*, reflects an underdog, have-not sensibility that is also resourceful and makes use of simple materials, including found ones such as Luján's cardboard, glue, and loose sand.[4] The protagonist in this

---

2 See Alfredo Mirandé, *Rascuache Lawyer*. Tuscson: University of Arizona Press, 2011.

3 Tomás Ibarra Frausto, "Rasquachismo: A Chicano Sensibility," in *Chicano Art: Resistance and Affirmation*, 1965-1985. Ed. Richard Griswold del Castillo, Teresa McKenna, Yvonne Yarbro-Bejarano. Berkely: U California P, 1991, p. 156

4 *ibid*, p. 155

novel survives by escaping from this sordid and *rascuache* world into nature. Thus, *The Stain* invites an eco-critical reading of a novel in which the role of nature is an antidote to the harsh world of modernity.

In her even more wildly imaginative novel *Phosphor in Dreamland*, Ducornet looks more like the García Márquez of *The Autumn of the Patriarch*, who also invented a vaguely Caribbean island as the setting for his novel. Her island is called Birdland and is the setting for a rewriting of not only García Márquez but Borges, Jonathan Swift, and the Chicano Tomás Rivera. Digressions and images of terror keep this *rascuache* world from ever resembling realism. In this novel, Ducornet invents a full-blown *rascuache* character, Nuno Alpha y Omega, an unorthodox young man also known as Phosphor, who is clubfooted with crossed eyes and who aspires to be a photographer and celebrated poet. With the classic hybrid Chicano name (indicated with the use of the "y"), Alpha y Omega, like *rascuachismo*, is linked to structures and feeling that is not serious and elitist but playful and basic. In a broader sense, *Phosphor in Dreamland*, like *rascuachismo*, finds its delight and refinement in what many consider banal and projects an alternative aesthetic—what Ybarra Fraust has identified as a "good taste for bad taste".[5]

As interesting and exotic as Birdland might be, the reader actually luxuriates in language and dreams more than any real state, for this one is clearly fake. The narrator's digressions, playful and entertaining *rascuache*-like footnotes, and terror prevent the American reader from falling into the stereotypical image of the Caribbean island as tropical paradise. Even though Ducornet seems more interested in language than the representation of society, she does adroitly satirize a hierarchical and superstitious colonial state.

Ducornet's dealing with the dominant hierarchy is a celebration not only of language and invention, but also the erotic and the body. When she attains momentum (which is frequent), language and body become transgressive and perverse. Her description of Phosphor embracing his lover, for example, is an incredible tour de force. Unexpected

---

5 *ibid.*

juxtapositions, surreal turns, and magical transformations permeate everyday life and virtually every page of *Phosphor in Dreamland*.

The more I think about Rikki Ducornet as a Latin American writer, the more I find her surfacing in the Southwestern United States near the border. Perhaps there is something irrationally magical about this, like the time I was reading *The Stain* for the first time, back in the 1990s, while travelling on a train through a desert portion of California. I paused to rest after reading a passage with a hare, gazed out the window with a few of the back yards in a rundown *rascuache* barrio, and saw an enormous hare. I sometimes warn undergraduate students against thinking fiction has anything at all to do with their real lives. But there was the hare . . . as in the case, similarly, in which I once saw a creature I had thought was a fantastic creation of Cortázar in the Jardin de Plantes in Paris—an axolotl.[6] Just as Cortázar somehow belonged in Paris, Ducornet somehow seems to belong to the Southwest. She lived for many years at the gateway to the Southwest, Colorado.

As metafictionalists who are highly conscious of language itself and whose writing constantly reaffirms the right of invention, Jorge Luis Borges, Salman Rushdie, Rudolfo Anaya and Rikki Ducornet have much in common. Rushdie, Anaya and Ducornet are all Borgesian writers who have crossed over to visit the territory of the *rascuache*. Ducornet is neither a mainline American writer nor really a Latin American writer. Her father was Cuban, so the most obvious ethnic marker might be Cuban American: Rikki Ducornet the Cuban-American or Latina writer. Given all of the above, I like to think of her as a Latina and *rascuache* artist of multiple talents and aesthetics.

---

6 García Márquez and a lot of other writers have claimed, at one time or another, that they are realists ("yo soy un mero realista") and that reality is more magical or strange or marvelous than fiction. In the case of the axolotl, I once strolled through the Jardin de Plantes in Paris, began thinking about the rare possibility that there might actually be an axolotl in the aquarium, and then discovered, in an eerie encounter, that the large human-like eye of an axolotl was staring at me once I entered the building with absolute skepticism that it would actually have an axolotl inside. The incident with the hare in California was also quite eerie.

Into Fox

JOANNA HOWARD

I remember first the long table: set with several pots of green tea, Turkish coffees and tea glasses or slender clay cups, and platters of baklava and little savory pastries or pistachio cakes from a Middle Eastern market where she walked, I believe, despite the distance, to gather delicacies to offer us, and I picture her in that elegant serape she wore in those days, black with red chevrons, carrying a round-bottomed market basket in the bright Denver sunlight, as if she was preparing a great feast for honored guests. Then I remember her at the long table, and us all along the sides on the wooden benches, packed in side by side, packed in, not quite like sardines, but there all in this one place. And although the house was filled with her drawings and paintings, and other wonders, carved masks and small statues and intricate shadow puppets perched on their sticks, and wool carpets of every color, and dark velvet cushions on the long wooden pews along the wall, and although there were sea shells as big as ravens, as big as the heads of dogs, and although there were the rough travertine floors with veins of gray and pink below our feet, and although on the counter behind her head, large flat baskets were filled with fresh mangoes and avocados and purple tomatoes, and behind that, on the shelves of the kitchen, earthenware crocks, and a rack of glittering spices in bottles, and mosaic canisters—sumac or fennel pollen or asafetida or Sichuan flower pepper—and square clasp jars of curling dried mushrooms of all the colors of rich soil, and the rust and ruby tones of the dried chilies— guaijillo, ancho, baklouti, and onward to darker colors, henna douglah, claret allepo, and the aubergine skins of urfa or isot—and although many things were labeled by hand in her looping script, the same she had used to write her many books, many more were unmarked and known only to her, by the site of their contents or upon recognizing a ribbon around the mouth of a jar, and perhaps they marked the moment for her that each was collected, or bought in an open air market, or carried with her from France or Morocco or Spain, or they were remembered by the dish they most recently created, or by the guests she chose to serve on that occasion, and so these small jars became portals into dozens of dishes, in a dozen more places, and moreover a dozen guests, on moreover a dozen tables, tables such as the one where we were all seated, the twelve of us. And although everyone wanted to look at everything at once, and to look everywhere at once, and look into the sitting room beyond the stone pillars, and into the kitchen painted scarab blue, and beyond the long table to the open glass that looked onto the little garden where crows gathered on the pebbles, and despite these spectacular distractions of what seemed like everything from everywhere here in this one place, it was *her* that we looked at, at the head of her table, her clear, lit eyes at times lavender in my memory, at times silver, looking up at us, or over the rim of her glasses, as she gripped a slender cup of tea in her hands and spoke to us of curiosity cabinets, and magical creatures and the stories of Scheherazade and Gilgamesh, and the animals deep in the zoo of our imaginations.

And we were not there for a meal, but we were replete with the flavors before us, in our cups and in our fingers, but mostly in the stories that she recounted, because we were *in class*, though unlike any class we had ever had before, and yes we wrote things and talked about the things that we had written as one does in a class, but I do not remember what we wrote or what we said about what we wrote, instead I remember her stories of stories, because she had read everything it seemed, and we had read nothing, though I thought I had done nothing but read for my whole life, so a part of me thought I had nothing left to read, or that I had read everything already, but she had read everything and then everything *else*, not only read everything and everything else, but read it in some hallucinatory, illuminated form, so that even stories that I thought I knew, or thought I had read came through differently, as though through another lens, or through one of her stereoscopes which lined the bathroom shelf. I would say of another person, 'she recommended to us' or I would say 'she advised that we read' but I will only say that she recounted, or retold stories. We knew she was good with language. We knew that from her books. But it was not only the language she gave us through her recounting or retelling, because she enacted them for us, over her glasses, at the head of the table, her arms lengthening out from the folds of the serape, with long pauses between speaking so as to let us digest the morsel just offered, long pauses during which she let her palms go flat on the wood of the table, and her shoulders would raise slightly so one bare, brown shoulder would appear, as her dark long hair fell over it, and she expressed or enacted in these glances and in these silent moments the feel of the thing just said, and gave with her eyes another facet, a depth or a duration, a part of the thing just said that was somehow beyond the words said, but was also the natural extension of those words, and it was like watching a great silent film star, in real time, in color, at arm's reach.

For example, I had read, or thought I had read, the Italo Calvino story 'All at One Point,' which she once retold to us, in drawing us toward it and drawing us into it. If indeed I had read the story before, whatever I had read was forever replaced with her bodily retelling of it, her becoming of the story, so that even now when I re-read it, or when I teach it, I hear it in her voice, and see her eyes and gestures, especially as she speaks the line she loved so well, "Oh, if only there were room, I'd love to make some noodles for you boys." And with her body she recounted to us the gestures of the woman who was at the beginning of the universe, where all things were at once in the same place, packed in, and so space and time were contained in a single, small point, and therein existed the fantasy of the woman of a name pronounceable only in the imagination, and voluptuous only in the imagination, because in the story everything is all in one point, and so there is no room for anyone to make noodles and there is no room for the volume of the body in general, and no room for the voluptuous body of the noodle maker in particular, and so the possibility of the action of the making of the noodles is also possible only in the imagination of the inhabitants of the single point who are the inhabitants of Calvino's story: and there it was, this fantasy of the desire not just to make noodles for the boys, but the desire to embody the making of such noodles, this great and generous act, of a great and generous hostess whose bounty is inseparable from her curvature and the movement of her body in space, as it was in my mind inseparable from the volume of her draped sarape over the curve of her slender shoulder before us, as she leaned over the table and mimed the rolling out of the noodles, and the heaping of the noodles in the bowl, and as she paused and bit her lower lip, and looked at us with her lavender or silver eyes, and it is almost now in my mind as if there was before us suddenly a great bowl of noodles, but disparate and finite in each of our hovering imaginations, so that we each saw different noodles, in soups and broths and sauces of all stripe and color, slipping out and curling across the long table, and still she waited, and paused in her retelling, and looked at us over her glasses, as each of us conjured our own images of the bowl of the noodles at the beginning of the universe, and then tried to imagine all the other bowls of noodles hovering before the others around us, and we saw before us all the possibilities of the universe in one small point, telegraphed by our imaginations from the end of a stick of spaghetti. Such was the table laid before us in her home.

And each of us in turn were served, our portions which were suited to us, and so she recommended books and stories and films and operas to each of us that we had never seen or heard of, and that indeed would change each of us, and in each instance, she turned her gaze, and gave it to one person, in one place. And so I will always remember when she turned to me and recommended the story of a lady who turns into a fox, by David Garnett, and in this small book, this ideally sized book, when the husband following his wife into the forest in the night sees only a vixen in his wife's nightgown, he stops, and the vixen stops, and she turns her head back to look at the husband over her one small shoulder as she slips out of her nightdress and into the woods. (This is not precisely what happens in *Lady Into Fox,* for the transformation takes place in an armchair, and the fox is left standing not in a nightgown exactly but in a little frilled bed jacket. We know from this from the language. The image of the vixen looking over the shoulder, however, is absolutely precise as depicted in the engraving or the woodcut.) And indeed, when I got my first copy of *Lady Into Fox,* there was the woodcut of the vixen in her nightdress, looking over one shoulder. However, while I have read it many times, and as much as a I love it, it will never be quite as much, quite as expansive as it was at the moment when she told it to us, and I felt, *to me,* turning her bare shoulder toward me, and then turning her head to look over her shoulder at me for this moment in which all the possibilities of the imagination seemed present, and her sarape dipping low like the strap of the nightgown, she was becoming vixen for us at the table and pulling me with her, into fox.

And so I suppose, it is not so much that I remember her class, or that I remember the stories she remembered and recounted to us, but I remember that her way of remembering was so much more memorable than whatever the thing itself was, even if the thing was already very memorable. And what I wanted to learn from her were not the things she remembered, everything and everything else that she had read and seen, but I wanted to learn the way that she remembered, the way that she read and the way that she saw, and then the way that she became. Because it seemed that in one single point she could find all the possible reaches of the imagination and take us into these reaches through her words and through her body, and so things that were magical were rendered more magical, and things that were impossible became possible, and things that were dull just simply didn't exist.

The Cabinets of Dr. Ducornet

MICHAEL J. EMMONS

In her essay 'The Practice of Obscurity', Rikki Ducornet recreates a moment when, as a child of eight in the Hudson River Valley, she played hide-and-seek in a friend's house. There she discovered

> a vast rectangular room, its west wall taken up with vertiginous windows. In the east the sun hangs high above the roof, and the room is heavy with shadows. The entire east wall is taken up with cabinets fronted with glass; glass spills to the floor like heavy water. The cabinets are old and pocked with bubbles; the glass is of uneven thickness. Like the restless objects of desire that elude Alice's eyes in the sheep's shop in Wonderland, the things in the cabinet are both appealing and enigmatic.[1]

Ducornet continues, describing each object in the cabinet as it gleams in the late afternoon light. She sees, suspended in specimen jars, a "modular chicken", a "natal lizard", "a fetal cat in levitation", "one preliminary lamb."[2] (Though it's never stated, her friend's father is likely a biology professor at Bard.) "All this announces the greatest treasure of all: the dizzying itinerary of the human fetus; it rides the afternoon across an entire shelf."[3] The development of both humanity *in toto* and each human *in utero* is laid out before her in suspended animation. Within the cabinet, all "that had been baffling, hermetic, unfolds, exquisitely palpable."[4] It's a moment of profound and exquisite revelation, the kind of moment that might well inspire a life-long aesthetic project.

It's no wonder, then, that the cabinet of curiosities has become the crucial metaphor driving Ducornet's literary output. In the title essay from the collection *The Deep Zoo*, Ducornet discusses the "potencies that, in the shape of dreams, landscapes, exemplary instants and so on, inform our imagining minds [. . .] For Bachelard they take the form of shells, a bird's nest, an attic; for Borges a maze, mirrors, the tiger; for Calvino moonlight, the flame, and the crystal; for Cortázar ants on the march and the cry of the rooster."[5] For Ducornet, the cabinet of curiosities, the wonder-room, the museum of natural history, the specimen jar.

A good portion of Ducornet's essay collections *The Monstrous and the Marvelous* and *The Deep Zoo* is dedicated to analyzing the concept of the cabinet of wonders, even as those books function—as the jacket copy to *The Monstrous and the Marvelous* states outright—as such *Wunderkammern* themselves. There on the shelves of her cabinets are the films of David Lynch and Werner Herzog, the poetry of César Vallejo and the fiction of Joy Williams, the paintings of Linda Okazaki and the wonder-rooms of Margie MacDonald. There's a genuine pleasure of kinship in seeing these treasures lovingly displayed: if you share Ducornet's enthusiasms, you feel less alone in your affection; if you've never encountered the artists she exalts, you're provided with an unimpeachable "aesthetic itinerary."[6] But more valuable yet is the perspective provided by tracking the metaphor through Ducornet's body of work and letting it reveal her innermost concerns.

The word *cabinet* appears in each of Ducornet's novels except *The Stain*. From the very beginning of her career she has employed the cabinet of curiosities—and its larger and smaller analogues, the wonder-room and the box of secrets, respectively—as a narrative emblem of arcane mysteries, a repository of secret histories. In the afterword to *The Jade Cabinet* (later expanded and repurposed as the opening essay of *The Monstrous and the Marvelous*), Ducornet notes that her childhood ambition was "to paint the museum scenery behind walruses and saber-toothed tigers", and that she longs for her "own poetic territory which would include a keeping garden for insects, an extensive zoological library (color plates intact!), a wonder room and a jade cabinet which would, ideally, contain a chimera of mutton-fat jade."[7] In a conversation with Michael Silverblatt conducted around the publication of *Gazelle*, Ducornet said, "I do believe in enchantment, and I do have a wonder-room at home, full of wondrous things."[8] And in the essay 'Walking to Eden', Ducornet admits that she is "*glamourized* (charmed, in other words), by museums. Whenever I visit a new city, I get myself, just as soon as I can, to its museum of Natural History. In this way I have seen the bones of Brazilian sloths in Italy and Italian fossils in France. Museums recur in these essays not by choice but by inclination."[9]

What's puzzling, then, given Ducornet's enthusiasm, is that with very few exceptions, the cabinet-keepers, the museum-enthusiasts, the curators, and the collectors in her fiction are malevolent and untrustworthy figures, all of whom come to tragic ends.

The Exorcist in *The Stain* is perhaps the most learned character in all of Ducornet's work, a scholar of arcane demon-lore and a passionate collector of bizarre relics. Like his literary contemporary Judge Holden in Cormac McCarthy's *Blood Meridian*, he's as charming as he is deadly, and only too happy to treat those around him like pieces in a game whose rules only he understands. The first of Ducornet's many antiheroes who hide a twisted sexuality behind a facade of piety, the Exorcist bends the Mother Superior of St. Gemmes to his will with a spirited session of toe-fucking, and molests the prepubescent Charlotte while she sleeps. The strangely birth-marked and feral Charlotte becomes for him another specimen for his collection; when he cannot obtain her, his mind shatters. He frames Emile, the novel's most sympathetic presence, for his murder of the mystical Téton twins. (The twins' hearts, at the novel's conclusion, end up two more artifacts in a cabinet, in the Convent of the Thorny Agony, "just to the left of Bernadette Soubirous' mummified corpse and to the right of the Divine Bridegroom's authenticated Thorn[.]")[10] Deprived of his beloved

Charlotte, the Exorcist becomes a sort of satanic werewolf, haunting the forests of the Loire, screaming the names of demons until a mob of villagers guns him down.

Ducornet continued her exploration of the darker aspects of the curatorial impulse with her next novel. The repugnant co-narrator of *Entering Fire*, Septimus de Bergerac, is a curator as well, a student of physiognomy and phrenology, racial taxonomies, the inscrutable rules of the anti-Semite's practice. His racism both colors and conceals his personal resentment toward his absentee father Lamprimas, whom he harrows across the globe, a terror campaign that results in the murder of Lamprimas' lover Marta Strada in the Sachsenhausen concentration camp. Septimus curates "an educational exhibition for the benefit of Frenchmen young and old": a museum of antisemitic caricature. The wonder of Ducornet's experience in the Hudson River Valley she twists here into something abominable. "The Museum of Natural History of Paris provided a splendid collection of bottled monsters; these would demonstrate the untold dangers of interracial breeding. What did it matter if some of the foetuses we exhibited were not human? Should an impressionable young person see a two-headed crocodile and take it for a Jezebel's *abortus*, all the better!"[11] Septimus, as prone to infantile excess as any of Ducornet's curators, creates his own antisemitic effigies out of wax, each image "more appalling than the next."[12] He takes his side show on the road, where he dies a broken prisoner of the McCarthy-era FBI.

A similarly grim fate awaits the major collector figure of *The Jade Cabinet*, Angus Sphery. Though he's neither the novel's most reprehensible character (that would be the stolid and murderous industrialist Radulph Tubbs), nor the most terrifying (that would be the insatiable, insectile *Hungerkünstler*), Angus is perhaps the purest incarnation of Ducornet's recurring motif of the collector whose drive to acquire and to curate estranges him from familial life.

Though his daughter Memory describes him as "a good man"[13] on the novel's first page, Angus's "insatiable desire for knowledge both worldly and divine"[14] leads him to one moral disaster after another.

Deafened by listening to the cries of Bedlam patients, he hopes to discover the "keys to the universal language"[15] in the gurgles of his newborn daughter Etheria. So as not to adulterate her language he never speaks to her, as a result she never speaks, and he attempts to abandon his flawed creation in a meadow.

Angus's study is one of the great wonder-rooms that populate Ducornet's work, and his daughters spend "so many delightful hours" there "among the butterflies and bottled bats."[16] Yet Angus never fails to put his pursuit of the universe's secrets, or simply of pretty objects, over his daughters' well-being. He trades Etheria to the artless Radulph Tubbs for a single piece—a cicada—from Tubbs's inherited cabinet of beautiful jade figurines.

Used as a bargaining chip in a struggle between a man with no imagination (Tubbs, crucially, hates the cabinet and its contents, and is in the business of removing Egyptian mummies from their underground cabinets and grinding them up to make bouillon) and a man with an imagination and nothing else, Etheria has only her silence for a weapon. The jade cabinet at Tubbs's manor the New Age, already an emblem of her father's betrayal and Tubbs's unearned prosperity, takes on a more sinister cast when Tubbs rapes Etheria with a jade dildo extracted from the cabinet's depths. The treasures of the jade cabinet, so coveted by Angus, only contribute to Etheria's agony. She flees the New Age, fencing Tubbs's jade to help finance her escape.

Etheria's position in the novel is quickly supplanted by the *Hungerkünstler*. The most precious and the most horrible of the treasures Angus Sphery acquires, the *Hungerkünstler*—a Czech hunger artist prone to incoherent, animalistic utterances and terrifying vendettas—destroys both him and Tubbs. Compared often to an wasp (an animal similar in many ways to the cicada), she first stings Sphery, forcing him to sell off his treasures to feed her appetites. Memory relates this story with horror:

> [He] sold the butterflies to buy the
> *Hungerkünstler* one dozen pairs of shoes, the

> Small Blues and Painted Ladies, the Great
> Peacock Moths and the Small Angel shades. . . .
> He sold his stuffed tanagers, his lyrebird, his
> Quetzal; sold his six hawkbill tortoise shells, the
> pearl in the shape of a pig, the skull of a wistiti . .
> . He sold everything, even the bottle of honey
> that had been procured from a hive built upon
> Thomas More's tomb, and the beautiful egg of a
> dodo. [. . .] But what is hardest to tell, and what
> shows above all else the piteous colouration our
> father's mind had taken: *he sold the jade:* the cane
> pommel once the pride of his youth; the cicada
> from Tubbs's cabinet and the chimera too; sold
> the earrings he had given to our mother
> Margaret Sphery to celebrate Etheria's birth![17]

Angus's collection of precious objects, once more important to him than his own daughters, is lost forever, but the *Hungerkünstler* isn't done yet. She murders Zephyra, the cross-dressing magician whom Radulph Tubbs (mistakenly) believes is Etheria returned. Radulph never recovers from the death of his "wife," and is buried alongside Zephyra on the Spherys' land.

The curator figure in Ducornet's seventh novel *Gazelle*, the protagonist Elizabeth's father, shares many of Angus's qualities, though he's a far more benign character. *Gazelle* represents a major leap forward in the maturity of Ducornet's body of work, so it's fitting that its attempt to grapple with the *Wunderkammer* tradition isn't a fantastic figure like the Exorcist but rather an American professor, pedantic, timid, and cuckolded. Elizabeth describes him as "a closet warrior, a mild man and an intellectual, a dreamer of reason in a world he feared was chronically, terminally unreasonable",[18] and states that "[in] life as in chess, Father did not want to be touched, to be moved, to be seized; he was unwilling to be pinned down or cornered."[19] Abandoned by his friends, who cannot "follow the direction of his thoughts"[20] and his wife, who prefers the "gazelles" of Cairo to her hapless spouse, Elizabeth's father takes solace, as do so many Ducornet characters, in curios, lore, and games of strategy. This solace, however, is one that only he can appreciate. Charmingly, he appoints his daughter "Keeper of the Inkpot" and teases her that she "would be shipped off directly to the crocodile-mummy pits of Gebel Aboofayda"[21] for failing to keep his Mont Blanc well-filled, but he never notices his daughter's nascent sexuality or her destabilizing attraction to his friend Ramses Ragab. (Ramses, with his store the *Kosmètèrion* full of hundreds of bottles of perfumes recreated from ancient recipes, can seem at times like another in Ducornet's line of cabinet-maintaining magicians. Elizabeth's father even calls him "a performer of pneumatic magic" who surrounds "[himself] with djinn[.]"[22] But unlike those figures Ramses sells his wares, they're his livelihood. He lacks any fervor for hoarding.) He uses his games of war, with all their attendant esoterica, as a shield against the pain of his wife's betrayal, going so far as to shave his beard in the style of Amasis, king of Egypt, the war leader he role-plays. Yet he does not notice that Elizabeth has tattooed the hill of Osiris into her arm as a tribute to Ramses Ragab, let alone that the scars have become infected. What little he has left of Elizabeth's respect he jettisons by hiring a magician to return his wife to him. Though he calls it "a new sort of game, a game to keep my mind from wandering too far",[23] he becomes increasingly adamant about translating his fascination with the ancient world and its magical practices into an earnest attempt at using sorcery to win back a woman's love. The magician's spell works, to Elizabeth's father's great joy—but only temporarily. The Icelandic bombshell returns home just long enough to have breakfast, then hits the road.

In what is the most tragic of all his lapses, Elizabeth's father's vanity blinds him to his own geopolitical moment. After writing a book on ancient poisoning methods, he is "invited to Washington to give a series of lectures. His vanity, the chronic loneliness of the college professor abandoned to the trying anonymity of a rural campus of six hundred students and a miniscule endowment, ensured that he would accept with gratitude and kept him from inquiring too deeply into just who had invited him and why."[24] When Elizabeth's father learns the CIA is his benefactor, and that it has employed the esoteric practices he has uncovered against "tenacious and indigenous peoples" in "areas rich in resources American companies were eager to exploit"[25] he is disgusted and ashamed. His single-mindedness, the bane of any specialist, blinds him not only to his daughter's crises but to a monumental moral failure.

The unnamed psychologist protagonist of Ducornet's most recent—and finest—novel, *Netsuke,* is as rigorous a curator as Angus Sphery, though perhaps he has more in common with Radulph Tubbs, as he has, in his own words, "so little interest in aesthetic devices."[26] Or maybe the *Hungerkünstler* would be a closer analog, as both the psychologist and his lover the Cutter describe the psychologist as a wasp, boring deep into a fruit. The netsuke he collects are merely gifts from his wife Akiko, a true artist (the description of the triptych she is finishing, late in the novel, is powerful and convincing). The protagonist's true focus is in collecting lovers, a pursuit he undertakes with an immense, life-obliterating dedication. He calls his two offices "cabinets", and even nicknames them: "One of the cabinets I call Spells. I cannot enter it without my heart beating faster. The other I call Drear. If Spells is devoted to the pleasures of transgression, Drear belongs to all the rest[.]"[27] Spells is for the patients (he prefers the term "clients") he wishes to seduce, Drear for the untouchables who sustain him financially.

As his pursuits begin to overwhelm his life, the psychologist opens a third "cabinet", the New Spells, farther from his house, "his way of acknowledging the risk he is in and the essential part risk plays in his life."[28] Akiko decorates it, and a cabinet inside is dedicated to the netsuke. New Spells is where the psychologist enjoys his most striking treasures, his most desired clients, especially the death-haunted Cutter and David Swancourt, who lives a second life as a woman named Jello. In New Spells, the netsuke begin to merge with his lovers in his mind:

His life is speeding up. This is an old feeling and yet there is something new going on, unfamiliar. The new room, too, is unfamiliar, and the netsuke all so strange, buzzing behind the glass in a new Spells all their own.

He takes out the erotic ones. They nest in the hand like a breast, the smooth heel of a woman's foot, a delicate ear or elbow, the head of a cock, its root, the testicles, that delicacy, that weight. He can understand why people collect these, why they are so rare, so coveted. And then he notices that *all* the netsuke, not just erotic ones, have this quality—even the frog crouching on the body of the persimmon, the twinned gourd, its cut stern erect as a nipple, a wasp feeding on the cleft of a plum. He is like a voyeur, turning these over and over, examining their little dimples, secret moles, and discolorations. In his hands the netsuke begin to sweat. He thinks that the more they are fondled, the more they will be his.[29]

The psychologist moves into the third cabinet, becoming in a sense his own treasure. (The novel's epigraph is from the Surrealist poet Joë Bousquet: "I am my own hiding place.") Broken by his collector's compulsion and increasingly morbid—he watches snuff films as if they were "the unspooling of [his] most private nightmares"[30]—he begins a sadistic and futile affair with Jello. His life unravels at a terrifying pace. Betrayed by the psychologist's affair with Jello, the Cutter attempts suicide. Tired of the psychologist's abuses, Jello blackmails him. Chasing death as relentlessly as he has any of his partners so far, the psychologist dissolves his practice, and pilots the Studebaker containing both Akiko and himself into heavy traffic.

Corrupt zealots and anti-Semites, murderous sex addicts and

goldbricking fathers: the curators and collectors that populate Ducornet's work are a sordid bunch, especially considering their creator's sincere love of wonder-rooms, museums, the boxes of Joseph Cornell.[31] Yet this incongruity, baffling as it may seem at first, is vital to grapple with if Ducornet's astonishing achievement is to be fully understood. In the essay 'Optical Terror', Ducornet points out one of the *wunderkammer*'s more problematic aspects:

> The Enlightenment was preceded by the great voyages of discovery, which revealed a sprawling world, infinitely stranger than previously imagined. A World of Wonders reflected in *wunderkammern*, or cabinets of marvels in which the world's excess could be comfortably contained, as though so much savage and eccentric beauty—flamboyant birds, snakes broad as chimneys, pigs castellated with scales—could be assimilated in homeopathic doses only.[32]

In both her fiction and her essays, Ducornet never fails to remind us: a *wunderkammer* is no substitute for a *world*. Throughout her nonfiction she delights in tangling with the traditions of the cabinet of wonders and the museum, praising them in one breath and condemning them in the next. *Wunderkammern*, Ducornet argues,

> reveal an existential stance, an Alchemy in Reverse. Here the natural world is ordered in ideal display, ideal because isolated and disaffiliated from the real. As beautiful as these collections often were, they betrayed a rupture at the heart of things and revealed a wound that has never ceased to fester, a chronic blindness also, an incapacity to read not only the New World's body, but its metaphysical books of days

> and dreams and prophesies [. . .] It is as if God
> gave man a second chance at Eden, and man,
> that confirmed shopkeeper, could not dwell
> there but only sell there.[33]

Cabinets of wonder provide us access to the natural world, but at a dire cost. Their existence presents a grim implication: as long as a representative of the natural world is preserved in a *Wunderkammer* or a museum of natural history, its cohort can be safely destroyed. Museums, Ducornet notes in 'Waking to Eden', "have all too often abetted the vanishment of species, as have botanical and zoological gardens."[34] Equally important, they impose a false order and nomenclature upon a universe that has no need for it. In a discussion of the work of the animal collector Albertus Seba, Ducornet states that "naming and listing leads to a certain dislocation of the world."[35] She notes that when "Adam gives names to things of fire and breath, his singular power, his privilege, and his alienation are openly declared, and Eden's capacity to inspire and regenerate is compromised."[36] The narrator of *Phosphor in Dreamland* extends this concept, discussing "Alicia Ombos' study *A Swift and a Phosphorous Eye*" (really, Ducornet's essay 'Optical Terror', which shares much of its language with Ombos' study): "A species of distillation, [*Wunderkammern*] reveal an existential stance; Ombos argues: *an attempt to seize and fix a universe in constant flux. Their purpose is born as much from terror as delight.*"[37] The flawed curators of the novels are inheritors of this tradition of fear. They use their collections and their recondite studies not to preserve the world's wonders, but to validate their arbitrary hatreds, to retreat from their familial responsibilities, even to detonate their own lives. Their enthusiasm for collection becomes just another form of dogma, and dogma is Ducornet's greatest adversary. The objects in their cabinets, harvested without love, are fragments they have shored against their ruins.

But if Ducornet's *own* practice of wonder-collection, present throughout her autobiography and reflected exquisitely in her essays, has a representative in her fiction, it is Nicholas, the protagonist of *The Fountains of Neptune*. Awakened from a fifty-year-long coma and known colloquially as "the Sandman", Nicholas soon finds himself the sole resident of the spa at Paradis sur Loire. He transforms his surroundings into the enchanted Kingdom of d'Elir, a series of wonder-rooms as strange and marvelous as a Max Ernst painting. A self-described "curator of silence",[38] Nicholas, quite literally a child in an adult's body, has no difficulty seeing the potential for the fantastic in his eerie environment: "an obelisk lost among the trees; a staircase carved of shadow; the worn marble of abandoned floors soaking up a landscape reflected in windows desperately in need of washing. An empty cabinet smelling faintly of cordials. An attic as vast as a cathedral."[39] He chalks the borders of his kingdom on the floor of the spa, unconcerned with geography: "its Amazon embraces the Sahara, its Nile empties into the Mississippi; its Catskills sleep at the foot of the Andes."[40] He fills the spa with the sarcophagi of fictional monarchs, groves of aromatic trees, a bar in Thule he only ever heard about. With his imaginary friend (a term much too glib to describe the benevolent spirit who animates the last half of *The Fountains of Neptune*) Olivier, he reenacts great battles upon the floors of the Kingdom, using toy apes to represent armies of millions.

Though, as his ecstatic wanderings through the spa and the markets of Paradis reveal, Nicholas shares Angus Sphery's hunger for *weird old stuff*, he's less a curator in the vein of Sphery or Elizabeth's father than a creator in the mold of Simon Rodia or Henry Darger. He rejects a journalist's offer to introduce him to the curator of the Museum of Modern Art in Nantes, screaming, "'I HATE MUSEUMS!'"[41] For Nicholas, the Kingdom of d'Elir is far more than any dry collection of artifacts, or a distraction from the pestering realities of daily life, it's his singular artistic cause. An orphan by nature and a stranger to the twentieth century, Nicholas requires the Kingdom both to give himself a purpose and to serve as a rebuke to his old father-figure, the drunken bully Toujours-Là: "[If], as Toujours-Là believed, mindlessness rules the world, at least my own small corner is actively conceived. I say this with humility; simply, I am content to putter and paste, wanting nothing more than to occupy time and place *in my fashion*."[42] There is no terror, only delight, in his creation of one of the world's great *Wunderkammern*.

Toujours-Là gets the last laugh, however. Nicholas drunkenly recreates the vitriolic spirit of his long-dead tormentor, scaring Olivier off. Not long after, the townsfolk of Paradis sur Loire, terrified of Nicholas and his extraordinary project, destroy the Kingdom of d'Elir.

At the novel's end Nicholas, bereft of both Olivier and his mentor Dr. Kaisersteige, recalls Toujours-Là leading him to peek behind the bar at the Snail and Shark.

> There in the gloom under the counter among the bottles of the more expensive liqueurs was kept a fetal monster about eight inches high. Its oddly massive head covered with soft, red down sprung directly from its shoulders; the little person had no neck. Mounted in its jar upon a glass cross, it grasped the horizontal bar with both its fists, and knees and body bent, appeared to be riding a wheelless bicycle.
>
> It occurs to me now that, although the jar was undoubtedly smashed during the Second War, and the scraps of flesh reduced to dust at last, it still inhabits the keeping medium of my mind. That the Sandman is very like the floating monster, both of the world and not of the world, and—as long as I can hold fast the glass wand of reverie—somehow eternal.[43]

Ducornet has populated her novels with characters that appear to be self-portraits, who share aspects of her ethos and autobiography: Gabrielle in *The Fan-Maker's Inquisition*, Elizabeth in *Gazelle*, Akiko in *Netsuke*. But even without the above scene which connects him directly to her biography, it's Nicholas—the gentle visionary, both enchanter and enchanted, less a curator of trinkets than a creator of extraordinary worlds—who seems closest to her spirit. Maybe he'll use the time he has left to become a writer.

Ducornet has been inexhaustibly fascinated with *Wunderkammern*, but no cabinet, no matter how wondrous its contents, can compare to the kingdom of delirium that is her work. In *The Deep Zoo* she urges her fellow writers: "We must take care that our books do not resemble those seventeenth-century wonder-rooms or nineteenth-century parlors, with their meaningless jumbles of stuffed bears, kayaks, giant lobsters, and assorted stools."[44] What separates Rikki Ducornet's books from those wonder-rooms—and from the ones curated by her darkest characters—is that they have been crafted with joy, equanimity, wisdom, and love. The tradition of the *Wunderkammer* has waned, but her achievement, like the Sandman, is eternal.

Endnotes

1 Rikki Ducornet, *The Deep Zoo*, Coffee House Press, Minneapolis, 2015, p. 90.

2 *Ibid.*, p. 91.

3 *Ibid.*

4 *Ibid.*

5 *Ibid.*, p. 4.

6 Rikki Ducornet, *The Monstrous and the Marvelous*, City Lights, San Francisco, 1999, p. 5.

7 Rikki Ducornet, *The Jade Cabinet*, Dalkey Archive, Normal, 1993, p. 158.

8 "Gazelle", *KCRW Bookworm* podcast,http://www.kcrw.com/news-culture/shows/bookworm/rikki-ducornet-1, (accessed 23 October 2003).

9 Ducornet, *The Monstrous and the Marvelous*, p. 3.

10 Rikki Ducornet, *The Stain*, Dalkey Archive, Normal, 1995, p. 223.

11 Rikki Ducornet, *Entering Fire*, City Lights, San Francisco, 1987, p. 126.

12 *Ibid.*, p. 127.

13 Ducornet, *The Jade Cabinet*, p. 9.

14 *Ibid.*

15 *Ibid.*, p. 10.

16 *Ibid.*, p. 51.

17 *Ibid.*, p. 94.

18 Rikki Ducornet, *Gazelle*, Knopf, New York, 2003, p. 4.

19 *Ibid.*, pp. 4 – 5.

20 *Ibid.*, p. 5.

21 *Ibid.*, p. 13.

22 *Ibid.*, p. 33.

23 *Ibid.*, p. 96.

24 *Ibid.*, p. 70.

25 *Ibid.*, p. 72.

26 Rikki Ducornet, *Netsuke*, Coffee House Press, Minneapolis,   2011, p. 9.

27 *Ibid.*, p. 14.

28 *Ibid.*, p. 28.

29 *Ibid.*, p. 100.

30 *Ibid.*, p. 62.

31 "The Jade Cabinet", *KCRW Bookworm*, [podcast], http://www.kcrw.com/news-culture/shows/bookworm/rikki-ducornet-2, (accessed 14 June 1993).

32 Ducornet, *The Monstrous and the Marvelous*, p. 7.

33 *Ibid.*, p. 8.

34 *Ibid*, p. 3.

35 Ducornet, *The Deep Zoo*, p. 35.

36 *Ibid.*, p. 97.

37 Rikki Ducornet, *Phosphor in Dreamland*, Dalkey Archive, Normal, 1995, pp. 42 – 43.

38 Rikki Ducornet, *The Fountains of Neptune*, Dalkey Archive, Normal, 1997, p. 218.

39 *Ibid.*, p. 163.

40 *Ibid.*, p. 196.

41 *Ibid.*, p. 194.

42 *Ibid.*, p. 196.

43 *Ibid.*, pp. 219 – 220.

44 Ducornet, *The Deep Zoo*, p. 11.

Rikki Ducornet's Netsuke

BRIAN EVENSON

In English, we've decided that a whole range of narrative deviance and confusion can be designated as "unreliable narration" and piled in the same box, despite radical differences between the reasons for and types of so-called unreliable narration. Narrators who narrate unreliably because of a damaged perception are placed in the same heap as those who are deliberately lying, and those who are trying to hide something from us to protect others are seen as akin to those trying to hide something from us for their own gain. To say that a narrator is "unreliable" is to say very little.

The French, however, offer another term, one that has no equivalent in English-language literary criticism and which at very least offers a more specific stance and mood: *le narrateur infâme*. This infamous narrator is vile or despicable. He is someone whose narrative sets out to depict a picture of what the reader considers infamy, an infamy of which the narrator is necessarily a part. You have the impression, as a reader, of risking becoming implicated in the narrator's own vileness. To listen to a *narrateur infâme* is to undergo by proxy a descent into hell.

Rikki Ducornet's most recent novel *Netsuke* (2011) speaks from this place of danger. It begins in third person as we watch a man in his sixties running and stopping his run for a quick spontaneous fuck in the woods with a fellow runner he's just passed. He's the kind of man who fucks and runs on. If told this way, strictly from third person, this might soon become like other stories of philanderers we've read. But after just a few pages, Ducornet moves into first person, shifting to this man's perspective, where for many pages we largely (though not exclusively) remain. He is, as it turns out, a psychoanalyst, capable of being good at his job but more often incredibly transgressive. Indeed, he does the very thing that psychoanalysts are most forbidden to do: he has sex with his patients. Not just one patient but a number of them, both men and women, indiscriminately and with very little regret or remorse. And not just patients—anybody he runs across (quite literally in the first scene) who attracts him and is game.

He is someone who has arranged his life into careful boxes. His life is carefully partitioned: even his practice is split into two rooms. In one, which he nicknames "Spells", he sees those patients that he is fucking or on his way toward fucking. In the other, "Drear", he sees his normal, dreary, boring patients. He lives for Spells, for the rush and thrill of sex and transgression, but those partitions and splits have so eroded his soul over time that he's beginning to be a shell of a man, to not have a self at all. He's a deeply split individual, someone who knows he is headed for destruction and who as the narrative progresses seems less and less inclined to prevent it.

Indeed, he even seems to want to encourage it. He is, in his own words, *courting* annihilation, in a drive toward death that is sexualized. He leaves clues for his wife Akiko, a visual artist who for a good part of the novel remains unaware of his maddened sex life. He both longs to be discovered and longs to remain hidden, both does and doesn't want to hurt her.

Ducornet's style is lyrical in this novel, as always beautifully rendered, but it's also deliberately sparser than the lusher prose we find in her other novels. Instead, there's something more sober here, the style slightly stripped back, like a pocketknife whittling a branch to a sharp stick to make it perfect for puncturing an eye. It's a book that stands out from her other work as demanding a different style, a different approach.

What is most remarkable about this short novel is not simply the man's infamous narration, however, but Ducornet's ability to depict a difficult and damaged man in a way that both acknowledges his deeply flawed humanity—the private and originary wounds that have led him to an impasse that can only culminate, at the very least, in self-destruction—without diminishing his monstrosity. As such, it puts us as readers in a position where we are seeing a man at once charismatic and repellent with remarkable clarity, as someone both dangerous and oddly vulnerable, as someone whose face still offers its Levinasian appeal to us even while his vileness remains swollen and unreduced.

And just when we've begun to accept this voice, begun to become uncomfortably comfortable with it, Ducornet shifts again, bringing us back to the third person we began with. She remains with it for the last chapters of the book. All that dark intimacy fades into the distance. It's as if we've been ensorcelled, living in a sort of dark anti-Eden, and now are driven out into the lone and dreary world, faced to watch the final steps of his destruction from the outside, more objectively, with the spell broken. Thus the infamous narrative remains enclosed within a more objective third person story. He is allowed to speak, and to speak fully, but he is not allowed to have either the first or last word. If we consider that his profession is that of the "talking cure", the fact that he's not given the podium at the beginning or end, that his voice becomes one of many reported or quoted by the larger third person narrative voice, is quite significant. Whereas Nabokov's psychiatrist's voice at the beginning of *Lolita* feels tacked on, a concession to the publisher that a voice of reason should appear before the main narrative to tell people what to think, here we have a sense of a writer trying to balance the objective world and the people in it against one man's maddened interior, to allow the *narrateur infâme* to speak, but to keep him at the same time boxed in.

Netsuke is a book at once merciless and profoundly satisfying, one that engages the reader in a man's self-destruction and then ethically re-engages us with his wife and with the world outside of him. It's a tremendous piece of writing, unsettling, thoughtful and economical, dangerous, daring, and satisfying.

The Fragility of Validity

NADINE MAINOLD

Rikki Ducornet's Gazelle *inspired this piece, the voice of which would never have found expression without Elizabeth and her father's ivory chess set.*

Like a lover with an arsenal of mercurial excuses, my promise to call Mariana when I return to Rome some weeks later will remain unfulfilled.

I had finished escorting a group of American private school students and teachers from Paris through Provence as far as Nice, along the Cinque Terra to Portofino, inland to Pisa, *Firenze*, Siena, and finally *Roma*. Two of the teachers, a husband-and-wife couple from Seattle, pressed me to act as their personal guide for a separate tour they had arranged for their extended holiday, and we departed the morning after the students and other teachers had boarded their flight back to the States.

Dee and Mick had hoped, during the chaperoning of their students, to improve their grasp of the Italian language enough to address the demands of a self-drive exploration of the peninsula's central regions. Previous trips to other European destinations had sometimes resulted in ample opportunity to practice their command of Euro-zone languages when a tour leader exhibited insufficient competence, but being a native of the Veneto, I deprived them of that chance for this tour.

I was grateful for the work, despite operating illegally as a private guide, my license only allowing me to act as a group manager. Being

American, they overruled objections to accept what was a ridiculously high fee for the pleasure of taking them sightseeing along some of the less-travelled tourist routes. We first drove south to *Napoli* and the Costiera Amalfitana, and after a journey leading us through L'Aquila, Assisi, Bologna and *Venezia*, they insisted on visiting what remained of my family in the tiny, obscure village of *Lusiana* on the southern end of the *Altopiano dei Sette Comuni*; many of my uncles, aunts, and cousins had emigrated either to larger Italian cities or to Switzerland, the UK, the US, even as far as New Zealand and Australia. It was while working in a cousin's fruit plantation in northern Queensland that I had met my Colombian friend of the champagne-soaked kisses.

We spent the final two nights of their holiday in my parents' *palazzo* overlooking *Parco Sempione* in central *Milano*. I rarely see my parents and this visit is no exception; my mother is currently posted to the Italian Embassy in Hungary and my father works as a consultant heart surgeon wherever the Italian government sees fit to employ my mother in her quest to achieve Ambassador status. *Milano* fascinates me not the slightest, but Dee and Mick were delighted to attend a fashion show and visit the *Duomo* and the *Castello Sforzesco*. With the onset of travel fatigue, to be expected after so many weeks of journeying, I proposed they forego further sightseeing; instead we enjoyed a leisurely last lunch at L'Assassino before I drove them to Malpensa Aeroport, exchanging addresses and promises to remain in contact.

Dee and Mick had hired the vehicle for an additional day to provide me with return transport to Rome and I negotiate the afternoon snarls of traffic back to the *centro storico*, fortunate to capture a parking spot not far from my parents' building. Their apartment occupies the two upper floors and they rent out the remaining three: the ground floor to a partnership of accountants and the intervening levels as corporate housing for expatriate families.

The Eritrean cleaner my parents employ had already whisked through the guest bedrooms and tidied away any signs of our brief sojourn, leaving a collection of post on the marble mantelpiece of the entry hall, and I rifle idly through it. The only correspondence of interest is a pudgy brown package postmarked Mozambique and bearing my sister's elegant scrawl. I hesitate to open it; Cassandra and I are not close. We have never overcome sibling rivalry, although with maturity and hindsight we manage a cordial relationship. A successful photojournalist, she recently accepted an assignment to cover the politics and economics of Southern Africa. Insofar as my parents lament my incomprehensible decision to quit my partner-track legal career, they laud Cassandra for having made the switch from fashion icon follower to socially conscious chronicler. The irony of the situation underscores and fuels my animosity towards my elder sibling and my parents, content to hire domestic staff at unconscionably meagre salaries by virtue of ethnic origin and the discrepancy between labour supply in lesser developed countries and worker motivation in Italy. Northerners murmur, always behind cupped hands and in tones of sardonic and patronising amusement, that Africa's border lies immediately south of wherever one lives; a discrimination reflecting the same deep-seated prejudice informing Alex' curiosity regarding my sexual peccadilloes, as if the colour of a partner's skin lends him or her an added dimension of novelty, and which deters me from sharing the pot-pourri of experiences garnered during the years my mother was stationed in Ethiopia and Malawi.

Her first African assignment had seen us resident in Addis Ababa for three years, coinciding with my last year of high school and my first two years of university. During the former, I had secretly dated a *mulatto*, as the children of mixed marriages are named, shunned equally by both Italian and Ethiopian communities. Marco's paternal family had lived four generations in Addis, from the time of Italy's attempted colonisation, and his mother belonged to the educated Amharic elite that had deserted the country during Haile Selassie's fall and the pogroms of the Sino Soviet-backed Mengistu government. Marco's father worked for an international aid agency and had fallen in love with Marco's mother at a fundraising function in Geneva; she had returned long enough to bear two sons before assigning Marco and his brother to the care of poorer relatives while she alternated residency between Europe and Ethiopia. That Marco had a number of half-siblings was no secret amongst either community.

We met during a three-day school excursion to the Awash National Park, where Marco was working as the skipper of our white water rafting expedition, and not until twenty twittering co-ed students have donned life vests and stepped awkwardly or athletically in the snub-nosed orange rubber dinghies do I notice him; I look at shimmering hazel eyes as his hand on my waist steadies me on the craft and my stomach lurches. For the briefest instant, as he murmurs his name and smiles a welcome, his features shift from the bland professionalism of a guide to the quickening of interest I have learned to recognise as male appreciation. I sit at the prow, surreptitiously watching the play of his muscles while he helps the rest of my classmates, trying to discern any difference in the way he interacts with the other girls. He is friendly and courteous, making jokes and establishing an easy camaraderie, but each time our eyes connect, with the immutable acceleration of magnets colliding, we confess a flaring of concupiscent interest. By the time the excursion halts for a late afternoon lunch at our first campsite, adrenaline-charged and soaked with spray from the rapids through which we have passed, I am faint as much from hunger and exertion as the nausea-inducing apprehension twisting my innards.

Marco ignores me, or more generally, this group of status-sensitised students and the two teachers assigned us, directing his coffee-skinned *Habesha* assistants to unload supplies from the rafts dragged to a short sweep of sand-strewn shore where the river current stagnates as dark, mud-green eddies. We are to camp two nights in the National Park, the first here and the second at another site located further down the river, before returning via bus to Addis on the morning of the third day. The group is divided in two: one to pitch tents and one to cook lunch. I choose to struggle with canvas and rope and concentrate on hammering tent pegs in the dry, loamy soil of a sheltered area surrounded by scrubby, black-stemmed acacia jostling silver-barked gum trees. Large, smooth, ash-coloured stones border the campsite and we are cautioned against crossing these; the reason will become clear when we are joined at dusk by a number of rifle-bearing locals: they are the night-shift camp guards who will patrol the perimeter against lions.

Whether by chance or design, the tent I occupy with two other girls, both of whom I know well enough to share gossip and avoid disclosing personal drama, is sited opposite Marco's, discovered when we emerge from our respective quarters after dinner. We stand inert as startled gazelles, our gazes locked. He is naked to his waist, carrying a bundle of cloth and a wet case. Were he one of the boys in my class I would smirk and roll my eyes before sashaying off, claiming first right of the camp's washing amenities with a wilfully provocative sway of hips; instead my tongue flicks nervously over paper-dry lips, my breath stilled. I clutch my towel, flannel, and toothbrush.

"Um . . . I can . . . brush my teeth later." I half-turn away from him to lift the tent flap.

Marco smiles, inclining his head tactfully and gesturing at the pebble path. "It's better if you go now. Not a good idea to be wandering around alone after the fires are doused. I don't mind waiting."

I swallow and step in front of him, his torch lighting a path before my feet, feeling as though his eyes are burning a hole somewhere in the area between my shoulder blades. We reach the wet block and he opens the door to the shower chamber, ushering me inside.

"What's your name?" He lights a number of candles set in small recesses in the stone walls and douses the torch.

"Claudia." My toothbrush and flannel placed on the rock-hewn surface of the vanity sink, I turn and face him, gripping my towel as if a shield.

"Marco Avveduto." He extends his hand and I have no choice but to take it. His fingers are warm, the skin on his palm slightly calloused, and his grasp firm. My towel is dropped at the tremor his touch looses through me and we sink to the stone floor, but Marco is first to retrieve it. Wordlessly, he hands me the towel and steps outside, the door pulled shut behind him. The night sounds of the bush erupt in my ears as if an orchestra has commenced a wild *contrapunto* of intermittent howls, chirrups and rustles, his exit the downward stroke of an invisible conductor's baton.

Breathing shallowly, I engage the lock and glance at loops and whorls in the wood of the door, but all are intact. Fingers trembling, I remove my shorts and top, bra and bikini briefs, standing naked and staring at myself in the cracked mirror: dark shoulder-length hair, mahogany in the daylight, frames a fine boned face punctuated by sulky lips and sloe eyes. My body is shaped in part by the sport at which I have trained for years; running transfers easily between countries. My breasts are full, hips fuller, tapering to long thighs and calves. In the preceding twelve months I have begun to recognise, if not respect, my effect on the opposite sex, leaving me confused and confident, bashful and brazen.

A match strikes and a faint whiff of tobacco wafts inside the room as I turn on the water and gasp at the temperature, my nipples immediately shrivelling to the size of peas. I flannel myself quickly, goose pimples sprinkling my skin, and close off the jet of water. Dripping over the uneven stones, I reach for my towel and yelp: sitting atop a fold, almost invisible in the soft glow of the candlelight, is a scorpion.

"Claudia? What's wrong?" Alarm renders Marco's voice sharp.

"It's . . . it's fine." Grasping my toothbrush, I poke the scorpion, which immediately flips its sting over its body. I jump back, slipping on the wet floor to crash sideways against the door.

"Claudia!" Marco raps the wood. "What's happening?"

"It's just . . . just a scorpion." I pick up my underwear, willing to suffer water droplets rather than attempt dislodging the arachnid a further time. The memory of being stung by a scorpion as a child is painful. "Don't worry, I'm used to them. We have them in Italy, too."

"Claudia! Keep away from it—it's deadly." He rattles the door so hard the latch pops and the door swings open. "Are you alright?"

I yelp again, scooping up my clothes as the lean length of him fills the door frame. He averts his eyes and I back inside the shower recess, mortified at my state of undress and acutely conscious of his proximity. He reeks of the seductive scent of tobacco, the perfume of the cinnamon and cardamom ever-present in Ethiopian coffee, and the acrid tang of sweat. I oscillate between a stomach-cramping awareness of him and chagrin at that sensation and my demoralising nudity.

"Where is it?"

I point at the towel and he peers carefully at it, picking it up and shaking it. The offending creature has disappeared, crowning my humiliation, and Marco stretches the towel at head height and hangs it as a curtain across the shower. "Go on, I won't watch. The sooner you're clothed the sooner I can look for it." The dancing note of humour echoing through his voice, evidence he thinks I have fabricated the fact of the scorpion, prompts me to dress in seconds. I reef the towel from his hands and fold it in an untidy bundle, cradling it against my chest to prevent my hands from shaking.

"Thanks," I mutter, chin down as I sidle past him towards the door, to be stopped abruptly. His hand on my shoulder is a brand.

"Let me bring your shoes." He points at my feet. "I'm afraid the first aid kit isn't really equipped for scorpion stings." He steps briefly outside, returning with my hiking sandals, and kneels to place the shoes beside me. In that moment, as he looks up, his hazel eyes arrest my breath and double my heart beat, striking me with a gut-rending impulse to feel his tongue exploring my mouth and his lips pressing against mine.

He stands and brushes his hands. "I'll just be a few minutes. Don't walk back to your tent or I'll be worrying about you stepping on an adder."

Dismissed, I sit on a towel-swathed rock and stare at the stars, listening to him whistling and the water splashing against the walls. Images slide across my mind's eye: water misting the tautness of honey-dark skin, sluicing across his smooth, bare chest, along the breadth of his shoulders and down the muscled length of his arms, across the narrow-bridged nose and high cheekbones, running inside his mouth, dribbling down the cords of his neck, following the channels between his ribs, dividing in rivulets over his sculpted stomach and abdomen, disappearing in pubic hair snuggling a retracted penis, and plunging down his flanks. I shake my head abruptly, chewing my lip and wrapping my arms tightly around myself. I have giggled with friends over illicitly acquired magazines and had my share of gauche boyfriends and furtive, mechanical gropings in the darkened last row of a cinema. Once Cassandra took me aside, after a virulent argument with my parents about attending a hidden rave, to lecture me on the unwritten rules of how far, how fast, and how to retain sexual supremacy. Her gratuitous advice fell upon unresponsive ears, not just because her overture was yet another instance of her flaunting her ever-incontrovertible *savoir faire*, but because none of the boys from whom I had accepted the tag 'girlfriend' served more than providing me entrée to the clique of the high school where I found myself enrolled according to our expatriate location. Arousal, either at the sight of the masculine physique or elicited by the touch of a male, has yet to figure in my experience.

The door creaks open and Marco appears wearing a white T-shirt and pale linen chinos, his hair glistening in tight ringlets pressed damp against his skull, his mouth curling in a smile and his eyes twin pools of gleaming enigma. My stomach somersaults and I straighten, lowering my gaze and crumpling the towel around my flannel and toothbrush.

"Did you find it?" I match his pace, my eyes following the bobbing light of the torch illuminating the path back to the tented area.

"Yes. We're lucky it decided to make your acquaintance."

"Oh. Why?"

"I wasn't joking, Claudia. That species is lethal. Normally the park staff check this hut before a group of tourists arrives. This one must have been hiding for some time. Something about the way you smell attracted it."

"Is that meant to be funny?"

Marco laughs, a pleasant tenor sound hanging in the night air. "Not really. Scorpions have an acute sense of smell. That's how they hunt. You either had fruit wrapped in your towel or a stray lizard."

"So it's nothing to do with how I smell?" I toss my hair and raise an eyebrow, hand on my hip as I halt in front of him, arching my back, challenging him to retreat.

"Oh, it's everything, Claudia." Marco steps closer and my bravado flees. I point through the trees at the leaping flames of the camp fire where most of the class have gathered: someone is strumming a guitar and a harmonica warbles an accompanying melody.

"I don't want to keep you from the entertainment." My voice holds the timbre of a file rasped over wood and the cadence of an unbalanced metronome.

"You're not." He hands me the torch and gestures in the direction of our tents. "Just leave it inside the tent flap, please."

Infuriated with his blithe acquiescence to my withdrawal, I lean towards him and tilt my face upwards. "Of course. But I'd have thought you'd be interested in something other than same-old."

In such propinquity I can see the pupils of his eyes dilate in the reflected firelight and hear the slow intake of his breath, his lips twitching as he curls his fingers around my wrist, his thumb caressing the soft inner skin. I shiver, wanting to feel his thumb slide beyond that narrow band of my forearm.

"We can go back to the outside of your tent, Claudia, and no further. You're beautiful, but I'm not about to get my *culo* kicked out of here for messing around with a schoolgirl."

I gulp. Marco is no callow youth on whom to practice fledgling siren skills. His thumb on my wrist pools warmth from which a slow river flows up my arm, winds around my shoulders and chest, and sinks to my abdomen; he is infinitely more adept in the art of seduction than I, and no matter how I try to tempt him, he can and will refuse me. The thought is at once ignominious and, naturally, inflammatory. I moisten my lips with my tongue and pout, sighing and beginning to tug my wrist from his grasp.

"Oh, no matter, Marco. I wouldn't want to get kicked out of school for messing around with the hired help."

His fingers and thumb clamp around my arm and his nostrils flare as he snorts, a low-pitched laugh and something else that should feel threatening. He pulls me towards him and whips past me in an imitation of the rock'n'roll dance steps we have been learning at school in preparation for our graduation ball, to exchange our places and block my view of the camp fire. The expression on his now shadowed face is indiscernible.

"You really don't want to take 'no' for an answer, do you?" He leans me against the trunk of a smooth barked gum and bends his head, tracing his lips along the line of my jaw, breathing in the whorl of my ear and outlining it with his tongue, before kissing my neck down to the hollow of my throat and continuing up to my other ear. I tremble and the muscles of my legs become fluid; without the support of the tree I will fall, and he has not even kissed me.

Somewhere in the darkness behind us voices murmur and Marco stiffens, his head angled to one side as he listens. The words are unclear; he calls a greeting in Amharic and I realise the voices are those of the camp guards. He cups my shoulder in his hand and guides me to the path in the direction of our tents; my stomach churns like the rapids of the river we rode earlier, my pulse pounding like an untamed and galloping horse. I think of nothing remotely intelligent to say and too much that encourages trouble as we walk in silence to our tents. The open flap of mine shows two empty sleeping bags and one, off to the far side, filled with uneven bumps. I shove my bundle of towel inside and turn to face Marco standing with his arms folded across his chest, watching me.

"I guess . . . um . . . I'll be fine, now. Thanks."

"You know where I am if you need anything. Except . . . anything that might end up in fireworks." He lifts a finger and places it gently across my lips. "Sleep well, Claudia." He strides back along the path in the direction of the guards, the beam from the torch bouncing in front of him.

Inside the tent I rummage in my rucksack until I find the dynamo battery-less torch my parents gave me for the trip, before dragging my sleeping bag outside and winding the torch. It emits a thin stream of light with which I inspect the leaf-littered area beside the tent. Satisfied no scorpions are present, I stretch out the sleeping bag and lie upon it, searching out constellations in the sky memorised during childhood. The easiest collection of stars to find, and most appropriate considering where my mother's diplomatic career has herded us, is Cassiopeia. The obtuse-angled 'W' cluster is clearly visible against the layered sweep of a black sky studded with diamantine rivets of light.

At the sounds of footsteps crunching over gravel and a muffled giggle, I drop my gaze from the stars and stare at the path where a match flares, momentarily illuminating the face of the girl yet to take her place in our tent as she lights a cigarette. Everybody knows everybody who smokes, including the teachers, an activity only policed if made overt, and one I avoid because of the fear of ruining my running; I am good enough to compete, although Cassandra is always quick to label me an outsize fish in the small mere of our expatriate peers whenever I place. I watch the glowing tip of the cigarette zigzag in slow motion between my tent mate and her companion, recognised as her Brazilian boyfriend when they near the clearing. They finish the cigarette and step as indistinct shadows towards the tent, hesitating at the entrance before he follows her inside, and I am glad I have claimed a space to sleep beyond the confines of the tent. If the other girl awakes, a hissed discussion will ensue, likely resulting in the pair ousting the single because of the potential to be caught if they remain outside, or she will sleep, or imitate it, through their sound-strangled fumblings. Most of the senior girls are still, albeit only technically, virgins. Too many prostitutes and discreet opportunities exist in Addis to expect celibacy from the boys.

The implications of Addis' black butterfly economy had chrysalised and confronted me earlier in the year when my mother was selected for a three-month emergency stint in Rwanda and my parents agreed she should go alone. She could have refused, at an estimated and undesirable cost to her career, but my father had only ever supported her decisions, and when I arrived home from school earlier than planned one afternoon, I discovered the cost to my parents' marriage. Our residence is not as opulent as the Ambassador's, but my mother's position as Minister entitles us to more space than required, and the long hallway splitting the high-ceilinged, marble-tiled house allows sound to travel uninterrupted. I had dumped my schoolbag in the kitchen and was pouring a glass of water when I heard a grunting noise. The housekeeper was hanging out the washing and I had greeted the guard and the gardener after entering our compound gate; Cassandra is in London, studying fashion photojournalism, and the house should be empty. I pad along the hallway, my running shoes silent on the stone, suspicion seeping like poison through my mind, and stop and listen to the sounds issuing from one of the guest bedrooms, its door ajar: a female voice, high-pitched and breathless, in faltering English; my father, gruffly, *"apri la tua figa."*

I push open the door so hard it swings in an exploding arc against the wall and rebounds. In the second before it slams shut in my face I see my father in his unbuttoned linen shirt, his pants a puddle at his skinny ankles, kneeling over the naked body of a supine girl and forcing her chocolate-brown legs towards her fuzz-haired head as his white and flabby buttocks clench on a forward thrust of his hips.

I run to the kitchen and grab my bag, knocking over the water as I bolt from the house to the stables. Inside the cool gloom of the long, low building, surrounded by the snaffling sounds and ammonia aroma of horse, my lunch presses at the back of my throat, and I retch miserably in a bucket half-filled with urine-drenched sawdust and dung.

The rest of the afternoon was whiled away brushing down horses and mucking out stables and chattering in beginner's Amharic with the stable hands, trying to escape from and eradicate that image. I wanted to ignore it, pretend it was a figment of imagination, consign it to the coal pit of spike-painful memories buried and abandoned, and I refused to acknowledge its corollary: my complicity in discovering my father, since I could have drunk the water and headed for the stables without investigation, holding that spark of intuition in abeyance.

My father is waiting for me when I finally slink back to the house.

"Claudia!" His tone is peremptory. *"Vieni qui."* I halt in the archway of the salon where my parents usually entertain visitors of diplomatic significance and stare at him; showered and dressed impeccably, as usual, and seated on a chaise-longue. He waves at a chair opposite and I shake my head.

"We need to talk, Claudia." He remains seated and gestures again. "*Adesso.*"

"*Papà*, I have nothing to discuss with you." I spin on the ball of my foot, stopping mid-stride at his next words.

"It would be better if you didn't jump to conclusions like a child. Behave like an adult and I'll treat you as one."

I swing back, sneering in distaste and re-animated shock, my voice throbbing with disgust. "If that's behaving like an adult, I don't see the incentive to grow up."

"Claudia, I would have preferred that you had learned of this from your mother. But since it's happened this way, you deserve an explanation. *Vieni qua e sederti.*"

I am filthy, sweat-soaked and stinking of the stables, and we know it; sitting on the chair is a breach of my mother's etiquette of cleanliness, and mentioning her is incentive and impediment to gaining my confidence. "I'll shower and change."

He nods his assent. I wash and dress in jeans and T-shirt, and on my return, an ice-bucket from which protrudes an open bottle is standing on the drinks board. Two fluted glasses have been placed on the low table between the chaise-lounge and the chair I occupy, not the one my father previously indicated. He rises and lifts the bottle from the bucket, wipes water drops with a serving cloth, and pours bubbles of rose in the glasses. The housekeeper brings a tray of olives, buffalo milk *bocconcini*, and pickled vegetables, sets the tray on the glass table, returns the bottle to the bucket, and exits. My father passes me a glass of *prosecco* and raises his own.

"*Salute.*" After the perfunctory *chink*, he resumes his seat.

"*E allora, Papà.* What do you mean, Mama knows?" I sip the semi-dry sparkling wine, the produce of a cousin's vineyard in the Veneto, specially imported at the Italian tax-payer's expense and justified by my father, who claims he obtains the wine at a discount and never imports the full quota allocated to my mother's status.

"*Abbiamo raggiunto un accordo*, Claudia. I don't have affairs. I've never stood in the way of her career. But she cannot expect me to wait for her like a school boy while she fulfils her duties elsewhere. I don't ask her what she does. *E lei non mi chiede cosa faccio io.*"

"So who was that? If you're not having an affair?"

He raises one bushy eyebrow, his lips thinning. "*È ovvio, no?*"

My jaw drops and I blink, before gulping a mouthful of *prosecco* to regain my composure. The bubbles fizzle in my nose. "*Una puttana.*"

"*Si.* A pure transaction, Claudia. I need a physical release. A prostitute provides it. No messy entanglements. No-one is hurt and your mother is not threatened."

"No-one is hurt?" I splutter *prosecco*, shying away from the implication of that statement for the likelihood of conjugal bliss and instead retreating behind pragmatism. "*Papà, ma tu sei un medico.* What about HIV? It's rampant."

"*Precisamente.* Therefore, no exchange of bodily fluids. I make them take a test at the clinic first. As well as provide them, on top of their fee, with condoms and spermicides for use with their clients. They know they can always come to me if any other kind of trouble develops, providing they are discreet."

"*Seccatura? Che cosa intendi?*"

"I'm sure you're aware of the reasons behind unwanted pregnancies and the need to abort. They can't afford the children they have, or they are supporting siblings. *Spesso le due.* Not all men who use prostitutes are as considerate as I am. I provide them with income as well as a free termination service."

I am conversing with a stranger. That my father can sit here and discuss these women as objects is stupefying, but that my mother knows and condones it is a rank betrayal of the romantic view I hold of their marriage; whenever peers at school have spoken with a pseudo-cynicism of parental strife, I have always felt smugly aloof from such problems, and whatever else, my parents are supposed to represent ideal love. "How long have you and Mama . . . had this agreement?"

"*Non importa*, Claudia." He skewers an olive with a toothpick and chews it efficiently, spitting the seed at a napkin.

"And Cassandra—I suppose she knows?" The bitterness in my voice resounds and he shrugs, *tsk-tsking* impatiently and wiggling his delicate surgeon's fingers in disregard. "*E Mama* . . . so she has 'toy boys'?"

My father sets his glass carefully on the table and his hand, as he spears a calcareous-white cheese ball, quivers. He stands and walks to the drinks board without turning around.

"*Chiaro, è una possibilità.* She is an alluring, magnetic woman, Claudia. I would be a fool to think that she would not enjoy attention, that she might not find another man . . . attractive."

A light explodes behind my eyes and I sit stunned at what my father has revealed: he sleeps with prostitutes because he suspects my mother. I almost gag again and swallow the last of the wine, as much to keep bile from rising as to provide a means to escape further discussion.

"I have some essays I need to write, *Babbo*. I'll be down to eat when I've finished." I set my glass quickly on the table and leave.

The memory of him standing next to the sideboard, his head bowed, fades with the rustling of the tent flap and I crane my neck to see who will emerge. The Brazilian youth crawls out, tucking his singlet inside his shorts and lighting another cigarette, using the match as a torch and stumbling his way along the path to wherever he will sleep. I return my eyes to the blanket of stars above, too lazy to move and not wanting to be drawn in any post-grappling dissection of their encounter. The stars wheel slowly beneath fluttering eyelids . . .

A sudden alertness prickles all over my body in the same instant of cataloguing my surroundings and realising where I am. A low rumble, a mix of growl and snarl, issues nearby, followed by the sound of a rifle bolt being drawn back and the muted jabbering of the guards' voices. I freeze, my breath catching like a bubble of trapped air in my throat, my ears straining for the slightest snap of a twig and my eyes for the barest hint of movement presaging a lion or a hyena. A piercing whistle rents the night and the guards' voices move away. Long minutes pass until the nocturnal resonances of the bush resume a reassuring repetition, and I curl upwards to sit, exhaling in uneven gasps. I wind the torch unsteadily and shine the wavering beam at the bush, sweeping it in a low circle around the clearing, almost dropping the torch in panic when the ray falls upon a seated human figure. Marco.

He straightens, walking silently across before squatting at my feet. The torchlight dims and merges with the chiaroscuro effect of the starlight, silhouetting his profile.

"Are you just a magnet for trouble or do you have some stunningly good reason for sleeping outside? It takes a lion considerably more time to haul you off from the inside of a tent. Or didn't you realise that?"

His tone deliquesces my fear like acid searing flesh. "The tent was otherwise occupied. Or did you just bypass school and go straight to Lone Ranger status without ever going on an excursion?"

Teeth flash white as he laughs. "No, I . . . know what sharing a tent is like. You can't stay here, Claudia. Come on. Have they finished?"

I chew my lip, unwilling to be herded inside the confines of the tent and presuming he has only just returned. "How long have you been sitting there?"

"Not long. There's a very young male lion wandering around. Looks like he's been evicted from his pride. He's not in great shape. The guards have hustled him away but there's no point taking risks. You need to sleep inside."

The thought of the tent is stifling: lying wake imagining the exploits of my tent mate while Marco is sleeping scant and beckoning metres away. "Do you play cards?"

"Do I . . . what?"

"Give the guards time to make sure the lion doesn't come back. I'd feel safer. And they'll have time to . . ." I nod at the tent, grateful he is unable to see the blush spreading across my cheeks. Fabrication is not one of my strengths.

Marco extends his hand, helping me to my feet, and bends to roll up my sleeping bag. I follow him to his tent and he shines his torch inside, holding the flap open so I can crawl in, before he flicks the switch on a small hurricane lamp which bathes the tent in a soft glow. He folds my sleeping bag as a cushion and sits opposite me on his.

"Do you play backgammon?"

I nod, unsmiling and jubilant; I play obscure card games a mathematics teacher had taught me and with which few others are familiar, but my grandfather had been a backgammon enthusiast, mercilessly thrashing me until I learned to imitate his various tactics and score victories of my own. Before his death he had declared me his equal and given me a beautiful antique backgammon board, and my memories of him are amongst those most treasured from my childhood.

Marco extracts a board from the large tote bag at the back of the tent and sets up the pieces, chivalry dictating I toss the dice first to determine who will open play; his die is highest in value and he begins, his first moves revealing him to be a skilled player assuming I am not. I roll some high dice sequentially and opt for an obvious run home, confirming his preconceptions, and his throws of the dice remain low, enabling me to win the first game. I retain the opening move for the next game and win it, this time using a combination of bold moves and defensive positioning.

"Why did you suggest cards?" He has succeeded, barely, in interrupting my winning streak at the third game, and he is no longer smiling; we have agreed to the best of five and the next game is crucial for him.

"Because I didn't know you played backgammon and cards take less space in a rucksack?" Smirking, I feel supremely in control. Upending his assumptions has relaxed me; my stomach no longer flips when he looks at me and goose pimples have stopped rippling over my skin whenever our hands meet to exchange the dice. I have long since forgotten the real reason used to suggest a diversion.

"Or because you knew how long they were going to take?" He twitches aside the tent flap and peers briefly at the other tent, before turning to wink in patient collusion. "They should have finished ages ago but I haven't heard anyone go past."

This time the blush colouring me beetroot from neck to cheeks must be unmistakable in the lamplight. Marco watches me quizzically for a moment until realisation darkens his hazel eyes, the pupils growing so large I feel as though I am falling within the lambent depths. The hair on my arms rises and the tent seems to shrink, the ambience thickening with a crackling tension.

"There was no boyfriend, was there?"

"Wrong." I breathe in, tossing the dice, to be rewarded with two fives. "There was. But he had already gone and I didn't want to go to sleep. Your turn."

He accepts the dice and throws a three and a four. If I win, the best of five will fall in my favour and I have no excuse not to return to my tent; if I lose, we will play another game, implying he prefers me to stay even if courting danger. I lead with a high risk gambit, he pounces with his next throw, and I grind my teeth, deciding that losing is an embarrassment I have no wish to endure. We both remove each other's counters to the bar before I eventually concede defeat. He wins the opening move for the final game and establishes a defensive strategy; I counter with sheer luck and double sixes and he picks up the cup, pausing.

"Since you seem desperate to make my life complicated, I think it's time we evened up the stakes."

I lean back, resting on one elbow and pinching my lower lip with my other thumb and forefinger. "I can't imagine anything that would have the same effect."

Marco draws my hand away from my mouth and kisses my palm on the mound of flesh at the base of my thumb. I want to pull away, the sheer intimacy of his touch threatening to overwhelm me, and I want him to continue kissing me along the lines of the tremors that race up my arm and arrow to my stomach.

"You're not going out with anyone, are you? There's no boyfriend in that group," he nicks his head in the direction of the main campfire, "out there, no-one waiting for you in Addis?"

I nod, mesmerised. He is making love to my hand and I can think of nothing else.

"If you win, you choose where you sleep, for the rest of tonight and tomorrow night, and you choose whether we play backgammon, or cards, or . . . anything else. If I win, I choose where you sleep. But I don't mean just here at the camp, Claudia."

I am dumb. I can only stare at him, my body a quivering mass of sensations that begin and end with his lips dragging over the skin of my palm and wrist.

"When we arrive back in Addis, we see each other. Again. As in going out together. I don't want anything less."

I blink. I cannot keep a single rational thought in my mind, let alone two thoughts coherently conjoined.

"So? Do you agree or . . . shall we just stop right here and you go back to your tent?" He places my hand gently on my knee and holds up the cup, ready to shake it.

"I win, I choose. You win, you choose."

He throws the dice and two sixes roll up. "Yes." He hands me the cup after placing one of my counters on the bar. "If you throw the dice . . ."

I throw. I lose. I sleep in his tent with his arms around me and his breath warming my ear until dawn streaks pink and apricot highlights across the blue-black sky and birds sing a chorus of welcome to the milk-gold rays of the sun.

Marco proved to be pomegranate sweet and amarena cherry sour; I represented an unobtainable ethnic purity to him and he represented the illicit, partly exotic for me. When we sailed the calmer waters of infatuation, we revelled in an insatiable sexual tension, but we often stranded on the shores of cultural disparity and would withdraw, wounded, until kisses and caresses charted a course back to compromised harmony. My parents never knew of our relationship, but when Cassandra discovered I had stolen a packet of condoms from her in preparation for Marco's claiming of my maidenhead, she threatened to denounce us. I had no doubt she would do it and arranged to meet with Marco sooner rather than wait for a planned trip to the Red Sea to accomplish my deflowering, and Cassandra retaliated with the unerring accuracy of sibling intuition, thwarting me in the most brutal and blunt way she could: she paid a prostitute to visit Marco and in a foreshadowing of the photographic skill she would later demonstrate, snapped him in an equivocal embrace, hours before our agreed rendezvous. I never spoke with him again, nor did I ever forgive my sister.

I toss the post from Cassandra aside, since my parents are due to return within the month and little is to be gained in forwarding her mail to them in Budapest, and debate whether to stay a third night; I have been absent from Rome almost five weeks and the long-distance traffic will be no less a hindrance in the morning. As I stand in the hallway considering my options, my telephone chimes an incoming message from Alex: have I remembered Luca's birthday tomorrow night and do I need a lift and where have I been the last month? I wheel my travel trolley to the foyer before making a last-minute examination of window locks and the balcony doors of the salon and respond to him once I am seated in the car; after a flurry of messages we agree to meet at Tibertina in the early evening of the following day.

Many Marvelous Things

TOD RISE

In these characteristically beguiling and concise stories, adorned with illustrations by T. Motley, Ducornet plumbs her preoccupation with Rabelais, Swift, and Carroll—treating the reader to tales of bodily ingestions and emissions, the ecosystems of invented magical and grotesque creatures, and darkly humorous takes on sundered marital alliances. Opening lament 'The Wild Child' is narrated by an (un) repentant feral creature, wrested from her kingdom by religious insanity and incarcerated in a "cellar darker and colder than the bunghole of a corpse," before being finally liberated, toothless and de-liced, by her patron, to earn her keep as an example of tamed savagery: "I sit in the parlor on Wednesday to speak to pious ladies about the woods . . . They have taken my club and replaced it with a needle . . . Wind me up and I utter all the Holy Holies you wish."

Brutal erotic dreams are explored in 'Green Air': "A year unfolds reduced to letters of the alphabet and the colours of things dreamed: black ashes, a white body, the green weather within a room. In the final entry he is fucked by someone terrifying . . . she is a shadow as filthy as death, and collapses heavily on him. *A shroud?* he wonders. Has he been fucking beneath the shadow of death all along?", a topic tackled in a tense tone in Ducornet's remarkable and explosive novel *Netsuke*, the predecessor of which is the exploratory inversion (replete with its own scorpion sting) of 'Panna Cotta': "One day Lucinda rebels. An esteemed motivator, she cannot stomach to be held in thrall by another for long.

Without warning she tells him his cooking reeks of death, his kitchen is a morgue in which cadavers by the dozens are stacked—'Cadavers?' he gasps . . . Instead he must listen to her endless chatter about her own career; she speaks of it and her clients with a certain fevered animation. Her clients desire her . . . He pokes through scraps of paper in her desk drawers and although he feels a fool still his heart pounds because of the terrible danger he is in—desiring, disliking, and distrusting a woman simultaneously."

The One Marvelous Thing unfolds with sensory indulgence: Ducornet's universe is powered by exotic smells, tastes, appetites, and a cabinet of esoteric curiosities (*wunderkammer*) as in The Perlmutter Building of 'The Doorman's Swellage', dedicated to L.H.—Ducornet disciple Lily Hoang?—and peppered with delightful malapropisms 'overlapsed pessary', '*floor de leech*', 'all and Sunday' (the latter depicted graphically as the signature to the piece), and "[t]hat big potted plant—*watch your head!—*is a *vagus hippotamic* and as old as The Perlmutter herself. Don't touch it, sir! Harsh desert forage; its thorns are full of brine. It was shipped all the way from the high cliffs of Akhmar by Perlmutter's maiden mother-in-law, the philanthropod and ethnogaff: Lucy Strumpeter, whose book on nose mutilations—feel *that!—*is also bound in mole. That sappy greenness on the mantel is hers, as is the crystal dromedary, the crimp and the barometer. She was a tepid traveller."

Among other pleasures: satirical stories on artists, including the acerbic tale of an Estonian translation of a book gutted by one negative review on the eve of the author's promotional tour; the urban skirmish of two alpha females bent on the acquisition of 'artefacts' at bargain prices and ending with a delicately lesbian interlude in the eponymous fable; the institution of legalised slavery and the repository of broken dreams that is marriage between an Italian girl and her sculptor husband in 'Giulia on Her Knees'; the suggestively titled 'A Secret Life' homaging Robert Coover's *Spanking the Maid*, in which during a visit to Vienna young Gretel's subconscious absorbs daily experiences and transmutes these to nightly visions; and the wickedly amusing riot of language and profound insight that is 'The Ominous Philologist': "A pearl of poor quality is said to be botched; it is a *washpot*, the 'face of a woman dead for a week'; a *tossout*. In her clitoral frenzies, the bipolar Harishchandra insists that the botched pearl is a *tossup*; she is confusing *tossup* with *two bats*: the empty oyster and, by extension, the blown egg and the broken head. In this way does philology become a crime."

The flash fiction 'She Thinks Dots' is hilariously illustrated by Mr. Motley: the interplay between Motley's cartoonish artwork and Ducornet's stories is exceptionally droll. On heavily designed stories such as 'Koi', the inventive drawings complement Ducornet's deeply surreal imagination and talent for anachronistic oddity, and 'The Butcher's Comics', borrowing some of the stories from *The Complete Butcher's Tales*, is a beautiful marriage of text and art, culminating in a spine-chilling rendition of Ducornet's marvellous love-letter to Lewis Carroll, 'Brillig'. A reader triggered by the following sentences will find the collection a veritable treasure: "Only two decades earlier, he had stood in a similar line balancing a tray of bologna quesadillas and weeviled beans so horrible he had complained." And: "After all, the Dickmares are known to unspool and push their pistons forward with such alacrity, a subconical cavity will be stunned into service before it has the chance to ignite."

By the Grace of Rikki

G.N. FORESTER

I wrote to Rikki after reading one of her novels; I had lost interest in reading, had despaired of finding a writer whose work resonated in the manner of the novels of my youth (Aldous Huxley's *The Genius and Goddess* comes to mind). On opening that first book, I rediscovered the magic of reading; it was a gift beyond measure. The correspondence continued (miraculously, generously, for Rikki was working on her own projects while still finding time to respond regularly) as I eagerly explored more of her oeuvre, until confessing that I had scribbled poetry and prose maniacally for years until that juncture where I had had to decide either to take my writing seriously, or leave it buried in a drawer. Having had no courage to embrace life as a starving writer in a garret (I was living in a garret in Paris at the time, teaching English), the decision made itself.

Not until reading Rikki did the muse reawaken. Rikki, deeply sensitive and above all encouraging, immediately offered to read a chapter of a manuscript I had commenced and with which I was struggling. I took some days to respond; already star-struck, now awe-struck as well (as much at my own temerity as at her tolerance), before sending a chapter.

With a surgeon's delicacy and precision, she praised the strengths of the piece, and suggested areas for improvement. For those lucky enough to have been taught by Rikki, they will know the profound care she brings to appraisal, how she nudges understanding and supports insight, while still cultivating the essence of a piece of work.

An example of Rikki's extraordinary empathy (we were discussing incest):

> I must tell you about an experience . . . [he] wrote about a boy and his father. It was great writing and portrayed a loving, compassionate sexuality BUT when I suggested that despite the brilliance of the piece and the sweetness of the erotic world created, still hadn't the father abused his place of trust, didn't the father's seduction of the son IMPLY that the son was somehow powerless to seize the erotic world on his own, make autonomous choices as a sexual being? The same issue as the therapist who fucks his patient, becoming EVERYTHING? But love takes on many forms and I recall the film Loose Change, the boy with his mother: ONCE and it frees him; and I was convinced by the film. Not sure why; it was like a fairy tale; perhaps this freed them both from the father somehow . . . And it was evident at once that this was revolutionary for him, this was acute subversion and he was shaken, struck; he was thoughtful, he was . . . grateful! Astonished! AS writers NO TABOOS!!!!

I wrote a story for her after our next conversation, and her response was thrilling:

> So nice what you do here with the bike as a means to reveal the place, the school bus route, the world that spins out and away from here . . . including the seasons . . . wonderful. The drama so intense, from the parent's humorless rage to the escape into something that IS

shameful; two betrayals within an afternoon and both all about sex. Its enormous! Yet the writing demonstrates a capacity to look OUTWARD, it opens rather than implodes and leads to collapse; it has energy and vision . . .

Whether the manuscript remains lying in a drawer or dusted off and revisited, by the grace of Rikki, I am once again a writer, and a reader.

Postscript: An Email Interview with Rikki

EDITORS

Throughout 2013 while working on The Deep Zoo, Rikki Ducornet kindly and patiently answered a series of rambling questions and musings, elicited from reading her work and originally imagined with the idea of publication, the exchange ultimately finding a place in the Festschrift dedicated to her.

VP: When would be convenient for you to be interviewed?

RD: We could begin any time and I'd just fit it into my writing day . . . If this is helpful, the first four books form a tetralogy based on the elements: Earth, Fire, Water and Air; *The Stain, Entering Fire, The Fountains of Neptune* and *The Jade Cabinet.* (*Phosphor* is, among other things (!): LIGHT!)

VP: In *Gazelle*, you've indicated that the father is based around your own, and you mention elsewhere a recollection regarding the mother of a childhood friend while you lived in Cairo. Given the themes of *Gazelle* (transformation, betrayal/neglect by the parents, fascination with death, stifled development of the sensual persona) what was the impetus for creating the character of the mother—if not autobiographical, had you experienced an adult female figure which lent inspiration for the mother? How did she develop in the context of what you wanted to explore in *Gazelle*? Why is she so virulently driven by her fear of fading? What is your experience of that?

RD: I lived in Cairo for a year as a girl and the book is rooted in and inspired by that childhood experience; I went to school there and became well acquainted with the marvelous complexities of that city. At the time there was a small population (!) and hardly any cars; the city was full of trees and gardens and very safe. One could wander. I walked to school each day alone. As I have said elsewhere the mother was inspired by a friend's mother; this was one of those mysterious decisions that the book made; it was not my 'choice.' My friend's mother was wildly interesting and unsettling; she was larger than life. In some ways our mothers were alike: both were vain and sexy. I recall the two liked to trade clothes, that my mother traded a tube top for a pair of high-heeled sandals and bragged she had made a brilliant deal. The scene at the start of the book when we see the mother dancing naked and singing 'Lilac Wine' (that GREAT song by Eartha Kitt) happened—except that my friend's mother danced alone. There was no lover. This woman also had her body hair removed with hot caramel, and my father liked to joke that the caramels I so loved to eat in Cairo were all made from caramel that had been used in this way. "It is collected and filtered," he told me. "Nothing in Egypt is ever wasted." My friend's mother and mine were obsessed with being beautiful and remaining young—a thing that is not uncommon. Perhaps it has reached crazed proportions in our current culture, but the longing for eternal youth and beauty is, it seems to me, something that drives our species. We love the erotic power of youth, and mortality—finitude in other words—is hard to accept, especially as it announces itself with beauty's loss and the decline of Eros. I mention Cleopatra in the book; her laboratories have been discovered, places where she made face cream and perfume. Egyptian art is replete with images of beautiful people and as one entered the realm of the afterworld one's body was returned to full youth. Everything about the afterworld is like that— brimming with sap. Beauty and its loss is one of the book's themes. Beauty's loss is one of the things about being human that is especially difficult. We cannot help but identify with our physical bodies, and in youth the body is luminous with promise. I think we all respond to that beauty in others, that promise. I think we all are saddened when we look into a mirror, or the face of another and realize our own light is fading.

VP: Of all the male characters, only the magician and the butler are immune to the mother. Why these two? Ramses tells Elizabeth that the mistake he made was to love 'the three of you' . . . did he love the mother? Or, rather, did he really love either Elizabeth and her father since he, in a sense, betrayed both? Was he substituting the mother for Elizabeth because of her age, or does this romanticise the character of Ramses?

RD: Finitude, the loss of youth and beauty, Eros receding—all this is exemplified in the mother. She is clearly neurotic; she is famished and she is unfulfilled. This coupled with her narcissism makes her dangerous to her daughter. I don't think Ramses is witness to the ways the mother is so destructive to the daughter. But he is a man who is very susceptible to Beauty; he has devoted his life to it. And although he is aware of human weakness and vanity, he is also attuned to human fragility and sadness. (And the poetry of the ancient word is rich in these themes. Highly educated, this poetry has—or so I imagine— informed his perception of the world.) So it is clear when he describes the mother to the daughter, he is already somehow taken by a woman he perceives as something of a chimera—part beast, part woman, part goddess; an angel of love and a lioness; a tragic fallen angel (as, perhaps, we all are somehow). And the mother does not leave the father for Ramses; she's a slut and she needs men; she needs to wander the streets; she is fed by this danger, this adventure. Perhaps Ramses' fascination (and recall that we learn of this late; after we see the mother coming on to men in the street) reveals the nature of his own tragic flaw. Because he does love Elisabeth and her father; it seems to me this is clear. People often betray the ones they love and this, I think, is our greatest burden as a species. We cherish one another and yet the awareness of and delight in the other's profound reality is hard to sustain. Yet this betrayal is intolerable to Elisabeth. Not only because of her love for Ramses which is acute (and we see how alone she is, how haunted and how hungry; how Eros has blazed into her life) but because her mother's madness has betrayed Elisabeth's childhood—and this, seemingly, from the beginning. So she is especially fragile. This, also, is a thing Ramses does not know. But even if he did know somehow, Eros rules; it is hard to resist. It creates its own cosmos. It promises that we will, if only for an instant, live like the gods. It promises a taste of eternity. That we receive only a taste—this, too, is our tragedy. Nothing can be sustained. How loving he is when he returns to the house; how tragic he is, speaking to Elisabeth through a closed door!

VP: You've mentioned in interviews that the male Arab characters are life-giving—the warmth displayed towards Elizabeth seems typical of Egyptians, but not necessarily reflecting a religious/cultural aspect of Arabs. What made you see this particularly so as reflective of Arab culture? The incident of the lump of dung thrown at Sakkiet intimates the true position of local women in the society, and Ramses and his mother trying to bring a reluctant village populace towards a less hostile view of women—Ramses's mother is the only female character with any redeeming characteristics, if only partially. Would you say this level of ambiguity has been well understood in your readers, and has it had the effect for which you hoped in 2003 when you first commented on the male Arab characters in *Gazelle*?

RD: Egyptians belong to the Arab League and they speak arabic. So despite the richly various population, in my experience it is common to refer to Egyptians as Arabs.

VP: To what extent are the characters sharply defined when you (the writer) first meet them; how do they present themselves to you? Is it that you have an idea (a theme, since your work explores a number of correlated areas) and the characters grow from that, or a combination— ideas and characters—present themselves? Do you have something 'to say' per se, and the text develops from there? *Gazelle* is so intuitive in the sense of how you handled the thread—the three ages of Elizabeth and her memories—as a means to discuss what you've mentioned here (finitude, decrepitude, Eros, betrayal, fragility of ego) that it seems incredible to think you 'planned' this and it was not simply an organic development. Are you steeped in certain themes (as a result of your life experiences) that coupled with your painterly ability images present which you describe and in so doing, a story evolves?

RD: I have spoken a great deal over the years about my process . . . I am seized by the scruff of the neck; that I lean into the books, that writing is a process of revelation . . . I will say it again: REVELATION! Characters appear; one is inhabited. They demand a book. They clamor. They have big voices. They are driven; they drive me. It's like entering into a fever dream. I have no interest in writing what I know; what interests me is the process of discovery. The books tell me where they need to go. This has always (but for *Netsuke*—which wrote itself in two weeks) meant research; the writing is informed by the new knowledge which feeds the fever. Rigor and Imagination are the words that define my process. A fever dream, an inquiry into the nature of things, entering into a certain 'weather'; listening to a certain 'music'. When I wrote *The Fan-Maker's Inquisition* I read everything Sade had written including all his letters. This knowledge fed the fever that was his voice. The voice had its own energy and was irresistible. 'Hearing' him in French, I needed to find an equivalent music and weather in English. This happened almost at once. I would go downstairs in the morning and there Sade would be, fat and hot for conversation. It was uncanny and delightful; he proved a much better companion than one might have imagined. He was funny. He was unstoppable. The Fan-Maker opened the book wide so he could enter in.

VP: The best writers are those who leave no trace of their artifice in their work (meaning there are no seams or joins in the text or any clues that give the rise as to how a story developed). Some readers may lament a lack of conventional plot, but transition and change exists within *Gazelle*—it is Elizabeth's story of who she is and how she came to be—yet it seems so natural and spontaneous as though she appeared on the page without you having done anything more than paint her with words.

RD: *Gazelle* was driven by my rich memories of Cairo. It felt more like a deep, irresistible reverie than a fever dream. *Phosphor in Dreamland* was a waking dream; I was deeply in love and it was a fantasy written for my lover. I had thought I would be writing about my Grandmother's Cuba, but Cuba became Birdland and my grandmother appeared only briefly haunted by a sexed phantom smoking a cigar! *The Fountains of Neptune* began after a powerful liminal image just as I was falling asleep, of a child drowning but not dying; *The Jade Cabinet* owes its heat to Lewis Carroll—the writer with the greatest influence on my imagination. The curious thing about writing is no matter how much thought and work goes into it, still one feels like the instrument of something of immense mystery and vitality. Eros, I suppose. The Breath of Life. I have never understood writers who speak of boredom, although I do understand the risks of resurgent pain. Writing is all about mutability; the writer changes as she writes her book (as she is written by her book); if the reader isn't changed, well, what a waste of everyone's time! Maybe a bad book is like a bad marriage. No fever, the weather is oppressive, and the music has stopped.

VP: Have you read any of Pierry Louys and Lawrence Durrell? What were your thoughts? Henry Miller's *Quiet Days in Clichy* or *The Oranges of Hieronymus Bosch*?

RD: I read Pierre Louys many years ago, when I was living in France. And yes, Durrell; voraciously. I read his *Black Book* in Algeria! It was an important book for me; they all were. I read him in my early twenties. When I was around 17, 18 I read all of Henry Miller, and Anais Nin. I've not returned to them in a long time, but I was deeply taken by both; I'd read Sade's *Justine* at 16 (!) along with Swift (my father's way of introducing me to moral philosophy!), so I was prepared, perhaps overly so, for Miller!

VP: Were you to pick a Surrealist painter, who would be your favourite? What about the Expressionists?

RD: Max Ernst! He's up there with Bosch. I have been flabbergasted by Ernst, enchanted, inspired all my life. And the American Surrealist Joseph Cornell. Klee, Kandinsky, Ensor, Shiele.

VP: And Giulio Romano?

RD: Romano! So wonderful at the Hermitage after countless kilometers of crucifixions to see one of his vast, nearly life-sized, erotic encounters!

VP: Who is/are your favourite film directors(s)?

RD: Fellini, Bergman, Satyajit Ray come at once to mind, top of the list, Godard, Tavernier; Kathryn Bigelow is about to join their ranks. But there are so many; I love movies! Cocteau's *Blood of the Poet* was tremendously significant to me as a child; the film does not travel well in time, however. All Cocteau has paled but for *Beauty and the Beast* which retains its magic. Especially when coupled with Glass's wonderful music composed especially for the film.

VP: With respect to influences, who you would recommend reading? Which authors influenced you?

RD: Borges and Kafka have had a profound impact on my imagination. Borges translated Kafka's great short stories you know, and in the process fully became 'Borges'—fascinating story in itself. I discovered Borges in the late sixties, around the same time I discovered Jonas's book on Gnosticism. Jonas's book proved a marvelous way into the the great short texts of both writers, and above all Kafka's *The Castle*. My first novel *The Stain* is replete with Gnostic ideas: the world as a filthy inn, the soul imprisoned in the body's 'cage'; materiality as an aberration; the serpent as the first form Christ takes. Gnostic themes abound by the way . . . in all the books. Italo Calvino: A beautiful writer whose emblems I have made my own: the crystal—its every surface informing every other with light, this light is always restless; the flame that like the crystal animates what it illuminates—it, too is in constant mutation; the web, emblematic of the work of fiction in which all aspects are somehow inevitable and connected. When breathed upon it shimmers and quakes.

VP: With which other writers have you been compared (besides Angela Carter or Sylvia Plath)? With whom would you like to be compared? Would you see yourself as being the natural heir to Angela Carter? Anyone in particular?

RD: I knew Angela Carter; it was Robert Coover who suggested we meet. She was a marvelous writer and a very funny and delightful person. We discovered that many of the writers who had mattered to us were the same, Freud and Rabelais and Shikibu among them. Last summer I was invited to a Fairy Tale Conference in Ghent, Belgium; several scholars there suggested that now I was the "Fairy Queen." It was like being given a sudden warm shower of gold dust and honey. There is a brief moment in *Phosphor in Dreamland* which is offered as a tip of the hat to Angela. Robert Coover sent me *Omensetter's Luck* a million years ago and it was one of the books, maybe THE book, that had me wanting to write; I felt a deep kinship with its vision of Eros and human evil, the betrayal of the spirit.

VP: Let's consider misogyny (or perhaps better termed sexism) in living writers (male) who are lauded by the literary establishment. Are we on the cusp of a paradigm shift—younger female readers recognise the misogyny but are still seduced by the luscious prose; it seems that female writers receive less recognition, and therefore female readers tend to read male writers, because of a perceived lack of alternative. Do you have any thoughts on this?

RD: Some years ago now, the wonderful Marc Chenetier invited MacArthur Fellow Joanna Scott, Mary Caponegro, Jaimy Gordon (who won the NBA for her fabulous Lord of Misrule in 2010) and me to spend a week at the Sorbonne to meet with his graduate students in American Literature. Although our work was being studied at the Sorbonne and taken very seriously by a bunch of impressive and engaging students of literature, I recall we were asked the last day about the BIG books American men have a tendency to write; they wondered why ours were NOT BIG! I recall speaking of the male writers I deemed essential: Kafka, Calvino, and Borges, and the fact that they excel in short forms. I also suggested that perhaps the women writers had all suffered far too often the company of men who did not know when to shut up. We creatures with clitorises wanted the good bones of things *sans* all the fat. Women write as well and as lusciously as men and there are numbers of us out there being read and considered seriously both at home and abroad. Rick Moody is a champion of women's writing and was responsible for the historic proposal at the NBA, that the judges consider women and small presses with especial attention. It is clear that things have shifted dramatically with a vast expanded readership for innovative fiction—think of Kate Bernheimer's bestselling anthology for Penguin: *My Mother She Killed Me, My Father He Ate Me*—which is chock full of great contemporary women writers. This Sunday as I write to you, I have the *New York Times Book Review* in front of me with a cover photo of Karen Russell and a rave review of her new book written by the great Joy Williams—the author of *The Changeling*, one of the most extraordinary of American novels. NBA winner Katherine Boo takes up page 8 speaking about the books she loves; her *Behind the Beautiful Forevers* is one of the best books one could ever hope to read. (And I have not even spoken of all the amazing literature in translation.)

VP: What are you reading now?

RD: I have been reading all over the place. I may have mentioned Robert Calasso whose every book is a revelation; I keep rereading *KA!* His retelling of the Hindu myths. Just read Eleni Sikelianos' new book of poetry: *The Loving Details of the Living and the Dead*; she's a terrific poet and this is a beautiful book; Laura Mullen's *Murmur*; Mo Yan's *POW!* (like reading a contemporary Rabelais!); Andrew Solomon's amazing *Far From the Tree*; Oliver Sacks' *Hallucinations*; Laird Hunt's *Kind One*; CD Wright's *Deep Step Come Shining*; the amazing biography of Leonard Cohen: *I'm Your Man* and also *The Holy and the Broken* on the song 'Hallelujah', and Cohen's first novel *The Favorite Game*. (On a Cohen jag having seen him perform brilliantly in Seattle at the age of 78; women of all ages mewling in the audience) . . . about to read Bin Ramke's new book *Ariel*. So I have been reading all over the place. This will change when I get back into my novel; I'll be reading for and around the book as it unfolds and directs me. But this is what the past two months have been like, in part . . . and there are others; it's been a busy time to catch up on so much. . . . Friends have just dropped in with Valentine's Day cake and stories; one friend has a sister-in-law visiting who is a nun and believes there will be a female pope; I have been told the pope who is about to step down likes to wear red shoes which is uplifting; we got off on the little candies made in Flavingy—an anise seed dipped in white sugar said to have been a favorite of the whores of Venice as it perfumed their farts.

VP: Female pope? No, never! They bleed, they breed, they betray the sins of the fathers perpetrated upon the blasphemy of the sons! Licorice root (suck its sweetness and see!) blackens the tongue and stains the faeces and repels viral invasion but to scent the breath of the anus the Ayurvedans would recommend cardamom!

RD: The breath of the anus! This exchange recalls dinner conversation with Angela Carter! In Subzathrastan the anuses of noble brides are packed with cardamom for three hours each and every fortnight by small boys called fuaz (the process referred to as: fuazeem); they wear saffron yellow sleeves and sing; the retrieved cardamom is used to flavor the tea of the Ham Fuaz who rule the land discreetly from the ritually designated backroom of the Subzathrastan gymnasium known as the Potoor (but actually called the Vat).

VP: How delightfully exotic. A sub-continent location? Hopefully they feed them cacao beans as well! To return to *Fan-Maker*—it is a work of art on so many levels; re-reading the mud vs. crystal paragraph: Sade laments the Church likening humanity to mud, where he celebrates the brilliance and lucidity of human intellect as the basis for pleasure. You make him, for all his faults and frailties, less the monster and more the man. Human history is bloody and little has changed.

RD: Yes, so TIRESOME, to say the least, our species' vicious monkey ways . . . Subzathrastan—the last autonomous principality to the north west of eastern Kerala, south of the western foothills of Faz; it is so small that in a recent interview Al Gore called it the "shoebox state"; he apologized last Thursday. (Probably wise to be sure your cardamom comes from elsewhere.)

VP: The same (be sure of origin) is said for civet-shat coffee beans and goat-digested argan oil—would that make us coprophages, despite the fact that the beans are not actually digested? We can learn from the dead less than the living (for Elizabeth, bodies, for critics and readers, authors).

RD: You coprophage! Do you know *A History of Scatology through the Ages?*

VP: To be added to the reading list. Dogs in Africa were kept as much for hunting as they were for consuming shit (they adore human shit). While living in Cairo, the Ministry of Agriculture and the Ministry of Environment established compost worm colonies to cope with organic refuse. Because Egypt has insufficient water, it was suggested to use the worms to render human faeces to pathogen-free fertiliser (requiring three weeks rather than the standard six months of windrow composting with its inherent problems), thus making water-based flush toilets unnecessary. The idea was received with wonder and rejection. A human produces enough faecal matter in one year to manure enough food crops to feed that same human for a year, but sadly attitudes to human derived manure (and our institutionalised methods of recovery of the nutrients prevent ecologically friendly and sustainable alternatives) . . . Turning to dreams, you've said elsewhere dreams are profoundly significant for your creative output.

RD: My first book, *The Stain*, was kicked off by a dream of such power I leapt out of bed at four in the morning. I had never written a novel, I never imagined I would; it was a wild ride and as exhilarating as it was terrifying. That book is deeply informed by my life in the Loire Valley—that landscape, those voices, the persistence of ancient dogmatisms and superstitions that informed every day conversations with neighbors. The place I lived in, a small village, was deep in mystery and poetry, too. A lot like La Folie, the village in the book. I began to write seriously there. The second edition of the *Butcher's Tales* were written there for the most part, although that book was begun in Canada.

VP: In a recent dream the protagonist and a previous lover succeeded, on the second attempt, of murdering the grandmother, and were playing cat-and-mouse with police and family to distance themselves from the death and thereby inherit, unimpeded, the grandmother's fortune. Stuff which in your hands might be spun to gold. The qualities of the dream state: events repeat infinitely, time stretches to infinity, and the tunnel only ends when the consciousness of a wakened state is regained. Immensely disorienting unless the dream state is welcomed as a creative resource. The reality of the grandmother's death, is, of course, much different.

The last wayward grandchild, far from the family home, finally stumbles to her bedside. Lustrous eyes that seem to have stolen every shade of blue from the world peer at the newcomer. The grandmother smiles, murmuring odd noises beyond becoming words, hands fluttering on the blankets. The grandchild kisses her goodbye. The next day the family attends again the bedside of the grandmother. But when the grandchild enters the room, late, and looks at the the grandmother, her eyes are still pools of water reflecting slate-pale skies, leached of colour, and she utters no noise nor shows recognition. The heart still beats, blood pumps through the veins, but "she" has forsaken the body and is no longer "grandmother". The grandchild flees the room, crying, "She's gone, don't you see, she's already gone," and the following morning the grandmother dies.

Three days after her death, the grandchild wakes abruptly, the house still and quiet, the dawn not yet broken, aware of the grandmother, in no tangible way, not a concrete apparition, no fleshly thoughts or words or feelings, but as an abstract sense of her, her presence. With the first twittering of birds outside the window, the presences fades. At breakfast, one cousin asks the other about experiencing anything strange on waking. "She was here." Each nods. "She wanted to say goodbye." They look at the grandmother's son, whose eyes, so like those of his mother, blur, his chin falling to his chest. "Yes, I know. I felt her, too. She's gone, now."

The grandchild refuses to attend the funeral because they dress the body and paint its face and such a ceremony seems barbaric. The grandmother has already been farewelled.

RD: Such a beautiful description. I was beside my father when he died, and I remember so vividly what you describe—the moment when the one one knows so well has left and their body has lost its meaning. Aunt Rose and Uncle Friedle is the first story I ever wrote. It came to me in Canada in the bathtub. I sent it to my mother who was in England dying of cancer. She received it and in her very last letter to me wrote: "Some nightmares are best kept to oneself." That was the last thing she had to say to me. The next thing that happened was that I dreamed she was dead and walking down a country road dressed in yellow. She was holding her own ashes in the palms of her hands and looking down at them with bewilderment. That's how I knew she had died.

When Lina [Gerard DeGre's mother] died I was in Algeria. I dreamed I was standing by her bed and she said "This is it, God be damned!" Later that day I received a telegram saying she had just died in a hospital in Mexico. And her last words were: (in Italian) "The comedy is over." And in English: "God be damned."

The only other time I have dreamed of the death of someone close to me was my dear friend the illustrator Martin Provensen. Somewhere in the Hudson Valley he was walking towards me smiling and when he reached me said: "Ah. You are a funny one." I was in France when he died; he died at his home in the Hudson Valley where he lived with Alice. They did many extraordinary books together, books I adored as a child. Martin was one of the most wonderful people I ever knew, and a great storyteller.

VP: Do you have early memories of your parents?

RD: I woke up early one morning—I was six—and found my father in the kitchen, just back from a party on campus. He was standing by the kitchen table with a big glass of orange juice in his hand and he was wearing a tux, a cummerbund, spats and a black silk top hat!

VP: It must have been unbelievable to grow up on campus! Sometime around the Red Scare, NATO forming, the Korean war. Events that would probably seem insignificant at age six, but conversations around you might have mentioned these. Your father must have known Mary McCarthy, intellectuals running Europe (Blücher, Hauser, Hirsch, Werner Wolff), Bellow, Ellison, Weiss.

Did you know of this, written by your mother, dated 1965?

Gerard DeGre, Secretary-General of the International Model General's Club, was born in 1915 and has been engaged in one form of war game or another since he could walk. By the age of 12 he had accumulated close to 1000 Mignots and Britains - but made the mistake of giving his entire collection to his kid brother. For the next 10 years Gerry was interested only in strategic map games, and during this period developed a few board games of his own; some of them remarkably close to Stratego and L'Attaque others were variants on Chess. He still possesses a remarkable collection of chess sets including one in carved ivory representing Romans vs. Egyptians during the Cleopatra period!

During his early twenties, Gerry developed a keen interest in Naval War Games and soon built up a considerable fleet of 1:2400 scale which he always proud to show visitors. His interest in naval war games continued unabated through his military service as a Naval Lieutenant during WWII.

In 1946 Gerry joined the faculty of Bard College, Annandale-on-Hudson, New York, where he is now Professor of Sociology and Social Philosophy and where he met Joseph Morschauser when the latter was a student there. The Bard College collection of rare books included a copy of H. G. Wells' LITTLE WARS and it was the discovery of this book that set Gerry off and back to military miniatures. The fleets were put in drydock and a considerable outlay was made for Authenticast 20mm WWII tanks and figures. Wells' rules were adapted to the mid-twentieth century and for several years Britains' 4. 7 guns were trained on the guidons of tanks, armoured cars and heavy infantry!

The turning point away from armor (land or naval) came with Jack Scruby's "War Game Digest" and the new phase of painting 19th century regiments began, and with these a whole new set of rules for melee, rifle fire and related problems with which we are all concerned.

Gerry now has several French armies and can put into the field full divisions for 1815, 1870 or 1914. In addition he has built up Greenwood and Ball-Scruby forces of the 1870-1890 period: British, German, Italian as well as an Imperial Russian Army of 1812

(Scruby, Hinton and Rose figures). He is presently developing a 1900 WWI Imperial Russian force from hand-painted figures imported from Spain. All of Gerry's figures are 20mm which he maintains are the ideal size for war games. The table top countryside consists of sections of two ping pong tables in a "U" shape, the cities made up of 19th century European buildings, most of them converted from Faller HO kits by his wife, Muriel, whose main passions are trees and cafes.

Gerry has a continuing interest in the Theory of Games, and is always experimenting with new approaches to his hobby, often to the dismay of his opponents (like George Scott of Poughkeepsie) who find the rules changing from week to week. This experimentation runs all the way from complex game theory matrices to the use of tiddly-winks for artillery fire (which has become the rage among some english hobbyists). He is perhaps best known to the fraternity as the originator of the "simultaneity principle" (both players writing their moves on paper ahead of time), the "matrix systems" of melee and rifle adjudication which provided the answer to the dice roll as the "king of battles", and the "unit system" of mounting 20mm figures in groups of twos and threes was perhaps first developed by him.

A project which he has devoted considerable time and expense ha been the organization of the MODEL GENERALS' CLUB, the international society of wargamers which now includes impressive lists of inernbers from the USA, England, France, Italy and Mexico. The international society is made up of a number of local Model Generals' Clubs and serves as a focus for communication and consultation. Gerry is Secretary-General of this Club, as well as the director of its research activities at International HQ at Annandale-on-Hudson, NY. His hope is to have an organization which will some day include all active model wargarners throughout the world. Both the WARGAMERS' NEWSLETTER and TTT carry reports on MGC's activities, and WN has already published MGC articles on

> *DUEL THEORY and SQUIDGE AND SQUOP (Tiddlywink artillery fire). The old WAR GAME DIGEST included a number of Gerry's research reports for the Model General's Club.*
>
> *Last year his daughter, Erica, married Guy Ducornet, a member of the French society of collectors and an avid wargamer —"beginning," says Gerry with a grin, "a dynasty of wargamers." Since Guy is also on the Bard faculty, there is a family "battle" at least once a week when, for some reason or other "Guy's French Cuirassiers always seem to kill at least three times their number. But," says Gerry, "next time—maybe my newly painted Russian Sumski Hussars will send them reeling back to Paris!"*

RD: Fascinating. I had no knowledge of this. (Interesting she does not mention his passion for CARS. Somewhat like Toad in *Wind and the Willows!* POOP! POOP!) Fascinating what she says about trees and cafes. . . She must have been thinking of Paris. My mother was so in love with Paris! When my father and I went to Cuba to see his family, she opted for Paris. They did know Mary McCarthy, Blücher (my favorite teacher!) and my father set up what became known as the 'Common Course' for incoming students; a wonderful course in the history of ideas. We knew all these people (and Hannah Arendt, Blücher's wife, sometimes came to campus, too). My parents' ashes are buried beside them. Guy has a book out, *Annanadale Blues*, about his time at Bard and working with Ellison. I babysat for Saul Bellow. Gore Vidal was a close friend of my mother's; she ran his political campaign for the House. And Werner, a BIG person in my life. Werner had a little preschool when I was the age for that and he loved me and nurtured me; I became his special child I think, [he] invited me whenever he invited my parents to his ****MAGICAL***** apartment on campus. I am currently reading his book on Easter Island. I have a painting of his and when he died, Kate gave me his shells and his oil paints. How I loved them both!

At some point the wars took over and my father got swept up into game theory and abandoned all else. Jane Urquhart has a sweet story to tell [about] my father asking her: Would you like to come down to the game room and sea my ocean? (Or something like that). (NOW you know how BIG the wars were—and see right into the opening chapter of *GAZELLE!*) Gosh, perfect stuff for a critical work! HOW did you find this?

And on my mother? An attempt to put it all in one small box:

She had been beautiful, talented; she had somehow survived her own mother, Old Piano Legs, who managed to bring the world to a halt whenever she opened her mouth. I imagine Frances was a screamer as my mother was, exacting and irritable and mostly unaware that the world could be delightful and interesting. (She didn't scream at me, but she wheedled and nagged.) I recall a visit to her little home in the suburbs of Florida at a time when land crabs by the tens of thousands were in migration. Those crabs were a wonderful subversion and diversion. They were the best thing that ever happened to me in her company. Charlie, mother's father, had come to the states at the age of twelve (from Russia) and at once ran away to the circus where he started his new life in the New World shoveling elephant shit. He was loving and laid back and fun and after he died of stomach cancer (he was a hard candy addict) I learned he'd had an affair with a neighbor and as Frances said it: ". . . went over to her place to eat her stew." (She meant it literally.)

My mother was a talented painter, not a gifted writer, longed to be a novelist and when she finally found a publisher for her novel, the editor who had accepted it threw himself out of a window before the contract was signed. She did get a cookbook deal with Doubleday and I shudder to think of it because I did the corny illustrations [*The Jack Sprat Cookbook*]. She was a good cook (who lied about her pie crusts which were frozen) and gave great dinner parties. Once in Cairo she had some dresses made with a very handsome brocade made with silk thread. She wore one to a cocktail party only to discover that brocade she had chosen was the material used for the wrapping of corpses. Once when I was a small girl she told me that she had looked in on me as I slept, that my hands had been crossed over my heart, that I "slept like a corpse." (This fact could, in some small way, explain my deep fascination as a child with Egypt and its mummies. My favorite book as a kid, along with

Alice and *Wind in the Willows* was *Gods Graves and Scholars*.) She once covered the walls of my room with posters from MOMA; it was enchanting. She once gave me a box of Victorian novels for Xmas.

When I left home I packed all my books and love letters from high school and diaries and the sculptures a lover had carved of wood including one of my naked body; as soon as I left the country she got rid of all of it; the statues she burned. All this had been precious to me and there was no need to get rid of it; she had wanted to get me out of the house, relentlessly pushed for my premature marriage (she thought I was a sex pot who needed to be bridled); she was very taken with all things French including Guy—so that was part of it—poor Muriel, she had energy and courage but she was also cramped somehow, somehow bitter and thwarted. There was a great deal of sun in her and charm and lust for life, but I was the vessel for her anxieties and I think always perceived as flawed . . . yet, at the same time, as a dangerous competitor.

But there are other things: she allowed me to act in plays as a child on campus and once in school where I played the Bad Seed (I still wonder why I was chosen for the part); I think she always saw me as that: a bad seed or at least a bewildering seed. Yet in her way loved me, at least sporadically; she was one of those mothers who want to hug after they have been screaming. She left me alone a great deal which mean I learned to be autonomous, but also meant I was somewhat strange. If it had not been for my father I think I would have crumbled; his marvelous bounty of affection and whimsy and eagerness to share ideas assured that I thrived. We painted together, she made sure I had dance lessons, piano . . . but Mrs F. used a ruler on my fingers and I lasted less than a week. (Her son, David, was the first male (we were not yet teens) to kiss my hand.)

She painted a series of four wonderful paintings called *Post Atomic Objects* and then stopped. She believed in poltergeists and saw balls of fire bounce about the bedroom. She smelled good: of Magie perfume. She brought me back watercolors from Paris and for herself a tiny black embroidered evening bag. She wore negligees. I once saw her in her bubble bath and found her beautiful without all her makeup and frizzed hair. She looked a little like Lucile Ball channeling Rita Garbo and my father liked to take pictures of her in cheesecake poses. I think she was something of a vamp, but she was also a prude; for a time we had her girlhood piano in the house and she'd sing Broadway tunes. Cole Porter. Autumn Leaves.

She was a terrible gossip. It humiliated her that she had never gone to college (she supported my father when he went to City College) yet prided herself in her careers—as a fashion illustrator and, later, a radio show host, then TV, then journalism; she loved to do things for the community; for the life of me I can't think of a time when we were really friends; I think I could never trust her after the incident with the blue egg. But she saved my life when at the age of six I thought I was a mermaid and had grown gills and she pulled me from the water. She was open-minded for a woman of her time. I know my father adored her, that they were real lovers and companions for many years. But it grew rocky; she was demanding; she was deeply dissatisfied. Her Jewishness plagued her also; a certain humiliation there and deep anxiety. A large number of her family vanished during the war—a thing I learned from a distant relative after growing up. I recall her generosity with others, I think she was romantic, would have loved to live abroad; I realize now she must have battled with her own demons.

VP: As to no mention of cars in the article (great laughter at POOP POOP!) that may have been because the piece was written for a war game magazine, Jack Scruby's *Table Top Talk*. It was found by simply searching on Erica De Gre and Erica Degre; it was the former that turned up the page on a gaming discussion forum where your father was mentioned, and reading through the entire thread, someone had kindly copied the page from the magazine. *Annandale Blues* is a must-read as well . . .

RD: . . . X is a lunatic. Sometimes the March Hare; sometimes the Mad Hatter and sometimes, the RED QUEEN! Be ready to go down the rabbit hole. Bring a parachute and wear a helmet. Track shoes. Carry a rubber hammer. For:

> He thinks that he is very sane,
>
> the years they pass; its still the same.
>
> He raves and raves but then he's sweet
>
> (but briefly when he's on his feet).
>
> Should he stand on his head
>
> run for the door: the flag is red

VP: To focus now on some of the factors that have provoked your brilliant analysis and convergence of images in stories: key events and relationships in your life, from a philosophical perspective. You've been married twice . . .

RD: . . . [A] wealth, aesthetic and philosophical, that was shared, and travel, ideas. . . My second husband, such a tragic figure BUT he was, before he became ill, tremendous fun, imaginative and full of life; he made me think of Zorba the Greek. He sent me these astounding letters, in the voice of someone else; they are Calvinoesque. [We] shared Mexico, we shared sailing and the complexities of divorce! [In a letter to Steven Moore, Rikki writes triumphantly of handling a 43 foot sailing yacht by herself.] Both my husbands had suffered brutal child abuse, and this impacted on their lives and mine, the lives of the children; I became so interested in Alice Miller and so on because I was needing to understand the repercussions of such betrayal . . . I had read so very much, thought about mental illness so much. And in the work of Russell Banks, for example. He read Alice Miller . . . Guy and I did some amazingly creative projects together and were and ARE still involved with Surrealism; there is a Loto game we did that is now very expensive on ebay when it shows up . . .

VP: Betrayal, particularly of children, features in much of your work eg Elizabeth in *Gazelle*, Nini in *Fountains*, Charlotte in *The Stain*, Septimus in *Entering Fire*, entire civilisations in *The Fan-maker's Inquisition* and *Phosphor in Dreamland*. From the opening pages of *Netsuke* a picture of betrayal: Is Akiko modelled after you?

> *Akiko is witchy, clairvoyant. Her astonishing dreams*
>
> *are acute, surgical . . . She is in danger because I lie*

incessantly and the habit of these lies has blunted her gift and confused her . . . caused her to distrust her own intuitions. Yet I am in danger also, because I cannot help but offer her clues . . . sooner or later I will falter, offer her one clue too many . . .

Love believed true is but a reflection of longing, ensnaring lovers bound to reveal dishonesty.

RD: *Netsuke* is a novel informed by a wealth of experience. I don't want to seem evasive or coy, but I feel this sort of reading misses the book's intention. I understand the impulse—to want to know what is based on the novelist's life and what isn't—but such a reading cannot provide a way in to the book as I intended it. This book as all the others, was its own animal; it revealed itself along the way. Something of a fever dream. I hope it is received not as a set of keys but rather an experience in its own right. As the book's author, Akiko is a character I have an affinity with, but she is a creature of the imagination. Unlike the other books it was written in a flash; for two weeks I was seared, eating fire; the third and final week I raked the coals and put order to the flames . . . *Entering Fire* I was running over coals; *Netsuke* I WAS coals!

VP: Is *Netsuke*, in part, a farewell to some sort of relationship? Your novels never seem to be a vehicle, nor exude a sense of you creating characters to punish anyone you have known.

RD: *Netsuke* . . . no desire to punish but to understand what the inside of such a mind might look and sound like, at the time of a psychotic breaking apart. In *The Stain*, Sister Malicia was a payback! In *The Complete Butcher's Tales* there is a story called 'La Chincha'. There she is, my grandmother, my father's mother Emelina Carmen Dionesia (who I called Lina). I have some great photos of her. Foxes is also about her: its a dark glimpse into her sorry downfall. She had been an extravagant and beautiful woman. When she got old and fat she turned the mirrors around so that they would all face the wall. In the same book (most of these stories are the first things I ever wrote) are 'Shoes and Shit' and 'I Will Never Forget You Ernie Frigmaster'. These are BOTH about my mother's father: Charlie Harris.

The Butcher's Tales is full of stories rooted in the real world. The first ones were published in Canada by Fiddlehead Press in a book called *From The Star Chamber* by Fred Cogswell. That book was precipitated by my mother's cancer, the terrible death of my husband's brother and the events taking place in Greece, a *coup d'etat* in which people were being swept from the streets and tortured. One woman who survived her torture miscarried her child. I read an interview she gave and was so deeply troubled I wrote all night. That book is a first draft and was not edited, yet it holds on . . . beginner's luck. A kind of heat . . . it came from a very real, very deep place. (And I was listening to the music of Laura Nero; somehow she is part of what set things off.)

VP: In which of your other books, if at all, do you have a female character that plays with words (such as Sade does in *Fan-Maker*) or something Joycean (eg *Finnegans Wake*) in thought/inner dialogue?

RD: *The Jade Cabinet*, narrated by a female character, Memory. She's a Victorian, but she uses language with real playfulness and has a unique sensibility for a woman of her period. I guess I've always felt that my primary interest as a writer IS language and madmen are a fascinating vehicle; I've never thought of myself as a 'woman' writer; I've turned down invitations to be in anthologies of women's writing because I think it's stupid (I know that is not addressing your question, but somehow it matters); I think the creative process transcends sex and all the rest; one of the books I love best is Murasaki Shikibu's *Genji* which has been called 'Proustian' because of its psychological acuity and complexity. *Genji* is a deeply human book; Shikibu's intimate and searing investigation of male betrayal and acute and seemingly very modern understanding of sexual angst is perhaps 'feminine' and she wrote in woman's Japanese—but I'm not sure her sex explains the book's extraordinary power—just as Proust's masterpiece is not determined by his gender. Your question is interesting; if I capture Sade's voice in *Fan-Maker*, in other ways it is one of my most straightforward books in terms of language compared to *The Stain* or *Fountains*, say: I was reading Bachelard: *Water and Dreams*. That philosophical reverie was behind this. ALL waters, from 'meteors' (ie snow and rain) to the blizzard. Water in all its forms informs the book. REFLECTION as one's reflection in water and day dreaming. Sade was a great vehicle as was the Nazi [sympathiser] in *Entering Fire*. Such creatures give one lots of room. Maybe the Hunger artist in *The Jade Cabinet* is one of the strangest moments because Memory is dealing with a madwoman, or when she writes about Baconfield the architect . . . The wildest writing over all is *Phosphor in Dreamland* I think, but again the voice is male. . . The power in my infancy was my father; my mother destructive and often clueless . . . Language was his domain although my mother had a radio show and longed to be a novelist.

VP: With respect to the feminist label, women's collections can be deceptive. The creative process transcends gender in those who are comfortable with their sex and sexuality and the ambiguities between. There is a (natural) backlash amongst women writers/academics/public figures to reject "femaleness" in favour of "maleness" in order to redress the problem of a power imbalance; an inherited cultural phenomenon arising through the squabble over resources and typically such squabbles are solved by physical aggression, not with intelligent aggression. However, the adoption of the physical aggression (and the second stage, intellectual aggression—if aggression is viewed as behaviour resulting from fear, lack of control, or adequate access to resources) characteristics does not take the struggle for recognition beyond the boundaries already set by the victorious aggressors; the rules and the game need re-definition, and it is writers who transcend the whole issue that can demonstrate a way forward, simply because their own gender (while important) is not important in writing a gendered character. If a writer cannot recognise without prejudice and bias what are the intrinsically "male" and "female" aspects, her/his characters will conform to stereotypes and the voice of the character will not be authentic, particularly if the writer fears the other gender (consciously or not).

Sade is authentic because you go beyond your female skin to enter his. Few male writers inhabit a female character the way you capture

Sade as a male. Even Durrell—despite that (Proustian) exploration—his female characters still suffer his wrestling with daemons of his own making (and Darley was written as a male in the Quartet, Sylvie was written flawed in the Quintet, and Bruce and Pierre were gay, not female). It is the same with *Netsuke*; a sense from the beginning that the psychiatrist is male (and not because white collar professions are still perceived as the province of the male) but because you explore that character with an empathic lens. *Genji* is written similarly, as you note, because of the period constraints, but it is precisely because of that sensitivity that it achieves its power, as does Proust in his writing.

RD: I also do not like the label feminist; it aggravates me as does 'black' writing and so on . . . But demonization, objectification, all of that is such a deeply human issue; perhaps—it seems so—a primate issue! I once wrote about the Bloody Countess Bathory just as a reminder that abusive authority is a human issue not just a male issue.

VP: Have you had your work translated in German or Italian?

RD: *Fan-Maker's Inquisition* came out in German; *Gazelle* in Italian (a disaster!). I'd love to be well-translated in Italy. Here's the thing; *Gazelle* was picked up by AvantPop Collection Immaginario. The editor left and was replaced by someone who:

1. Asked an Italian friend for a translation of the first chapter, then got another translator who both used that chapter in their own translation, AND

2. did it so quickly that the book was out within two months of a signed contract, AND

3. was so quickly printed there were things printed twice, AND

4. *Gazelle* was called: *E sia acqua sabbia e cenere* (!?)

5. FURTHERMORE the editor invited me to Milan (I was in Paris for the book fair) and changed his mind without telling me.

This is the only time I have ever had a bad experience with a publisher; it was crazy!. . . Just had the great news that two books will be published in France in October [2013]: Cambourakis and Gallimard. (I hope one of them will invite me to Paris!). Cambourakis is republishing *Entering Fire*, and Gallimard *The One Marvelous Thing*. Guy has translated many of my books; he claims it is not easy, in fact; for one thing the vocabulary is much smaller in French and for another the 'tone' is not easy to catch . . . and then there is the problem of equivalents in humor. He gave up on *The Fountains of Neptune*! His first translation, of *Entering Fire*, missed the book's humor entirely, but then he did it over and it's a brilliant translation. As are the others. They are amazing!

VP: From an interview with Steven Moore, apparently he discovered you? How did that happen?

RD: Steve is great; a smart, good guy . . . But he didn't discover me; I was already published; Chatto and Windus in Britain did my first two novels, but I had already published in Canada and had a reputation (I fled from there, I realize now I was always fleeing! I felt 'unready')! I don't recall any editing done with Steve beyond copy editing as the books were 'done' and Dalkey did reprints or if the book was unpublished it was ready to go with barely a tweak. I always send off a finished ms. (Nothing wrong with working with an editor; I just polish by the moon before I send anything off.) I think Steve may have written asking for a book and saying he was interested in a long term thing . . . Joyce Carol Oates had made an offer on a new book but she only published one book not more. So I went with Dalkey. I was impressed with Steve's passion!

As for publishers ALL my experiences have been really good; City Lights's publication of *Entering Fire* led to the Lannan (!) and Coffee House's treatment of *Netsuke* has been fantastic. The BIG mistake my agent insisted upon was leaving Henry Holt where I received big advances and was told I had a home forever; they were not counting on sales but something bigger. My agent decided after two books to go to Knopf—I argued about this knowing I had a real place with Holt, but being my agent after all I relented; I got a great advance for *Gazelle* from Knopf but it was a one night stand most likely. But I am so in love with Coffee House I feel well served and they had the rights for Spain and Turkey and sold the book in these countries.

VP: Why do you write?

RD: WHY? As Borges says, I'm paraphrasing: as tigers have stripes and roses their fragrance, so the human species has poetry . . . wired to do it; wired to do it. PURPOSE? Adventure! Knowledge! Revelation! Language is a vehicle if Eros.

VP: And if no-one were to read you?

RD: Maybe it's akin to the hunger for love; what if nobody loves you? We're wired to love, too . . . Maybe it's waiting to pounce in an unexpected form; maybe a writer needs to get lost in the poets who once enthralled; maybe a writer needs to write her own *HOWL* about whatever has eaten her heart; maybe we all need a new version of *HOWL!*

ZIM
October 23 1991
GOBBLER BEAD
DEAR NICK BANTOCK,
WHENEVER I RECEIVE A PARCEL FROM MY friend KRISHNA MURTI the Cosmologist, I OPEN it EAGERLY. This time his gift went beyond my wildest expectations: He had sent me your enchanting GRIFFIN AND SABINE. WHEN I CAME UPON THE first SEALED ENVELOPE, I FELT A SUDDEN RUSH of EXCITEMENT; the Act of OPENING it produced A REAL SHIVER! For days now I have been lost in delicious conjecture: what is the true NATURE of Griffin's unique Love, the muse SABINE? Is she PRANA? A PHANTOM of the Mind? Autonomous ANIMA? CHIMERA? IS SHE A WHIM? DELIRIUM? IS SHE AN HALLUCINATION? WHATEVER SHE IS, she's ONE of the WORLD'S GREAT ANIMATING ELEMENTS!
HERE on ZIM, I draw for the Local MUSEUM. In keeping with your EXTRAORDINARY CORRESPONDENCE, I've chosen to illustrate my LETTER with Zimbic curiosities.
(How I wish I could own the entire collection of Sabine's gorgeous STAMPS!) With ADMIRATION + AFFECTION, Rikki DUCORNET
VIEW out THE WINDOW
PHALLIC AZURITES of BOG LAKE
A SKIAGRAPHIC SKINK

Bibliography

Novels

The Stain (1984)
Hardcover, Chatto & Windus/Hogarth Press, London, 1984.
Hardcover, Grove Press, New York, 1984.
Paperback, Borgen, Volby, 1985. (tr. Chili Turèll).
Paperback, Dalkey Archive, Illinois, 1995.
Paperback, Metaekdoti Publishers, 2005.
Paperback, Sphinx, Göteborg, 2007. (tr. Kristoffer Noheden).

Entering Fire (1986)
Hardcover, Chatto & Windus, London, 1986.
Paperback, Chatto & Windus, London, 1986.
Paperback, City Lights, San Francisco, 1987. Reissued 2001.
Paperback, Éditions Deleatur, Angers, 1993. (tr. Guy Ducornet).
Paperback, le Serpent à plumes, Paris, 1999.
Paperback, Cambourakis, Paris, 2013.

The Fountains of Neptune (1989)
Hardcover, McClelland & Stewart, Toronto, 1989.
Paperback, McClelland & Stewart, Toronto, 1989.
Hardcover, Dalkey Archive, Illinois, 1992.
Paperback, Dalkey Archive, Illinois, 1993. Reissued 2015.

The Jade Cabinet (1993)
Hardcover, Dalkey Archive, Illinois, 1993.
Paperback, Dalkey Archive, Illinois, 1993. Reissued 2009.

Phosphor in Dreamland (1995)
Paperback, Dalkey Archive, Illinois, 1995.
Paperback, le Serpent à plumes, Paris, 2000. (tr. Guy Ducornet).
Paperback, Sphinx Bokforlag, 2012.

The Fan-Maker's Inquisition (1999)
Hardcover, Henry Holt. & Co., New York, 1999
Paperback, Ballantine Books, New York, 2000.
Paperback, Deuticke, Frankfurt/Main, 2001. (tr. Verena Stalder).
Paperback, le Serpent à plumes, Paris, 2002. (tr. Guy Ducornet).
Paperback, Ediciones del Bronce, Barcelona, 2002. (tr. Albert Borràs).
Paperback, AST Publishers, Russia, 2004.
E-Book, Dzanc Books, Michigan, 2013.

Gazelle (2003)
Hardcover, Alfred A. Knopf, New York, 2003.
Paperback, Fanucci, Rome, 2003. (tr. Anna Martini).
Paperback, Anchor, New York, 2004.
Paperback, J. Losfeld, Paris, 2007. (tr. Guy Ducornet).
E-Book, Anchor, New York, 2007/2013.

Netsuke (2011)
Paperback, Coffee House Press, Minneapolis, 2011.
Paperback, Odeon, Prague, 2012. (tr. Martin Pokorný).
Paperback, J. Losfeld, Paris, 2013. (tr. Marie-Hélène Dumas).
Paperback, Blackie Books, Barcelona, 2013. (tr. Ismael Attrache).

Brightfellow (2016)
Paperback, Coffee House Press, Minneapolis, 2016.

Short Fiction

The Butcher's Tales (1980)
Paperback, Aya Press, Toronto, 1980.
Paperback, Atlas Press, London, 1991.

Haddock's Eyes/Les Yeux d'eglefin (1987)
Hardcover, Editions du Founeau, 1987. (tr. Pierre Yvard).

The Volatilized Ceiling of Baron Munodi (with Guy Ducornet) (1991)
Paperback, Éditions Deleatur, Angers, 1991.

The Complete Butcher's Tales (1994)
Hardcover, Dalkey Archive, Illinois, 1994.
Paperback, Dalkey Archive, Illinois, 1995.

The Word "Desire" (1997)
Hardcover, Henry Holt & Co., New York, 1997.
Paperback, Owl Books, 1998.
Paperback, Dalkey Archive, Illinois, 2005.

Two Fictions (with a tip of the hat to Borges) (2002)
Paperback, Obscure Books, Wisconsin, 2002.

The One Marvelous Thing (illustrated by T. Motley) (2008)
Paperback, Dalkey Archive, Illinois, 2008.

Poetry

From the Star Chamber (1974)
Paperback, Fiddlehead Poetry Books, New Brunswick, 1974.

Wild Geraniums (1975)
Paperback, Actual Size Books, Kent, 1975.

Bouche à Bouche (with Guy Ducornet) (1975)
Paperback, Soror, Paris, 1975.

Weird Sisters (1976),
Paperback, Intermedia, Vancouver, 1976.

Knife Notebook (1977)
Paperback, Fiddlehead Poetry Books, New Brunswick, 1977.

The Illustrated Universe (1979)
Paperback, Aya Press, Toronto, 1979.

The Cult of Seizure (1989)
Paperback, Porcupine's Quill, Ontario, 1989.
Paperback, Skylight Press, Cheltenham, 2012.

Essay Collections

The Monstrous and the Marvelous (1999)
Paperback, City Lights, San Fransico, 1999.

Desirous (with Brian Evenson and M.E. Warlick) (2008)
Paperback, Pierre Manard Gallery, Massachusetts, 2008.

The Deep Zoo (2015)
Paperback, Coffee House Press, Minneapolis, 2015.

Children's Books

The Blue Bird (adapted from Madame D'Aulnoy) (1970)
Hardcover, Alfred A. Knopf, New York, 1970.

Shazira Shazam and the Devil (with Guy Ducornet) (1970)
Hardcover, Prentice-Hall, New Jersey, 1970.

Editor

Shoes and Shit: Stories for Pedestrians (with Geoff Hancock) (1984)
Paperback, Aya Press, Toronto, 1984.

Artworks & Illustrations

A comprehensive list can be found at www.rikkiducornet.com